A Strategic Guide to
Technical Communication

A Strategic Guide to
Technical Communication

Heather Graves and Roger Graves

broadview press

LIBRARY AND ARCHIVES CANADA CATALOGUING IN PUBLICATION

Graves, Heather, 1958-
   A strategic guide to technical communication/Heather Graves and Roger Graves.

Includes bibliographical references and index.
ISBN 978-1-55111-814-7

   1. Technical writing. 2. Communication of technical information.
I. Graves, Roger, 1957– II. Title.

T11.G738 2007   808'.0666   C2007-901990-0

BROADVIEW PRESS is an independent, international publishing house, incorporated in 1985. Broadview believes in shared ownership, both with its employees and with the general public; since the year 2000 Broadview shares have traded publicly on the Toronto Venture Exchange under the symbol BDP.

We welcome comments and suggestions regarding any aspect of our publications—please feel free to contact us at the addresses below or at broadview@broadviewpress.com
www.broadviewpress.com.

NORTH AMERICA
Post Office Box 1243,
Peterborough, Ontario,
Canada K9J 7H5

Post Office Box 1015,
3576 California Road,
Orchard Park, New York,
USA 14127
TEL: (705) 743-8990
FAX: (705) 743-8353

EMAIL:
customerservice@
broadviewpress.com

UK, IRELAND, &
CONTINENTAL EUROPE
NBN International, Estover Road,
Plymouth, UK PL6 7PY
TEL: 44 (0) 1752 202300
FAX: 44 (0) 1752 202330

EMAIL:
enquiries@nbninternational.com

AUSTRALIA & NEW ZEALAND
UNIREPS University of New
South Wales
Sydney, NSW 2052 Australia
TEL: 61 2 96640999
FAX: 61 2 96645420

EMAIL:
infopress@unsw.edu.au

Broadview Press acknowledges the financial support of the Government of Canada through the Book Publishing Industry Development Program (BPIDP) for our publishing activities.

Cover design by Lisa Brawn
Interior by Em Dash Design

Printed in Canada

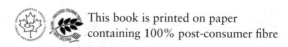 This book is printed on paper containing 100% post-consumer fibre

Contents

Preface

Note to Instructors

First, thank you for selecting *The Strategic Guide to Technical Communication* as your course text. This book should provide a comprehensive introduction to your students of a variety of approaches and strategies that they can use to create effective technical documents and presentations. This book does not follow the standard organization of many texts with the theory and conceptual information in the chapter and then a variety of exercises and assignments collected at the end. Instead, the exercises and assignments are placed within the chapters, following the discussion of the relevant concepts or points. The idea is that students should read the chapter prior to class and, when they get to class, you can quickly summarize for them the main points to which they should pay attention, and then you can assign an exercise that will reinforce the theoretical concept and get students started working with it. Theoretical discussions about writing are useful, to a point, but they really become relevant when the ideas are applied to a particular text or situation. The exercises embedded in the chapter serve to show students how the ideas may immediately and usefully be applied to their own situations.

There are also several different kinds of exercises and assignments in the book. IN-CLASS EXERCISES are short assignments intended to be done by students in class in 15 or 20 minutes. They ask students to use the main ideas just discussed in the previous section and to think critically about those ideas. Sometimes, the exercises complicate a simplistic view of writing; other times, they have students become comfortable with a strategy that they will need to use in a longer, more formal assignment later in the class or term. LAB ASSIGNMENTS are slightly longer than in-class exercises, but they are still intended to be completed (or at least worked on) during a class meeting. For instructors who book a computer lab for some or all of their class meetings, these assignments get students busy working with the central technical and writing principles covered in this book. If you do not use or do not have access to a computer lab for your technical communication class, the lab assignments are still useful for getting students started applying the writing strategies to a particular problem. The assignments may be finished and handed in at the end of class, or they may be taken home and finished before the next class. Students can bring the finished version to the next class meeting or email it to you, depending upon your preference. The third type of assignment in this text is the MAJOR PROJECT, which is a longer, more formal assignment that has students consider the main concepts from the chapter (or chapters) in order to produce an effective example of one of the main genres of technical communication. Assign the major project at the beginning of a particular unit of study and have it due the following week or at the end of the term, depending upon your course plan and schedule.

Consider having your students work collaboratively on both the in-class and the lab assignments. Given the collaborative nature of much technical communication, group activities provide your students with opportunities to work with others, to discuss the course content, to hear others' bright ideas that might spark greater creativity in their own, and to get to know each other in ways that promote a positive learning environment. Collaborative work of this nature generally results in better written texts for you to read and less grading or marking time because the in-class and lab assignments result in 6 or 7 papers for quick review rather than 25 or 30 individual efforts. We do recommend limiting the groups for in-class work to four people because more members than that can mean that some contribute very little to the activity. Two or three to a group forms a useful and productive unit. We have also used the major projects as collaborative assignments with good success. If you decide to do so, limit the size of the group to three people. We do not expand the requirements for collaborative projects, nor do we grade the collaborative assignments harder. We find that negotiating the group dynamics is an excellent additional lesson for students, and the finished project can provide them with evidence for future employers that they work effectively with other people. The advantage to you is that you have fewer final projects to grade during the last weeks of the term.

You may have noticed that we cover persuasive writing twice in this volume: in Chapter 4, "Writing technical prose," and in Chapter 6, "Writing winning proposals." The first discussion is a general one about persuasive writing—how to make a case for your viewpoint when you need to—while the second discussion focuses on persuasive writing in proposals. In Chapter 6, the strategies are adapted to the proposal genre, and consider, for example, how to create and where to locate your ethical appeal. Understanding where and how to build your case results in an effective, well-written, and successful proposal. The chapter on proposal writing lays out for students how to adapt the earlier general discussion to the specific demands of the proposal genre.

Depending upon the goals of your course and the length of your term, you may decide to cover the chapters in the order in which they are presented in this text. Do not feel that you have to, however. With the demands of a short term—in some cases a ten-week quarter—adapt the order of the chapters to suit the needs of your students and the assignment schedule. When we taught this course in the quarter system to computer technology and information (CTI) students at DePaul University, we had to limit the course content to instructional documents. This meant we included only the status or progress report (from Chapter 7, "Reporting technical information"), along with the how-to (Chapter 8) and usability (Chapter 9) sections, with the major course project being an instructional manual due at the end of the term. After covering the introductory chapter in week one, we would dive right into the instructional and usability chapters so that students could begin the major project; then we would fill in the other areas, such as research, document design, ethics, style, and online documentation as the term progressed and as time permitted.

Other instructors at different institutions focus their course around writing technical reports, in which case they would defer the how-to and usability information until later in the term or refer students to it for additional help rather than teach it directly, depending upon the needs of their students. If your term is longer (13 to 16 weeks), you might find you have time to cover both instructional and report content fairly thoroughly. In the section that follows this introduction, look for the alternate tables of contents that suggest ways to order course material depending upon your term length and your course focus.

While this volume contains eleven chapters, several of the chapters contain information that will likely take you longer than a week to cover in class. For example, Chapter 7 ("Reporting technical information") contains discussions about status or progress reports, laboratory reports, white papers, and recommendation reports. You could easily spend a week on each of these genres if you wished to focus your technical communication course around technical reports. Similarly, Chapter 4 ("Writing technical prose") and Chapter 5 ("Designing documents and page layout") could be assigned at least two weeks in your syllabus. In fact, you could easily spend three or four class meetings on discussions of style, argumentation, and the use of definition and description in technical prose. Similarly, the design principles outlined in Chapter 5 take at least a week for most students to grasp before you move on to talking about page layout and designing a grid. To be honest, learning to use the design principles takes several weeks but, if you introduce the concepts early in the term, your students can gain practise as it progresses, and you should be able to see significant improvements in their ability to create an effective design by the end of the course.

Similarly, you can spend several weeks covering the information in Chapter 2 ("Leading and misleading the reader") and Chapter 3 ("Researching technical subjects") since students benefit greatly from opportunities to develop their interviewing or surveying skills through multiple chances to try out the strategies and revise their efforts. When covering the information in Chapter 2, you would likely want to spend a week on the discussions of ethics and plain language and another week on creating effective visuals. Students benefit from chances to work with others while they learn how to use a graphing program or practise the conventions for creating effective visuals. We have found that hands-on exercises in the computer lab help students to learn a great deal in a short time; they can interact with each other and experiment with new techniques while having the instructor present to give quick feedback or help them out with a tip or shortcut. We have also found that students can teach us (and each other) many tips and shortcuts for using technology.

Note to Students

First, thank you for purchasing this book. It should provide you with ideas and strategies to help you create effective technical documents. This book takes a rhetorical approach to technical communication. This means that instead of setting up a list of rules that you should apply uniformly to all writing situations, this book introduces you to the bigger picture of how the words you write can affect the people intended to use them. By understanding who your readers or users are and what they need in a technical document, you can adapt your knowledge to their situations to provide them with what they need and can use. This book should help you do this by outlining some specific strategies that you can use, demonstrating ways that they might be used, and summarizing the challenges that certain documents or genres present to the writer. The exercises and assignments in each chapter will help you practise the strategies and apply the concepts that you need in order to make good decisions about how to write a document, and then they will guide you in developing a good working draft. When you test your document with members of your target user group, you should receive feedback that will help you revise the draft into a usable and effective piece of work. Since the key requirement of technical communication is that it provides the information that its target users need, we can measure the success of a document by the productive experience users have with it. Your goal, as a writer of technical documents, should be to present usable information on a specialized (and usually technical) subject matter to readers or users who lack knowledge or experience in that area. If you are not already an expert in the area or subject that you need to write about, your first task is to learn enough about it so that you can direct the learning and experience of others. This book will help you figure out how to educate yourself as well as facilitate the learning of others.

Alternate tables of contents for different types of technical communication courses

TEN-WEEK QUARTER

The quarter system, as you may know, requires you to hit the ground running and not let up until the ten weeks end. Many instructors frontload critical "need-to-know" course content into the first three or four weeks, and then include the "nice-to-know" content in the later weeks of the quarter. Distinguishing between "need-to-know" and "nice-to-know" requires some ruthless decision making.

Ten-week quarter: Technical manual version

WEEK 1: INTRODUCTION TO BASIC CONCEPTS OF AUDIENCE, PURPOSE, AND GENRE

Chapter One: Thinking about audience, purpose, and genre

WEEK 2: WRITING TECHNICAL PROSE AND RESEARCHING TECHNICAL SUBJECTS

Chapter Four: Writing technical prose
- Defining, describing, and explaining
  Extended definitions: How is an operational definition different from a set of instructions?

Chapter Three: Researching technical subjects
- Interviewing
- Secondary research: Finding print and online sources, especially "Citing and paraphrasing researched sources"

WEEK 3: INCORPORATING DESIGN INTO TECHNICAL DOCUMENTS

Chapter Five: Designing documents and page layout
- What is document design?
- Strategic solutions: Four design principles
- Designing a layout grid

WEEK 4:   WRITING GOOD INSTRUCTIONS AND MANUALS
Chapter Eight: Writing how-to documents: Instructions, procedures, and manuals
- What makes instructional documents good?

WEEK 5:   USABILITY TESTING
Chapter Nine: Testing and reporting document usability
- What is usability?
- Planning the test
- Designing the test
- Conducting the test
- Reporting your results

WEEK 6:   INTRODUCING THE MAJOR PROJECT (A TECHNICAL MANUAL)
Chapter Six: Writing winning proposals
- Why write proposals?
- What is the standard generic format for a proposal?
- How do I incorporate persuasion into the format to create a winning proposal?

WEEK 7:   USING VISUALS AND ETHICAL ISSUES IN TECHNICAL COMMUNICATION
Chapter Two: Leading and misleading the reader: Ethical issues of technical communication
- Ethics at work
- Writing ethically: Plain language guidelines
- Using visuals ethically to communicate effectively

WEEK 8:   DIGITAL TECHNICAL COMMUNICATION AND STATUS REPORTS
Chapter Ten: Taking technical communication online
- Either "Sharing documents electronically" or "Writing online documents."
Chapter Seven: Reporting technical information
- Status or progress reports

WEEK 9:   CREATING EFFECTIVE ORAL PRESENTATIONS
Chapter Eleven: Presenting technical information orally

WEEK 10: STUDENT PRESENTATIONS
Class presentations on major project

Ten-week quarter: Technical report version

WEEK 1: INTRODUCING THE MAIN CONCEPTS OF AUDIENCE,
PURPOSE, AND GENRE

Chapter One: Thinking about audience, purpose, and genre

WEEK 2: COLLECTING INFORMATION AND CONDUCTING RESEARCH

Chapter Three: Researching technical subjects

WEEK 3: ELEMENTS OF EFFECTIVE TECHNICAL PROSE

Chapter Four: Writing technical prose
- What is style?
- Defining, describing, and explaining

WEEK 4: PROPOSAL WRITING (FOR MAJOR PROJECT)

Chapter Six: Writing winning proposals

WEEK 5: MAJOR PROJECT (WHITE PAPER OR RECOMMENDATION
REPORT)

Chapter Seven: Reporting technical information
- White Papers or information reports
- Recommendation reports

WEEK 6: ETHICS AND USING VISUALS

Chapter Two: Leading and misleading the reader: Ethical issues in technical communication

WEEK 7: PAGE LAYOUT AND DESIGN

Chapter Five: Designing documents and page layout

WEEK 8: STATUS OR PROGRESS REPORTS AND WRITING TECHNICAL
PROSE

Chapter Seven: Reporting technical information
- Status or progress reports

Chapter Four: Writing technical prose
- Argumentation: Constructing a persuasive case

WEEK 9: ORAL PRESENTATIONS AND SHARING ELECTRONIC FILES

Chapter Eleven: Presenting technical information orally

Chapter Ten: Taking technical communication online
- Sharing documents electronically

WEEK 10: STUDENT PRESENTATIONS ON MAJOR PROJECTS

Student oral presentations based on major project

THIRTEEN-WEEK TERM: TECHNICAL MANUAL VERSION, WITH ONE REPORT

WEEK 1:   INTRODUCTION TO BASIC CONCEPTS OF AUDIENCE, PURPOSE, AND GENRE

Chapter One: Thinking about audience, purpose, and genre

WEEK 2:   WRITING TECHNICAL INSTRUCTIONS

Chapter Eight: Writing how-to documents: Instructions, procedures, and manuals

WEEK 3:   TESTING TECHNICAL INSTRUCTIONS

Chapter Nine: Testing and reporting document usability

WEEK 4:   PAGE LAYOUT AND DESIGN

Chapter Five: Designing documents and page layout

WEEK 5:   PROPOSAL WRITING

Chapter Six: Writing winning proposals

WEEK 6:   ELEMENTS OF WRITING EFFECTIVE TECHNICAL PROSE

Chapter Four: Writing technical prose

WEEK 7:   CONDUCTING RESEARCH AND COLLECTING INFORMATION

Chapter Three: Researching technical subjects
- Interviewing
- Survey research
- Secondary research: Finding print and online sources

WEEK 8:   REPORTING TECHNICAL INFORMATION

Note: Cover one or two of the four genres discussed in Chapter 7, depending upon the focus of your course. In other words, if you are teaching the technical manual, predominantly, then you might use only the section on status or progress reports and, during this week, have students learn about and then write a status report on their major project.

Chapter Seven: Reporting technical information
- Status or progress reports

WEEK 9:   DIGITAL PRESENTATION OF TECHNICAL INFORMATION

Note: Depending upon your focus, you might do one or the other of the sections in this chapter. Having students actually prepare documents that will be used online is quite time consuming, and it will generally require more than one week of class time.

Chapter 10: Taking technical communication online
- Sharing documents electronically" and/or "Writing online documents"

WEEK 10: ETHICAL ISSUE AND USING VISUALS
Chapter Two: Leading and misleading the reader: Ethical issues of technical communication

WEEK 11: ELEMENTS OF WRITING EFFECTIVE TECHNICAL PROSE
Chapter Four: Writing technical prose

WEEK 12: ORAL PRESENTATION OF TECHNICAL INFORMATION
Chapter Eleven: Presenting technical information orally

WEEK 13: STUDENT PRESENTATIONS
Oral presentations by students presenting their major projects

SIXTEEN-WEEK SEMESTER

WEEK 1: INTRODUCING THE BASIC CONCEPTS OF AUDIENCE, PURPOSE, AND GENRE
Chapter One: Thinking about audience, purpose, and genre

WEEK 2: INTRODUCING ETHICAL ISSUES
Chapter Two: Leading and misleading the reader: Ethical issues in technical communication
- Ethics at work
- Ethics for students
- How is ethics related to technical communication?
  Copyright, trademarks, and patents
  What is not copyrightable
  Rules for copying images

WEEK 3: CONDUCTING RESEARCH TO WRITE ABOUT TECHNICAL SUBJECTS
Chapter Three: Researching technical subjects

WEEK 4: STYLE AND ARGUMENTATION IN TECHNICAL PROSE
Chapter Four: Writing technical prose
- What is style?
- Sentence composition
- Figurative language
- Analysing prose
- Argumentation: Constructing a persuasive case

Chapter Two: Leading and misleading the reader
- Writing ethically
Plain language guidelines

WEEK 5: DESIGNING TECHNICAL DOCUMENTS
Chapter Five: Designing documents and page layout

WEEK 6: INCORPORATING VISUALS INTO TECHNICAL DOCUMENTS
Chapter Two: Leading and misleading the reader: Ethical issues in technical communication
- Using visuals ethically to communicate effectively

WEEK 7: WRITING EFFECTIVE PROPOSALS
Chapter Six: Writing winning proposals

WEEK 8: WRITING INSTRUCTIONAL DOCUMENTS
Chapter Eight: Writing how-to documents: Instructions, procedures, and manuals

WEEK 9: TESTING INSTRUCTIONAL DOCUMENTS
Chapter Nine: Testing and reporting document usability

WEEK 10: REPORTING TECHNICAL INFORMATION, PART 1
Chapter Seven: Reporting technical information
- Recommendation reports

WEEK 11: REPORTING TECHNICAL INFORMATION, PART 2
Chapter Seven: Reporting technical information
- White Papers or informational reports

WEEK 12: REPORTING TECHNICAL INFORMATION, PART 3 AND ACCESSING TECHNICAL DOCUMENTS ONLINE
Chapter Seven: Reporting technical information
- The laboratory report
Chapter Ten: Taking technical communication online
- Sharing documents electronically

WEEK 13: WRITING DOCUMENTS TO BE USED ONLINE
Chapter Ten: Taking technical communication online
- Writing online documents

WEEK 14: STATUS OR PROGRESS REPORTS
Chapter Seven: Reporting technical information
- Status or progress reports

WEEK 15: PRESENTING TECHNICAL INFORMATION ORALLY
Chapter Eleven: Presenting technical information orally

WEEK 16: STUDENTS PRESENT SOME ASPECT OF THEIR MAJOR
PROJECTS
Student presentations of major project

Acknowledgements

First, we have to thank the hundreds (maybe thousands) of students whom we have taught at Illinois State University, DePaul University in Chicago, and the University of Western Ontario in London, Ontario for motivating us to develop the teaching materials that form the basis for this book. The students at DePaul University were especially helpful because they refused to just talk about technical communication but insisted on doing it and on learning ways to do it well. These demands forced us to take a strategic approach to teaching technical communication, to developing specific strategies that improve the design of documents, that create a compelling and well-supported argument, and these strategies are laid out in this text. We also appreciate the generosity of the numerous students who gave us permission to reproduce their work in this book. We felt it was important to include examples of what contemporary students, enrolled in a technical writing course at the postsecondary level, could reasonably be expected to achieve in response to the assignments in this text. We could not have met this objective without our students' support and enthusiasm.

We would also like to thank Chris Tardy at DePaul University for testing the manuscript for this book in her technical communication class in the winter quarter of 2006 and for providing us with useful feedback that helped us to improve it. With her contribution, we were able to "road test" the manuscript at both American and Canadian postsecondary educational institutions to ensure it reached its target audience and achieved its purpose in both situations.

We would also like to thank Anne Brackenbury and Julia Gaunce at Broadview Press. Anne inquired about this project and then pursued it with her editors at Broadview to discover their level of interest in it. We also appreciate Julia's editorial support through the process of developing this text. Thanks also to the board of directors at Broadview Press, who decided to take Broadview Press's offerings in a new direction with the acceptance of our manuscript. We also want to thank reviewers Gisele Baxter, John Killoran, Tania Smith, and Warren Clendinning who gave us valuable suggestions at both the proposal and manuscript stages of the process. With their feedback, we were able to make some significant changes and additions to the book to make it more useful. Thanks also to Judith Earnshaw and to Piper-Lee Bradford for their effort and time producing this book. We are also indebted to Karen Taylor for her careful and respectful editing of the manuscript. We especially appreciate how tactfully she corrected our unclear and sometimes infelicitous phrasing. Thanks also to Lil Allain who proofread with great care to help to make the final version as clear and error free as possible. Thank you to Liz Broes and Matthew Jubb who did a wonderful job choosing the fonts and designing the interior. We also wish to thank Laura Cardiff, Michael Denny, and Anna Del Col for their excellent work putting together a terrific website to support this project. Finally, thanks also to our children, Erin and Eric, and our extended family who will, no doubt, be pleased to hear that this book is finally finished.

CHAPTER ONE

Thinking about audience, purpose, and genre

No matter how many technical skills you have, you still need to deal with people at a level they can understand, so communication skills are just as important as technical skills.
—Paula Anthony, Tech support team leader

What is technical communication?

Technical communication refers to the activity of preparing and publishing specialized information in a way that allows non-specialists to understand and use the information to accomplish some task. While the information can be presented verbally in an oral presentation, a class, or even over the telephone, it most often takes a written or visual form. Here are some examples of technical communication:

- computer manuals (print versions and help screens)
- assembly instructions for appliances, equipment, furniture, toys, and games
- research articles that present scientific or technological discoveries
- magazine articles that explain how to complete a process— preparing yellow chicken curry or a dovetail joint
- training films that demonstrate a process
- instructions on how to register online or create an email account

In most cases, readers of technical communication come to the information to learn or to do something that otherwise they could not do. If effective, the technical communication should make it possible—and even easy—to comprehend the information and to act on it to perform the task. Technical documents generally share this main purpose: to inform.

How does it differ from other types of writing?

All writing takes place in a specific context, and all writing involves these elements: a writer/speaker, a message, and a reader/listener. Two of the main differences between technical communication and other types of communication are that 1) its subject matter usually requires some type of specialized knowledge and 2) it provides a bridge for

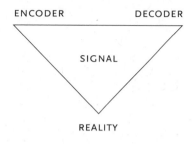

FIGURE 1.1
Kinneavy's communication triangle.

James L. Kinneavy, A Theory of
Discourse *(New York: Norton, 1971),
61. Reprinted with permission.*

the lay or non-specialist reader to complete an action successfully. It also incorporates visual elements where they help readers more easily accomplish the task. Some people call technical communication "instrumental" because it works as an instrument or tool for people to get something done.

Figure 1.1 shows one way to think about the relationship between writer, reader, and text in any kind of writing. In this diagram, reality forms a third point on the triangle, which shapes the relationship between the writer (encoder), the reader (decoder), and the text or document (signal). In technical communication, usually the text represents a version of reality that the writer has prepared for the reader. Different kinds of writing focus on different aspects of the communication triangle. For example, writing that focuses on the writer/speaker is called "expressive," and examples include personal letters, diaries, and journals. Writing that focuses on the reader/listener is called "persuasive," and examples include advertising and editorials in newspapers. Most technical and scientific writing focuses on "Reality," including textbooks and reports. Finally, writing that focuses on the text itself (the words) is called "Literary"; examples include the kinds of literature you study in English classes: poetry, fiction, and drama.

One aspect of the communication process that this triangle omits is context, which we might represent by drawing a rectangle around the triangle that also includes writer, reader, and reality. While context is important in any piece of writing, it is especially important in technical and professional communication because it affects how the reader or user understands and responds to the document. Ignoring the context can ensure that your writing is unsuccessful: for example, you create an instruction booklet for operating a chainsaw, and you bind it like a novel using ordinary paper. The operators' context for using this booklet will likely be outdoors with no place to set down the booklet or any way of keeping it open at the required page. A rectangular card, laminated in plastic, might be a more usable format for this booklet, one that recognizes the context in which the chainsaw operator will need and refer to your instructions.

FIGURE 1.2
Beale's model of communication.

*Note: This model is from Walter H.
Beale,* A Pragmatic Theory of Rhetoric
*(Carbondale: Southern Illinois UP, 1987),
114. Reprinted with permission.*

How does the communication triangle help you to think more about the writing situation for particular documents? The following exercise, in which you analyse the different aspects of some sample documents, will give you a chance to find out. Focus not only on aspects that make it easier to think about the different components of the communication situation but also on features of communication that the triangle does *not* give you a way to think about.

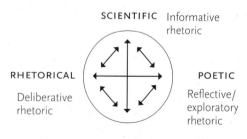

One of the problems with the communication triangle is that it makes it too easy to think that these different areas (writer, reader, text, and reality) are entirely separate—that, for example, newspaper reports are entirely about describing reality and not about trying to persuade you to adopt a particular position on the topic. The point is that rhetorical genres often—maybe always—overlap. A better way to show this overlapping is demonstrated in Figure 1.2.

You will notice right away that Beale's categories for writing are different than those in the communication triangle. Beale discusses the purpose or aim of different types of writing. The aim is to attempt to explain the type of relationship created between the writer, the reader, reality, and the text. For example, poetic writing (or discourse) relates primarily to the writer and has as its goal the writer's self-expression or self-exploration. The reader reads poetic discourse to explore the writer's personal vision. In contrast, writers of instrumental discourse seek to relate readers and reality: they provide information to help readers perform a particular action. This type of document becomes a tool to accomplish something. Writers of rhetorical discourse have as their goal the persuasion of readers—changing their minds about a particular issue or belief (or at least prompting them to consider the writer's viewpoint, however briefly). And finally, writers of scientific discourse seek to relate readers to reality in a different way than instrumental discourse by informing and educating them about complex technical ideas.

Notice the addition of the arrows to this diagram: they indicate that any particular piece of writing—a newspaper report, for example—can sometimes have dual aims. It may *inform* you about some event while also trying to *persuade* you to condemn or applaud those events. In fact, some people argue that it is impossible for a piece of writing to have only one function. This view raises the possibility that every piece of writing does double work. For example, as a consumer, when you compare the assembly instructions for two different brands of bookshelves, you may decide to buy the one that presents the process as easy and pleasant (a persuasive goal) as well as clearly showing you how to do it (the instrumental goal). The instructions may start with a paragraph that describes the innovative features of the bookshelf design (informational and persuasive goals), while also including a list of tools you need for the assembly (an informational goal). How many different types of goals can you identify in several different writing samples? The following exercise helps you think about the ways that a document can pursue different aims at the same time.

IN-CLASS EXERCISE 1.1

Applying the Communication Triangle to Sample Documents

Assemble a collection of print documents, some that are examples of technical communication and others that are examples of professional or business communication. For example, here is a selection of possible documents:

- the user's manual for an appliance such as a CD player
- a flier that arrived in your junk mail recently
- the installation guide that came with the mini-blinds (or other DIY product)
- a brochure that you picked up in the grocery store or the doctor's office
- a letter from a non-profit organization asking for donations
- the bill from your cell phone or land line

Now, analyze your collection of documents individually from the perspective of the communication triangle:

- Who is the writer?
- Who is the intended reader?
- What are the purposes of the document?
- What form does the document take?
- In what way does the content of the document represent reality?
- What characteristics do these documents share?
- What limitations do you see to the communication triangle as you seek to apply it to the selection of documents that you collected?

Analysing Documents with Multiple Aims

Assemble a second collection of documents that includes a broader range of sample documents: add a short story or poem, as well as a newspaper article; a magazine article; a set of instructions; a business letter or two; some advertising fliers or brochures; a scientific report, if you have one; a magazine or newspaper editorial; a business form, questionnaire, or bill. Study these different types of documents from the perspective of Beale's model, illustrated in Figure 1.2.

- What is the main purpose or aim (i.e., rhetorical, scientific, poetic, or instrumental) of the document?
- What kinds of secondary aims does it have?
- Which other categories might it also fit well into?
- How easy is it to assign a primary category to each document?
- What kinds of documents make it difficult to determine a primary aim or purpose?

Creative vs. technical writing

Many people who don't know much about technical communication beyond their experience as a user struggling with poorly written assembly instructions or a badly organized computer manual view technical communication as dull and uninspiring. When asked about it, they often contrast technical writing with creative or fiction writing. They think of the latter category as innovative, imaginative, and artistic, while they consider technical writing to be dry and unimaginative. And poorly done technical writing can be all of these negatives—and more. But effective technical communication can be innovative, imaginative, artistic—in a word: creative.

Often, technical writers get to use a product before anyone else, and they are challenged with the job of creating documentation that enables others to quickly and easily use this product. The writer decides on a useful format; figures out how best to illustrate the product, when visuals would be helpful; designs a page layout that will make the process or the product attractive and easy to use; and produces text that is clear, unambiguous, and easy to read. While producing such prose is not usually introspective, the way that journal or novel writing might be, it is still an intriguing and creative process, a process that will change people's lives in small but significant ways. When users understand the basics of how to use a machine or computer program, they can move towards greater skill and increased opportunities to expand those skills and take on new challenges. The technical writer becomes a partner in this process, helping users to develop and improve their knowledge and skill.

Who are these "users"?

In technical communication, it is much more accurate to think of your reader as a "user" rather than as the member of an audience. "Audience" is actually a metaphor, taken from theatre and referring to the multitude of people who sit in the seats to observe a performance. But audience is an inaccurate metaphor for technical communication because it implies an inactive relationship between the writer or performers and the reader or spectators: sure, the spectators may cheer, or boo, or laugh at the performance, but they do not interact with the script in the way that users of technical communication do. Users are active participants in the performance of the technical communication text: they are much closer to the actors' role than the audience's role because they make the writer's words come alive by using them to do something, instead of just passively taking in the information.

Another way in which users of technical communication differ from the audience for other types of writing is that writers of technical communication rarely write for a "general audience" or "general user." In fact, writing that directs itself to a "general audience" in technical communication is usually poor writing. It's poor because it assumes that everyone has the same level of knowledge about the subject matter, the same background and experience, the same attitude towards the information that they are learning, and so on. One way to visualize some of the critical differences between users of technical communication is to imagine yourself as a new employee for a roofing company. If you have never laid shingles before, then on your first day of work when a co-worker points out to you that the first layer of shingles must be laid backwards—that is, the un-notched edge is laid parallel to the edge of the roof—you will be relieved and grateful to hear this tip. However, after you have been working for this company for several months and you have participated in all aspects of roofing several dozen houses, such a "tip" will irritate or offend you because you already know how to lay the first row. While such basic information was essential for you to learn as a novice roofer, it is unnecessary and distracting to hear it when you have become an experienced roofer.

In fact, experienced or advanced users will often reject a set of instructions or manual that provides too much information that they already know: they tire of sifting through known material to find the things that they do not know. At the same time, first-time users of, for example, a software program may become frustrated and angry with instructions that omit the most basic steps—maybe, to hit the enter key after selecting a particular command. They may lack the experience to figure out this point, which is obvious to everyone who is not a first-time user. As you can see from these examples, the needs of users can vary widely.

The challenge for technical writers becomes how to learn what their users already know, what they need to know, and how to provide it for them where and when they need it. The first step becomes to learn about your users before you can begin to create effective documents for them.

WAYS OF THINKING ABOUT USERS

Before we consider specific users, here are some ways to think about how to group users. For example, if you are writing a users' guide on how to create cascading style sheets in Macromedia® Dreamweaver® software, think about who might open this guide and why? Obviously, anyone who owns a copy of Dreamweaver and who wants to create a cascading style sheet would use this guide. And this kind of person could very likely be your PRIMARY AUDIENCE—that is, the group of users that you hope will choose your guide and use it to successfully create the style sheet. Your primary audience is the major group of users who will receive your message, in this case, follow your instructions. In using your instructions to successfully create the style sheet, they will fulfil your purpose in creating the guide—to show users with some prior knowledge of Dreamweaver how to use this more advanced function.

But is this the only group who may open your guide? In fact, there are other clusters of users who may also consult your guide. For example, consider users who have created dozens of style sheets in Dreamweaver in the past, but who have not used the program in several months: they might open your guide to refresh their memories on how to get started. They may not actually follow step-by-step through your instructions. Instead they will skim through them, filling in the details that they have forgotten. This type of user, in this case, experts, will form a SECONDARY AUDIENCE for the guide when they use it as a reference rather than a how-to. This is a second group of users, those who have a different level of knowledge and experience than your primary users, but who may also consult your guide.

There are three other groups that may also use or affect the use of your guide. When you are first assigned to work on a project, your boss or instructor becomes an INITIAL AUDIENCE, that is, the individual who will review and approve your efforts on the project, in this way affecting whether or not your document ever reaches your primary audience. Another group that can affect whether your project ever reaches its primary user is the GATEKEEPER AUDIENCE. This individual is often a supervisor higher up in the organization who will give final approval on your guide, that is, make the decision about whether it will be published. The gatekeeper audience might give you feedback about ways that your guide needs to contribute to the organization's image, resulting in revisions to its style or arrangement. This supervisor may shape the document without ever using it or learning the process that you are teaching.

A fifth group that might also affect your document is known as a WATCHDOG AUDIENCE. The watchdog audience might be a government or regulatory organization that is unconnected with you directly but that reviews and comments on the products that your organization creates. This type of audience may or may not have the power to prevent your guide from being published, but its members' comments evaluating your work may affect the reputation of your employer. For example, if your guide fits its target audience well, then reviewers might post glowing reviews about your guide on amazon.com or indigo.ca, resulting in dramatic increases in sales, and attention and imitation from other technical writers. This watchdog audience might propel your guide to the new industry standard through its evaluation and approval.

Write a paragraph or two describing the different groups that might view your résumé and list two or three goals that these groups might have in viewing your résumé. Assess how important you think each group might be in deciding whether to invite you for an interview. Describe how you might revise your résumé to make the information more accessible that each group might want.

While you may have to negotiate through the initial and gatekeeper audiences as you develop your guide, the main group that will shape its details and organization will be your primary users. Their background knowledge and expertise will drive your design decisions and the level of detail that you provide in your instructions. The big question then becomes, "How do I learn what I need to know about my primary users?"

How do you learn about your users?

There are several strategies that you can use to start to learn about the group of users for whom you intend to develop your technical document:

- Take an inventory of what you do know about your target user group
- Create a profile of the characteristics that distinguish your target user from other types of users
- Interview individuals who fit into your user profile
- Observe individuals who fit your profile using similar types of documents
- Analyse earlier versions of the document to assess how the user was characterized there to note changes, useful strategies, and mismatches with your profile

Of these strategies, some are more accurate and valuable than others: interviewing members of your target user group is generally the most valuable because you can ask questions and receive feedback that is valid; you can test your assumptions about your users' preferences, approaches, and understanding. Taking an inventory about what you already know about your users can be reliable or not, depending upon your previous experience and knowledge of this group. If you have already conducted interviews and observations of representative members of your user group for an earlier version or similar type of document, then your inventory will likely be most reliable.

On the other hand, if you have a vague idea of your users, and you consult your own preferences and experience as representative of your users in order to project what they may be like, your profile could be wildly inaccurate. Similarly, relying too heavily on the user profile assumed in earlier versions of a document could also miss your mark because the earlier writer neglected to build an accurate portrait of the knowledge, experience, and needs of the primary users or because the product or process you are describing has become much more familiar, over time, to the general public.

To build an inventory of the characteristics that you know about your primary audience, consider such factors as:

- Level of experience with the subject matter of your document
- Educational background, both generally and specifically in subjects related to your topic
- Experience with and attitude toward learning new things
- Experience with and attitude toward technology generally and your topic specifically
- Relevant demographic characteristics such as age, sex, race, socio-economic background or class, culture, and first language.

If you do not have information about many of the points above, then you will need to do some research to find out where your primary users will fall in the spectrum of these different factors.

INTERVIEW USERS

One method of research is to conduct interviews with some representative users to find out about their attitudes and levels of expertise. You might also take advantage of this opportunity to gather information about their preferences regarding the design and arrangement of instructional information that will be useful to you when you get to the design stage of your project. For example, if they are accessing online help, do they like to have a screen shot illustrating the written instructions or do they become impatient waiting for the image to load? Would they find it more helpful to be able to access a screen shot if they need more information but otherwise have just the text appear in the help screen? For detailed information about successful interviewing, please see Chapter 3, "Researching technical subjects."

OBSERVE USERS

Another way to gain valuable information about how your users actually use a technical document is to observe them in the course of their work as they use a similar product. This activity is similar to a usability test (discussed in detail in Chapter 9, "Testing and reporting document usability"), but the goal is to collect more general information about patterns of use of instructional (or other) types of document. For example, how carefully do users refer to the documentation (or do they refer to it at all)? Do they follow step by step from the beginning of the activity, or do they skim pages until they find the specific step or point that they need? If they don't even open the manual, you might follow up with questions about why they prefer experimenting over reading the manual. Their answers might help you design a better arrangement or presentation that helps them find the precise information that they need.

INTERVIEW EXPERTS

If you cannot gain access to representative users, then an alternative strategy is to talk to co-workers, fellow technical writers, or knowledgeable peers who do have expertise in this area and who are willing to share it with you. When interviewing them about their impressions, you can test your assumptions about your users against their knowledge and experience. While this option isn't as reliable as talking to actual primary users, it is definitely more effective than guessing.

CREATE USER PROFILES

When you have gathered your inventory of information about your users, use it to create user profiles. User profiles are concise sketches of specific individuals who share characteristics of your primary or target user group. Spend five or ten minutes generating a series of profiles of specific (invented) people who represent various viewpoints from your primary users. See Figure 1.3 for two profiles of potential users for the guide to creating style sheets discussed above.

Develop these profiles to help you think specifically about your users: to consider their attitudes, to see them as real people who will interact with the text and illustrations that you develop. When you are deciding on specific design or organizational choices for your project, you can make better decisions if you have a concrete idea of who will use this document.

Reaching your primary users

One way to identify useful strategies for reaching primary users is to look at what other writers have done. Through the choices they make in designing and organizing their information, they illustrate the assumptions they have made about the needs and interests of their users. The following exercise will give you a chance to look at the ways in which several web designers have adapted their information to what they perceive as the needs of their target users. As you explore the different websites, think about which strategies might be useful in your writing.

WHY ARE YOU WRITING?

Another essential component of the writing situation besides audience is purpose or aim: what do you hope to achieve through cre-

---

IN-CLASS EXERCISE 1.4

Write a User Profile

Write a user profile of yourself as a reader of this chapter. Include whatever demographics you think are relevant, as well as personal characteristics that affect your reading and reception of the information in this chapter.

SAMPLE PROFILES

Gina – 45-year-old administrative assistant, BA in history in 1982; self-taught software programs including Word, PowerPoint, and Excel; makes minor changes to department's web pages on Internet to update announcements, etc.; basic user of Dreamweaver but eager to learn more. Ambitious and not afraid of technology.

Karl – 27-year-old financial analyst, MBA in 2002; proficient user of various web-based software; owns a small consulting firm supported by website; paid consultant to develop website for him two years ago, but now needs to update it; wants to do this himself. Novice user of Dreamweaver; concerned about whether he can make the changes that he needs to by himself.

FIGURE 1.3
Sample user profiles

ating the document that you are writing? You may have one main purpose or several important goals that you want your user to understand after reading your document. For example, in a memo to co-workers, you might want them to learn that they have one month to review their benefits selections and make any changes they want. The goal of your memo will be fourfold:

    1. to get them to read your memo and understand it;

LAB ASSIGNMENT 1.1

CHARACTERIZING YOUR USERS

Choose your own favourite website plus two of the websites listed below, and explore these sites. Using the questions that follow, try to figure out what assumptions the content developers are making about their users' needs. See if you can develop a profile of the type of user that each of the websites addresses through its content and presentation.

    a. http://nsr.mij.mrs.org
    b. http://www.useit.com
    c. http://www.marijuana.org
    d. http://www.guinness.ie
    e. http://whitehouse.gov/kids
    f. http://www.royal.gov.uk

Generating ideas for your profile
- Who is visiting this website?
- What special characteristics do they have?
- What is their background in the subject matter?
- What attitude toward or level of interest do the site designers assume the user has in the subject?
- Why do you think users will come to this website?
- What tasks might users perform based on the information in this website?
- What legal issues are there regarding this subject matter that the website designers had to address?
- Is the content of the website directed at a cross-cultural audience? How can you tell?
- What level of technical knowledge does the website assume in the reader/user? How can you tell?

Creating a user profile for each website
Write a paragraph or two about each website in which you create a description of the target users implied in the answers to these questions. Try to include as many different topics as you can to help yourself think about ways in which the users may be different or similar.

Strategies for reaching target users
Now compare the general descriptions using these questions to get started:

- Based on your analysis of these websites, what are four or five ways that users may differ from one another?
- How do these differences affect the kind of information that is included in the writing prepared for them?
- How do these differences affect the visual presentation of the information?

2. to persuade them to review the attached booklet (or visit the informational web page) that outlines their possible choices;
3. to motivate them to visit the website (or review the attached form) and make any changes they want; and
4. to do all this before the deadline (e.g., March 31).

If you review these four goals again, you will notice that persuasion and motivation figure centrally in your purpose for writing the memo. If your readers are uninterested in the subject of your communication or they consider themselves too busy to devote time to this activity right now (as they try to hit an important project deadline), they may put the memo aside with a casual glance or without even looking at it. So one of the rhetorical challenges of your writing assignment is to get readers to pay attention to your message; another rhetorical challenge will be to encourage them to take a moment to think about their benefits and then review and make changes to their current selections.

Perhaps you are preparing a report for a client after inspecting the home upon which they have made an offer, conditional to you certifying that it has no major structural flaws. Because the inspection took several hours and you are charging the client several hundred dollars for the report, you want the report to be long enough to reflect both the cost of the inspection and the care with which you conducted it. Therefore, one of your purposes in writing the report is to demonstrate that you did inspect every inch of the property carefully. Another purpose is to show that you have identified any possible problems that they will need to fix. A third purpose is to inform the potential home-owner of where the problems lie so that he or she can decide whether to remove the condition or withdraw the offer. Finally, you want your client to be satisfied that the cost of your inspection was a worthwhile expenditure.

To achieve these purposes, you will likely write a report of at least 100 pages in which you transcribe the notes that you took during the inspection into a coherent description of the current condition of all major systems in the house, as well as the drainage features of the landscaping around the house and in the yard. Much of this text will be boilerplate—that is, text written previously that can be adapted with minor changes to the current inspection. But sections of it you will write specially, giving details about the client's house. For example, you will emphasize the fact that some areas of the roof have been patched with roofing cement, that some shingles are curling a bit on the south slope, and that you recommend they replace the roof within the next two or three years.

Clearly, the writer's reasons for composing a particular document are often complex and multiple. One goal that often characterizes technical documentation is education, its primary purpose being to instruct the reader or user. After all, that is why many of us consult instructions or user manuals—to help us figure out how to operate a new appliance or use a software program. And while the goal of instruction may be primary, most texts will also have secondary goals that the writer is hoping to achieve: to inform, to satisfy, to please, to persuade, and so on.

Kitty O. Locker has noted that all business communication also has the partial purpose of building goodwill—that is, the writer hopes to establish with the reader a sense of cordiality with the writer's organization. This is also true of technical communication in that the documents created to support technological developments also foster good or ill feeling in the target user groups. Technical documents that instruct users quickly and painlessly in how to accomplish the tasks available using the associated product can only foster goodwill, increasing users' desires to try the company's other products based on the positive experience with this one. Unfortunately, building goodwill has not always been recognized as an important component of effective technical communication, with the result that many people view instructions and manuals as difficult or even impossible to follow.

What is genre?

Examine the document in Figure 1.4 below. What kind of document is this? If you recognized it as a set of instructions, you already know one of the major genres of technical communication. Of course, there are others.

If you brainstorm a list of characteristics that make this document distinctive, you will likely notice the headings that group various kinds of information (e.g., ingredients, steps for preparing), the numbers or steps in a process, and the single action in each numbered step. These characteristics are the conventions of a well-written set of instructions. Of course, you can probably think of a number of instructional sets that you've tried to use that lack some of these conventions; likely they were also challenging or frustrating to try to follow.

Some documents that you write as a technical communicator are exclusively technical (e.g., an operational manual or a technical report), while others include genres from business or professional writing (e.g., proposals, letters, and memos). Although the word "genre" was originally viewed as a descriptive term classifying documents into neutral groups such as résumé, technical report, or user manual, more focus on the term has led to a more accurate and perceptive definition. In *Genre and the Invention of the Writer*, Anis

LAB ASSIGNMENT 1.2

LINKING PURPOSE AND AUDIENCE

Select a document that you've written recently (for example, a job application letter, a report, an essay, a letter, an email message), and reflect on the audience and purpose for this document. Then write several paragraphs answering the following questions:

- Who was your primary reader?
- Did you consider other possible readers? Who were they?
- What did you know about the primary and other readers when you began writing?
- Were you aware of one primary purpose or goal that you were trying to reach with this writing?
- What other goals do you see that you also had in drafting this document?
- What rhetorical or writing strategies did you use to achieve your goals for writing?
- Can you think of other strategies that you might have used to be even more successful in reaching your goals?

Bawarshi defines genre as "typified rhetorical strategies communicants use to recognize, organize, and act in all kinds of situations."[1] This definition underscores the characteristics of genre: the structural and rhetorical conventions (i.e., "typified ... strategies"), the organization and presentation of content, and the goals and function of the genre. Genres are used to accomplish actions, and, by selecting one genre over another, we convey specific information that immediately helps readers to understand the purpose of the document.

For example, if you mail an application letter and résumé in response to a job ad that appeared in the newspaper, the recipient of your application will immediately recognize both as employment application materials and place them with the others for consideration by the hiring personnel. The genre of job application documents invokes a typical format for each document and an expectation by both the sender and recipient. It requires particular activities on the part of the sender and the receiver. For example, the sender expects some acknowledgement that the application was received: ideally he or she would like to get a telephone call requesting an interview. The recipient expects that the package will showcase the sender's relevant skills and experience.

If you radically alter any of these documents, perhaps enclosing a poem instead of an application letter, you risk the recipient misunderstanding and misclassifying (or throwing away) your application materials. Unless the advertisement specifically invites innovative approaches to the application, this apparent ignorance or flouting of basic conventions is risky. You are unlikely to receive serious consideration for the position unless you follow the conventions and meet the expectations of the individuals who will make judgments about your suitability as a prospective employee.

1   Anis Bawarshi, *Genre and the Invention of the Writer* (Logan: Utah State University Press, 2003), 17.

MARINATED PORTOBELLO MUSHROOMS

marinade:

1 tbsp chopped fresh basil
1 tsp chopped fresh garlic
2 tsp balsamic vinegar
2 tbsp olive oil
Sprinkle of freshly ground pepper and salt

Other Ingredients:

Six Portobello mushrooms
Feta cheese (enough to put some on each mushroom)

to marinate mushrooms:

1. Mix marinade at least two hours ahead.
2. Pour half of marinade into a large, flat dish (or a plastic bag).
3. Place mushrooms smooth side down on top of marinade.
4. Drizzle rest of marinade on top of mushrooms.
5. Refrigerate until needed.

to cook mushrooms:

1. On a pre-heated barbecue (or on a broiler), grill mushrooms for about 3 minutes on each side.
2. Baste with marinade.
3. Turn stem side up.
4. Fill each cap with feta cheese to taste.
5. Cook for another 3 minutes.
6. Serve hot.

FIGURE 1.4
Example of the genre of instructions

WHAT ARE THE MAIN GENRES OF TECHNICAL COMMUNICATION?

Technical writers expect to produce at least some of the following genres:

- Procedures or instructions
- Manuals
- Reports on technical subject matter
- Specifications
- Proposals
- Letters
- Memos
- Oral presentations

Of this list, the last four genres are broader than just technical communication: they are the primary genres of business and professional writing, and they are the main building blocks for conducting business.

WHY DOES GENRE MATTER?

To be considered an educated and experienced professional in your field, you need to know about and be able to produce the principle genres of your field. If you understand the conventions of the genres that you need to write and you have mastered the ability to meet those conventions effectively, then you will be considered a "good" (and maybe even the best) writer of technical communication. Once you understand and can use the conventions of a genre, you can focus on the writing itself, making the content and presentation as effective as possible. Understanding the basic generic conventions of how to structure instructions helps you to focus on the process of creating the text. Some important purposes of this text are to introduce you to the requirements of the basic genres of technical communication, to provide opportunities for you to practice these genres, and to build up a portfolio of samples of your best work that will help you to demonstrate your skills and abilities in this area so that you can develop your career options in the area of writing professionally.

WHAT ARE GENRE SETS?

"Genre sets" refers to groups of documents that go together. For example, if a software development firm publishes a request for proposal (RFP) to document a new program that their engineers have developed, you may respond to their request with a proposal outlining your technical communication consulting business's plan to create the reference and operations manuals for the project. The RFP, the proposals that are written in response, and the documents that are created as a solution to the problem outlined in the RFP all make up a "genre set." Similarly, when you responded to the job advertisement with your application letter and résumé, you were creating another genre set. In other words, one initial document will set in motion the need for other documents to be created in response. It is the interrelation of these different documents that serves to transact some types of business in the writing professions.

HOW ARE THE DOCUMENTS IN GENRE SETS
INTERDEPENDENT?

Let's look at an example of a genre set that you may already be familiar with: the job advertisement, the application or cover letter, and the résumé. Unless you are writing an unsolicited or prospecting letter of application looking for employment, your application materials are usually prompted by an advertisement, published on a website or in a newspaper. The details of the advertisement are what prompt you to respond to it, because your qualifications match well with the needs expressed in the ad or because you would like to move into a related field of expertise or perhaps because the position represents a promotion from the skills that you are using in your current job.

Examine the advertisement for a horticulture assistant reproduced in Figure 1.5. This example is typical and includes information on the job title, the location, the duration (if not full-time permanent), a description of the position, the qualifications, and the contact information. If the job seeker likes the sound of the job description and sees a match between the major qualifications listed and his or her experience and abilities, then you know what happens next: he or she will send an application. Note the italicized text in the qualifications section. These are the major qualifications required for the position: excellent communication and interpersonal skills; diplomacy and tact; sound judgment, reasoning, and analytical skills; minimum supervision on individual and team initiatives; organization and recordkeeping skills; experience or background in food safety, hor-

---

JOB DESCRIPTION

POSITION: Horticulture Assistant, Food Industry Division
DURATION: May to September (approx. 18 weeks)
LOCATION: Stratford

The Ontario Ministry of Agriculture and Food, Food Industry Division, is currently seeking enthusiastic summer staff to assist with the delivery of programmes related to food safety for foods of plant origin. Successful candidates will collect samples of produce (including maple syrup and honey), conduct surveys, gather information and participate in food safety and regulatory projects under the general direction of our professional staff. If you wish to develop skills and knowledge related to the horticulture industry and food safety and have a valid driver's license, then this is the job for you!

QUALIFICATIONS:

- Excellent *communication and interpersonal skills* to work with a broad range of ministry clientele;
- Well-developed *diplomacy and tact*;
- Sound *judgment, reasoning, and analytical skills*;
- Ability to work with *minimum supervision* both on *individual and team* initiatives;
- Excellent *organization and recordkeeping skills*;
- Regulatory experience or a *background in food safety, horticulture, or a related* discipline would be an *asset*;
- Computer skills should include software programs related to *word processing, spreadsheets, and email*;
- Must have a *valid Class G driver's license* as extensive travel is required for this position.

Mail résumés and cover letters to Lindsay Meyer, Administrative Services Rep, Food Industry Division, 5th Floor, 1 Queen St.,
Guelph, ON N1H 4Y2

FIGURE 1.5
Job advertisement for a horticulture assistant.

ticulture, or related discipline; word processing, spreadsheets, and email; valid Class G driver's license.

Of these qualifications, note that background in food safety, horticulture, or a related field is "an asset" while a valid Class G driver's licence is "required." Calling the regulatory experience or background an **asset** means that having this prior experience gives you an edge over other applicants, but, even if you do not have this background, you will still be considered for the position. In contrast, stating that a valid Class G driver's licence is REQUIRED for the position means that NOT holding one disqualifies you from consideration. If you understand the conventions of phrasing job qualifications, you recognize the distinctions being made in this ad between credentials that are "nice to have" and "absolutely must have." You also understand that applying to a position when you lack a required skill means that you may not be considered for the position at all.

WHAT ARE THE CONVENTIONS OF THE APPLICATION LETTER?

Examine the sample application or cover letter reproduced in Figure 1.6. There are two types of highlighting added to this sample: bold and italics. The bold type emphasizes the match between the job's described requirements and the applicant's credentials. The italics underlines the conventions of a cover letter including statements that 1) apply for the job; 2) state location of job ad; 3) summarize primary qualifications; 4) refer to enclosed résumé; and 5) give contact information. (In Figure 1.6, the numbers in brackets correspond to the numbers in this list of conventions. Note that Timbercroft provides specific detail in the second paragraph of the letter that develops the qualifications summarized in 3.) The letter also echoes specific phrases from the job ad to describe the previous work experience and job responsibilities to create a direct link between the language of the ad and the argument presented about the qualifications (italicized in both documents). One thing that this application letter does NOT do is indicate some knowledge of the organization. If Timbercroft had visited the website of the Ontario Ministry of Agriculture and Food, Food Industry Division, then she could have included a sentence or two about the responsibilities of this area and how her prior experience would help her contribute to meeting these responsibilities. This addition would strengthen the quality of her letter by showing some knowledge of what the Food Industry Division does.

WHAT ROLE DOES THE RÉSUMÉ PLAY IN THIS GENRE SET?

The third document required in this genre set is the résumé. Many word processing programs offer the option of using a template for

March 15, 20XX

Lindsay Meyer
Administrative Services Rep
Food Industry Division, 5th Floor
1 Stone Rd
Guelph, ON
N1H 4Y2

Dear Ms. Meyer:

I *am applying for the job*(1) as a Horticulture Assistant for the summer in Stratford, Ontario. I found out about this job from the *Jobmine site at the University of Waterloo.*(2) I believe that I am well qualified for this job based on my *background in science, my previous work experience, and my personality.*(3)

I am studying biochemistry at the University of Waterloo and am currently taking Applied Microbiology, a class that includes sections on **food and water regulation and safety**. My interest in this class prompted me to apply for this job. *As you will note from the enclosed résumé,*(4) I have been previously employed as a sales associate for Talbot's, an upscale women's clothing store with a wide range of clientele, and as a receptionist in an optometrist's office. Both of these jobs have required me to deal with a **huge range of people**, sometimes in difficult situations, while continuing to be **professional and represent the company or doctor well**. Out of these experiences, I have developed **good communication and interpersonal skills**, as well as the ability to **work with other people as a team**. Especially at the optometrist's office, I had to keep track of patients' files, letters to and from the doctors, booking appointments, and the inventory of glasses waiting to be picked up. All of these things required me to be **organized and keep good records**.

In addition, I have fairly extensive experience with the Microsoft Office Suite of **Word and Excel, and with a variety of web-based email services and programs**. I have been driving for three-and-a-half years; I have **my G licence** and a **clean driving record**. I am a mature and responsible person who is capable of working well **without supervision and in a variety of situations**.

To contact me, please either call or email me. I can be reached at either my *home phone number, 519-050-1234, or my cell phone number, 519-050-5678, or my email, ttimber2@mysite.com.*(5) Thank you for your consideration of my application, and I look forward to hearing from you to talk about the ways in which I can contribute as a horticultural assistant this summer.

Sincerely,

Toby Timbercroft

Toby Timbercroft

Encl: CV

FIGURE 1.6
Sample application
or cover letter.

professional documents. The templates offer several "fill-in-the-blank" forms for letters, memos, résumés, reports, and other genres. These templates are useful because they highlight the major conventions and categories of information presented in each of these genre types. They are also useful because they illustrate ways in which the format forces you to configure your past experience in particular ways, highlighting some and obscuring some.

Examine Figure 1.7. It uses the "elegant résumé" template from Microsoft Word®. Note how it emphasizes your name, placing it at the top and centre of the page in a large font size, while de-emphasizing your contact information, placing it at the bottom of the page in a small font size. The template includes as the first heading, "Objective," cueing the user to draft an objective as a required element of the résumé. The career objective is a brief description of the position that you would like to obtain. Note that it is NOT a complete sentence, nor does it use "I." In fact, career objectives (especially if you are a student searching for a summer job) are not essential and, when poorly written, can undermine your attempts to present your credentials.

The other major groupings cued by the template are experience, education, and interests. The experience section emphasizes the previous responsibilities and job titles that you've held, as well as enabling you to illustrate a continuous record of work. However, if you have not worked continuously, then the format of this type of résumé highlights this fact because it places the dates of work on a single line, as well as the job title and location. The reader need only scan the dates to note any gaps in your work history. At the same time, if you have a consistent work history and impressive job titles, the format of the résumé emphasizes these facts as well. Note also that the work is listed in reverse chronological order—that is, your most recent experience appears first, moving backwards through history. If you compare the template in Figure 1.7 with the other choices—e.g., "contemporary résumé" and "professional résumé" in Microsoft Word®—you will see that the elegant format *somewhat* de-emphasizes the dates of employment, placing them in the left column of a three-column table that highlights the place and location of the job and "burying" the dates in a block of text. They still stand out in this format but not as much as in some of the other templates, which place the dates in their own column, surrounded by white space.

Note also that in the job descriptions, the résumé uses sentence fragments and bullet points to highlight your main responsibilities for that position. It is bad form—and creates a poor impression—if you use complete sentences and paragraphs describing your responsibilities.

The next section, "Education," discusses your academic history. The convention of the résumé is also to list this history in reverse

TOBY TIMBERCROFT

OBJECTIVE

To obtain a full-time summer position that allows me to apply my knowledge of science to solving practical science problems.

EXPERIENCE

Receptionist

June XX–August XX   *Dr. Molly Springbank, Optometrist*   *Burlington, ON*

- **Booked appointments**
- **Prepared patient files**
- **Rang up sales of contact lenses, glasses, and handled appointments (cash, credit, debit, cheque)**
- CHECKED PATIENTS' HEALTH CARDS
- ANSWERED THE PHONE

Sales Associate

October XX – May XX   *Talbot's Clothing Store*   *Oak Brook, IL*

- **Assisted customers in choosing merchandise**
- **Assisted with store security**
- **Rang up sales (cash, credit, debit, cheque, gift certificates)**
- SET UP AND STRAIGHTENED STORE DISPLAYS

EDUCATION

University of Waterloo

September 20XX –
Waterloo, Ontario

- WORKING TOWARDS A B.Sc., MAJOR: **Biochemistry**
- **Dean's List** FOR FALL 20XX
- EXPECTED GRADUATION: 20XX

Oak Park River Forest High School

20XX–20XX
Oak Park, Illinois

- HIGH SCHOOL DIPLOMA AWARDED
- HONOUR ROLL
- EDITOR OF SCHOOL'S LITERARY MAGAZINE, CREST
- ENGLISH DEPARTMENT AWARD (20XX)

INTERESTS

- HIGH LEVEL OF EXPERIENCE WITH **Word, Excel, email**, CASH REGISTERS, AND CALCULATORS
- FLUENT IN FRENCH AND ITALIAN

FAX 519-050-1234 ◎ ttimber2@mysite.com
7 Summit St. ◎ St. Agatha, Ontario ◎ N0B 2L0 ◎ 519-050-1234

FIGURE 1.7
Sample résumé template.

MAJOR PROJECT 1.1

THE JOB APPLICATION PACKAGE

Go online or look through the classified section of a newspaper to find an advertisement for a position for which you are currently qualified. Prepare an application package responding to this ad, consisting of an application letter and a copy of your résumé. Use your current qualifications to apply to this position—the point of this exercise is to help you make a strong case for your existing expertise and experience. You don't want to make up qualifications because it is always a good idea to be accurate and truthful in the information you present in this genre set. If you make up information or misrepresent yourself, you could find the interview most unpleasant; if these fabrications are uncovered after you obtain the job, you could well be fired.

If you wish to, you may use a word processing template for your résumé, but be aware that your reader may review hundreds of application packages for this (and other) positions, many of which will use the same template that you choose, so your résumé will not stand out, at least from a design perspective. You might review the discussion in Chapter 7, "Designing documents and page layout," to help you create a design for your résumé that will be professional *and* stand out from the rest.

As you create these two documents (the letter and résumé) pay close attention to the wording in the job ad, and try to shape your letter and your qualifications as they are represented in the résumé (and the letter) to respond to the information in the ad.

chronological order, listing first your most recent schooling or degree awarded. Once you complete an undergraduate degree, generally you omit your high school information as no longer relevant. Notice that the template privileges work experience by placing it first, but, for certain types of positions, you may want to put your education first, if it is most relevant.

The final section, "Interests," usually can include volunteer work, if you have done any, or special accomplishments or skills that justify giving them special mention. In the sample, Timbercroft has included the ability to speak two languages, as well as computer and related skills. Some individuals may include sports or hobbies that they enjoy. It does not, however, include personal information, such as your age, weight, height, marital status, or ethnic affiliation.

To summarize, the generic conventions of a résumé require you to provide a snapshot of particular types of experience that help to reveal aspects of your history. The résumé allows you to emphasize traditional types of employment or education that define you in a particular and traditional way. If your life has been fairly conventional, then you will find it easy to fill in the blanks of the template. It facilitates your self-presentation as an educated, experienced individual who can contribute to the needs expressed in the job advertisement.

However, if you have not led a conventional life, then the résumé becomes a more challenging genre to complete. It can highlight the ways in which your life has departed from "normal" and, at the same time, mark you as different. Some readers may find the differences intriguing; others may not. For example, if you were homeschooled, then that information will be emphasized in the "Education" section. It will be obvious if your employment history is non-existent or family-based. In other words, the framework of the genre of a résumé emphasizes two or three types of information to the near exclusion of others; on the positive side, it also organizes and presents in a clear and compressed way a great deal of information about you. The reader can quickly scan the lists to get a picture of some of your accomplishments and to decide whether he or she would like to speak to you in person. And this is one of the initial functions of a résumé: to get you a job interview.

As you can see from this analysis, the job ad, the letter, and the résumé all converse among themselves to provide a forum for you to display yourself to best advantage in showing how you can do the job.

CHAPTER TWO

Leading and misleading the reader
ethical issues of technical communication

Ethics may have been the last thing you thought you would encounter in a textbook on technical communication. After all, what have morals got to do with writing procedures? Well, it all depends on what the procedures are for. Steven Katz has reported on Nazi recommendation reports that explain how to improve the death vans used to exterminate Jews. As an employee, you might think encountering that kind of text, or agreeing to work on it, unlikely. However, at some point in your career, you may be asked or pressured to write something that is either less than wholly truthful or downright false. Or you may be asked to write about new ways to slaughter farm animals; if you are a vegetarian, that might present a problem for you since it asks you to help others to engage in behaviours that result in actions you disapprove of.

Ethics at work

"Whistleblowers" is the term given to people who not only refuse to go along with what they have been directed to do when they feel that those directions are wrong but also expose an ethical dilemma. Here are some examples:

- Allan Cutler reported on payments made to advertising companies for work that was never done to promote Canadian unity around the time Quebecers were voting to separate or stay within Canada.
- Mordechai Vanunu, a former nuclear technician at an Israeli nuclear facility, revealed to the British press that Israel had nuclear weapons.
- Bunny Greenhouse testified about the alleged overbilling by Haliburton Corp. to supply the US Army in the recent Iraqi war.

Learn more about the phenomenon of whistleblowing at this website: http://www.whistleblowers.org/.

The link between ethics and communication has been debated for a thousand years, beginning with Aristotle and his comments about the good character of the person speaking or writing and what they said about their topic. Quintilian, a Roman rhetorician, went so far as to say that only a good man (a virtuous, honest man) would be believable. However, recent history suggests instead that ethically-challenged individuals can be quite believable. The key here may be that they really believed what they wrote or said at the time they said it.

Ethics for students

Many large organizations create statements that reflect their values and offer guidelines for those who work for the organization, and sometimes even for those who work with them. For example, the University of Western Ontario offers the following student code of conduct:

> The University of Western Ontario is a community of students, faculty and support staff involved in learning, teaching, research, and other activities. The University seeks to provide an environment of free and creative inquiry within which critical thinking, humane values, and practical skills are cultivated and sustained. In order to foster and maintain this environment, all members of the University community are responsible for ensuring that their conduct does not jeopardize the good order and proper functioning of the academic and non-academic programmes and activities of the University or its faculties, schools or departments, nor endanger the health, safety, rights or property of the University or its members or visitors.
>
> *(Source: http://www.uwo.ca/univsec/board/code.pdf)*

This statement covers a lot of ground by using general terms such as "free and creative inquiry" and "good order and proper functioning" of all programmes offered by the university. One activity that would be headed off by this statement is the occupation of university offices by student protesters, something that did happen at some universities in the 1960s and 1970s.

While occupying the office of the president of your university may not be on your agenda, avoiding plagiarism should be. Most, if not all, universities have plagiarism policies to enforce academic honesty—ethics. It is important to the "proper functioning" of a university that those who study and work at it give credit to others for their contributions. All of us depend on the work of others to do our work; we read the books and articles that others have written in order to write our own essays and articles. Referencing systems help us locate relevant passages in texts others have written and make clear what are our own contributions to the academic conversation.

At university, much of the writing you will be asked to do will focus on you demonstrating what you know about a certain topic. One of the key functions of citation systems is to impress upon your readers that you know about (and have read) the important articles or books in the area you are studying. If you do not cite your sources, you lose the opportunity to impress your readers. More specifically, often there are differing positions within an area of study—conflicting positions, different "camps," differing theoretical approaches to gathering data. You can show that you understand that more than one approach will suffice and that you know what the approaches are through your references to these bodies of work. So references are not just ways to cover yourself from charges of plagiarism; they can also be ways to further impress your professors with what you know and the depth of your research.

Most discussions of plagiarism assume that students do it but aren't victims of it. As a writer, you should know that you hold copyright to your own work: your essays, reports, and manuals are works you have created. Consequently, you own the copyright to them. And while that may not seem like much in the context of writing a typical essay as a student, the documents you write in a technical communication course may very well hold value for others. Many students in our technical communication classes have written office procedure manuals for their workplaces, brochures, manuals for updating extensive websites they manage, procedures for running cross-generational housing complexes, and so on. These documents have real value to the organizations that the students created them for, and those students should have the rights to reproducing them should they have commercial value. Other students have published essays in magazines; while usually they sign away the copyright to those works, they should be aware of the value that these documents represent. As someone who is working to improve your writing skills, you should think ahead to creating a venue for your writing—perhaps a blog or a website. As the author of either of those kinds of publications, you are the copyright holder. You will want others to link to your site, but you will also want to prevent others from copying your work and using it on their site as if they had written it. As you become a better writer and seek a wider audience for your work, you become the person whose work is being used by others. Citation systems codify the established ways of using the work of others.

You can find all sorts of style guides that will tell you how to format references according to the Modern Language Association rules, the American Psychological Association (APA) rules, the University of Chicago Manual of Style (CMS), and the Council of Science Editors (CSE) style. Here are a few online sources:

APA	**Purdue University** http://owl.english.purdue.edu/handouts/research/r_apa.html	
	Long Island University http://www.liunet.edu/cwis/cwp/library/workshop/citapa.htm	
CMS	**University of Chicago Press** http://www.press.uchicago.edu/Misc/Chicago/cmosfaq/cmosfaq.html	
	Ohio State University Libraries http://library.osu.edu/sites/guides/chicagogd.html	
	University of Georgia Libraries http://www.libs.uga.edu/ref/chicago.html	
CSE	**University of North Carolina-Chapel Hill** http://www.lib.unc.edu/instruct/citations/cse/	
	Juniata College http://ia.juniata.edu/citation/cse/	
MLA	**Purdue University** http://owl.english.purdue.edu/handouts/research/r_mla.html	
	University of Wisconsin-Madison http://www.wisc.edu/writing/Handbook/DocMLA.html	

FIGURE 2.1
Websites where you can find more information about how to cite sources correctly, according to the documentation style chosen.

But in order to use these sources properly, you need to have made good notes while you were researching. That is, you need to have recorded:

- page numbers accurately,
- dates that you accessed a web page,
- quotations from the original sources accurately, and
- details of publication.

Without this information, you will not be able to write complete citations, and your readers will not be able to find the sources you send them to.

Providing a complete and properly formatted list of references is good, but even more important is working these references into your argument. If you can incorporate references into your writing through well-written summaries of the research you refer to, your writing will be judged to be superior. And if that isn't enough, it will also be a fair or ethical representation of the original article or text.

A good summary briefly (in a few sentences) communicates the gist of the original work to your readers. That is, you tell your readers what you think they should or need to know about the material written by someone else. Begin your summary by providing an overview of the original article, a fairly abstract or general statement of what it is about. Then write one or more specific statements that indicate what topic or statement within that general topic you think should be of interest to your reader. When you have explained in enough detail (this could be as little as a clause within a sentence or as much as several sentences or even a paragraph), provide a reference to the original article (the format will differ depending on which citation system you are using).

In the context of academic writing, this kind of citing and referencing is a basic building block of ethical work. You are immersed in a world of texts when you engage in higher education, and, to demonstrate that you belong, you need to refer to these texts and show you understand them. Doing this correctly proves your membership and establishes your credibility in the higher education community. For more information about citing and paraphrasing sources, see also Chapter 3, "Researching technical subjects."

How is ethics related to technical communication?

Technical communication changes the dynamic usually associated with plagiarism of essays and reports at school because technical communication fulfils a different function. The point of a technical document is not to show off what you know to an audience already familiar with what you are writing about. Instead, much technical communication aims to educate and inform readers about how to operate a piece of equipment or a software application. Instead of rehearsing already known facts, technical communication shows readers how to do things or how to understand things in a new way. As a result, the focus is less on demonstrating factual knowledge than it is on demonstrating the skilful use of ways of explaining or informing readers. Copying a paragraph from some other source doesn't answer the demands of the rhetorical situation of a good technical communication assignment: the level of knowledge of the reader is usually different from whatever source you might find, and so is the scope of what is being explained. The fact that much technical communication is done badly also makes it counter-productive to deliberately plagiarize.

Working technical writers, then, face ethical challenges that differ from typical academic contexts. One of these differences has to do with authorship. When a technical writer produces a report or manual for an organization, the organization owns the copyright to what is written. This text can then be "re-used" in other reports and manuals that the organization produces. This writing is sometimes referred to as "boilerplate" text or text that can be re-used in several documents. Much of the text in standard legal documents, such as wills, fits this description and use. So when you are writing documents that will come out under the corporation's name, the re-use of boiler-plate text does not fit under the category of plagiarism. However, technical writers face other ethical challenges.

One area of ethical choice involves how to give credit to others for work that is theirs. Copyright symbols, trademark symbols, and referencing systems (APA, MLA, and CMS) are some of the ways writers give credit to others. As a technical writer, you need to become familiar with the proper use of these symbols and referencing systems as a way to ensure that you do not appear to be taking credit for the work of others.

COPYRIGHT, TRADEMARKS, AND PATENTS

Copyright refers to the right to copy or otherwise reproduce original works yourself and the right to assign permission to make copies to others. This right applies to original works of literature, film, music, and art. Originality can be a hard concept to determine—think of re-mixes of old songs. Which part is original, and which part is new? Another difficult part of copyright is defining what a "substantial" part of it would be: one rule is that you can photocopy for reference one chapter of a book provided it amounts to less than 20 per cent of the book it was taken from. (Note that the right to "copy" less than 20 per cent of a book does not equal the right to re-use or reprint this text.)

You should label your own work with your (or your organization's) name, the year in which the work was first published, and the copyright symbol: ©. This labelling ensures your work will be protected in other countries that adhere to the Universal Copyright Convention, and where such a requirement is mandatory. Although this label is not obligatory in Canada (or the United States after 1989), the copyright symbol serves to remind others that the work is copyright protected. In this era of digital publication, you would be wise to adopt this as part of the standard way you create a document.

"Fair dealing" is the term used under the copyright laws of Canada to describe an exception to the small amount of a work that can be copied without seeking permission. Fair use includes making enlarged copies of print materials for visually challenged students. Non-profit educational institutions can make copies if the copies are used on campus for educational purposes. For a detailed description of many copyright issues, contact the Canadian Intellectual Property

Office (http://strategis.ic.gc.ca/sc_mrksv/cipo), or, for information concerning copyrighted materials and for licenses to reprint this material, consult the Canadian copyright licensing agency Access Copyright (http://www.accesscopyright.ca). Note, however, that many works are not available to be reproduced at a postsecondary educational institution in Canada, including:

■ unpublished works;
■ any materials intended for one-time use (such as workbooks);
■ commercial newsletters;
■ originals of artistic works (including photographs and prints);
■ print music, and;
■ works that are excluded. (Contact Access Copyright for further information or consult your licence.)

In the United States, copies can be made at non-profit educational institutions according to the Copyright Office's definition of fair use (http://www.copyright.gov/title17/92chap1.html#107). Despite these guidelines, the concept of fair use remains elastic. One person who used the name of an imaginary planet in a Star Wars™ movie was forced to surrender the web address to Lucasfilm or face a civil lawsuit from the company.[1] The website never had any copyrighted works on it; it was just that the name had been created as part of the series of films, and the company asserted that the name alone was something valuable that could be protected. Ironically, the name—Tatooine—was itself derived from a real city in Tunisia called Tataouine. If the creator of the website had used the real city's name, he could not have been sued. But protecting single words seems to be a new limitation on fair use. Trademarks refer to items that establish a brand: slogans, product names, packaging, and symbols. As a technical writer, you would probably encounter this in your references to existing trademarks held by your company or another company's products that work with your company's products; a reference to Microsoft Word® should have the trademark symbol affixed to it. Trademarks differ from patents in that they are not registered.

Patents refer to inventions such as new manufacturing products and processes. Usually, you would encounter them only by referring to them in texts that you write. Recently, some companies have patented human genetic sequences that they alter.[2] DEKALB® is a new type of corn developed by Monsanto, for example, and you should refer to it using the registered trademark symbol.

1 Anne Broache, "Free speech under Net attack, study says," *CNET News*, December 5, 2005, http://news.com.com/2100-1030_3-5983072.html

2 Human Genome Product Information, "Genetics and Patenting," U.S. Department of Energy Office of Science, Office of Biological and Environmental Research, http://www.ornl.gov/sci/techresources/Human_Genome/elsi/patents.shtml#2 (accessed Nov. 16, 2005).

WHAT IS NOT COPYRIGHTABLE

While the actual text of an article, novel, manual, or website is copyrightable, in Canada, some aspects may not be. For example, copyright does not apply to the following:

Titles for a song, slogans	"Rockin' in the Free World"
The idea for a plot	Woman elected president or prime minister
A work in the public domain	Hamlet
The facts in the article	Barrick Gold was up $1.06 to $31.26
The name of the program (However, this might be protected through a trademark registration.)	Microsoft Word™

FIGURE 2.2
Examples of items that cannot be copyrighted.

Source: Canadian Intellectual Property Office, "When Copyright does not apply," http://strategis.ic.gc.ca/ sc_mrksv/cipo/cp/copy_gd_protect- e.html#4 (accessed Nov. 16 2005).

RULES FOR COPYING IMAGES

Images add much to your work as a technical writer, but you may not have the time to create images or take photographs for the publications you produce. For many people, the web provides a tempting source of images because they can quickly select, right click and "Save As" to grab an image from someone else's web page. But remember that unless you have paid a fee to the photographer who took the photograph or the artist who created the image you want to use, you do not have permission to copy that visual.[3] If you lack a budget to pay for artwork, a better way to find appropriate images is to search for royalty-free images. A good place to start is Freeimages. com, a website that links to other sites with free photographs and clipart. If you are using Microsoft Office™ products, make use of the extensive collection of images available on your desktop or through links to Microsoft's website.

If your technical communication project has a budget, spend some of it to pay someone to create appropriate visuals or purchase some ready-made illustrations for your documents. As a student, however, it is unlikely that you have a budget. There are some ways to generate photographs fairly cheaply: consider buying a disposable camera and having the film developed onto a CD rather than prints. Enquire at the audio-visual office at your institution or organization about borrowing digital cameras. If you are documenting software procedures, use the "Print Screen" button on the keyboard to create pictures of what each screen will look like (For more information on how to create screen shots, see Chapter 8, "Writing how-to documents."). All of these techniques are free from copyright restrictions. But remember:

3   Canadian Intellectual Property Office, "Photographs," *Copyright Circulars* 11 (July 1, 1998), http:// strategis.gc.ca/sc_mrksv/cipo/cp/cp_ circ_11-e.html (accessed December 2, 2005).

if you took photographs to include in a brochure or newsletter for the company you work for, those photographs are owned by the company, not you.

Writing ethically

While it may seem obvious that what you write should be accurate and true, in practice there is considerable leeway between what may be factually correct and how you represent the facts in the documents you create. How many times have you read or heard references to the "spin" various political handlers put on a candidate's or politician's remarks? How often do you read headlines like these?

- "'Toxic attitude' poisons relations with U.S.: Envoy: 'Rhetoric not helpful,' Wilkins says" (*Ottawa Citizen*, Nov. 15, 2005, A1)
- "Martin draws a line on guns: PM heats up rhetoric on American policies" (*Toronto Star*, Oct. 25, 2005, A01)
- "Old rhetoric won't extinguish flames of riot in France" (*Morning Call* [Pennsylvania], Nov. 9, 2005, A13)

Each headline refers to *rhetoric* as a way of framing the topic that is being talked about. In each case, the authors take the position that this framing or way of talking about the issue will not result in progress towards a resolution of the problem under discussion.

As a technical communication student, you will have to make choices about how you want to frame the topics you write about. While the results are unlikely to be as loaded as the headlines quoted above, you will, nevertheless, decide on at least one main factor: how clear do you want to be in your writing?

Many people take it as a given that all writers should strive for clarity in everything that they write, and, at first glance, this would seem to be self-evident—when would you not want to be clear? It turns out, however, that there are many legitimate situations in which you would not want to be clear: bad news, for example, should usually be delivered after a buffer statement of some kind. It would be cruel to simply walk up to someone and announce that he or she was fired or failed a test or tell that a family member had died. On a résumé, you may not want to be clear about employment history if there is a gap in your employment record that would make you a less desirable candidate. In addition to these sorts of situations, many organizations often use language to hide the truth of a situation. They write in a deliberately vague way, use euphemisms, and organize information so that key components are buried deep within the fine print of a document. Plain language laws and initiatives came about as a solution to this kind of strategically unclear language use.

Pennsylvania's "Plain Language Consumer Contract Act" explains the need for plain language this way: "The General Assembly finds that many consumer contracts are written, arranged and designed in a way that makes them hard for consumers to understand. Competition would be aided if these contracts were easier to understand ... This act will protect consumers from making contracts that they do not understand. It will help consumers to know better their rights and duties under those contracts."[4]

Plain language definitions vary, but the essence of plain language is directness: write short sentences using specific, uncomplicated terms that your readers can understand quickly. This definition applies as much to government publications, legal writing, and scientific writing as it does to technical communication. Of course, sometimes trying to simplify language can create problems as in the examples in Figure 2.3.

4   Plain Language Consumer Contract Act (June 23, 1993), *P.S.* § 2202, http://members.aol.com/StatutesPA/73.Cp.37.html (accessed Dec. 13, 2005).

- SEEN DURING A CONFERENCE: FOR ANYONE WHO HAS CHILDREN AND DOESN'T KNOW IT, THERE IS A DAY CARE ON THE FIRST FLOOR.

- IN A LAUNDROMAT: AUTOMATIC WASHING MACHINES. PLEASE REMOVE ALL YOUR CLOTHES WHEN THE LIGHT GOES OUT.

- IN A DEPARTMENT STORE: BARGAIN BASEMENT UPSTAIRS.

FIGURE 2.3
Examples of simple but inaccurate communication

However, there are obvious differences between language that is inadvertently suggestive as in Figure 2.3 and language that seeks to confuse or discourage readers from understanding or asking questions. For example, Figure 2.4 presents some examples of phrases that are not direct and clear, together with their translations.

FIGURE 2.4
Before and after plain language

* *Management Working Group of the Interagency Committee on Government Information (ICGI), "Public Health Service, [US] Department of Health and Human Services, Brochure," Plain Language, http://www.plainlanguage.gov/examples/before_after/pub_hhs_losewgt.cfm, (accessed December 14, 2005).*

Before	Revised
Right of use means any authorization to use Outer Continental Shelf lands issued under this part.	Right of use means any authorization issued under this part that allows use of Outer Continental Shelf lands.
The Dietary Guidelines for Americans recommends a half hour or more of moderate physical activity on most days, preferably every day. The activity can include brisk walking, calisthenics, home care, gardening, moderate sports exercise, and dancing.	Do at least 30 minutes of exercise, like brisk walking, most days of the week.*

PLAIN LANGUAGE GUIDELINES

At its heart, plain language involves an ethical relationship between the reader and writer. As a writer, you must want to communicate with your readers clearly. To do this, you will take up their point of view and write what has been called "reader-based prose" or prose that is organized around what the reader needs to know. Rather than writing down everything you know about a topic to show off your knowledge or in the faint hope that readers will be able to sort through your text to find what they are looking for, you will take some time to investigate who is reading your work:

- What level of knowledge do they have?
- What is their cultural background?
- What is their income level?
- What do they want to know?
- What information will they use most frequently?
- What questions are they asking about the topic you are writing about?

Asking and answering these kinds of questions demonstrates your concern and consideration for your readers. The information you generate from this exercise will help you make decisions about how to organize your document and what kinds of vocabulary to use. See both Chapter 1, "Thinking about audience, purpose, and genre," and Chapter 9, "Testing and reporting document usability," for more information and specific guidelines for learning more about your readers.

Once you have gathered some data about your readers, you will be able to make decisions about how to organize that data in ways that respond to their concerns. One popular and effective way to organize information is through a series of questions with answers. If you've researched your readers' needs well, you can organize your document around the questions you know readers will have. Document design can also affect how easily your readers can find information; see Chapter 5, "Designing documents and page layout," for details about how to do this well. And, of course, how you write can make a huge difference in how easily your readers can understand your writing. The table below outlines some strategies that plain language advocates suggest you try. In addition, Chapter 4, "Writing technical prose," goes into more detail on writing style. Finally, use visuals according to standard practices so that your readers can tell if there are gaps in data. Chapter 4 goes into more detail on that subject.

Organization	Website Address
Copyright Central (includes links to works in French)	http://www.copyrightcentral.ca/
Access Copyright	http://www.accesscopyright.ca/home.asp
Canadian Intellectual Property Office	http://strategis.ic.gc.ca/sc_mrksv/cipo/welcome/welcom-e.html
United States Copyright Office	http://www.copyright.gov/
Copyright and Fair Use, Stanford University Libraries	http://fairuse.stanford.edu/
Copyright Society of the USA	http://www.csusa.org/
Plain Language	http://www.plainlanguage.gov/
Plain Language Commission (UK)	http://www.clearest.co.uk/

FIGURE 2.5
Resources on copyright, fair use, and plain language

Ten tips to make your writing easier to read	
At the word level	1. Use words that are accurate, appropriate, and familiar.
	2. Use technical jargon sparingly; eliminate business jargon altogether.
	3. Use active verbs most of the time.
	4. Use strong verbs (not nouns) to carry the weight of your sentence.
At the sentence level	5. Tighten your writing (eliminate unnecessary words).
	6. Vary sentence length and sentence structure.
	7. Use parallel structure.
	8. Put your readers in your sentences.
	9. Begin most paragraphs with topic sentences.
	10. Use transitions to link ideas.

FIGURE 2.6
Ten tips to make your writing easier to read

Using visuals ethically to communicate effectively

Using visuals effectively is an important component of technical communication. Perhaps you've heard the old saying "a picture is worth a thousand words"; in technical communication, a good picture can *replace* a thousand words of explanation. In fact, instructional material generally needs visuals to provide a clear and efficient means of learning the process. A visual included at just the right moment can make a lengthy description become crystal clear.

At the same time, visuals can serve to mislead or confuse readers and users, sometimes inadvertently and sometimes intentionally. For example, endless analysis and debate among engineers, technical communicators, and US government inspectors following the explosion of the space shuttle Challenger in 1986 worked to pinpoint the reasons that the decision makers misunderstood the risk involved in launching the craft during freezing temperatures. Some explanations suggest that the memo that documented the risk information was poorly written; others point to inadequate visuals that obscured rather than clarified the key information. Either way, the engineers who were aware of the risks failed to clearly communicate this risk to the administrators who made the decision to launch the shuttle in less-than-favourable weather conditions. Below-zero temperatures froze the O-rings, so they did not seal the fuel lines properly, resulting in fuel igniting during take-off and the resulting explosion and destruction of the spacecraft and crew.

In *Visual Explanations*, graphic artist and researcher Edward Tufte notes that "the [Challenger] rocket engineers and managers needed a quick, smart *analysis* of evidence about the threat of cold to the O-rings, as well as an effective *presentation* of evidence in order to convince NASA officials not to launch."[5] He argues that, while the engineers presented the data in a series of charts, their presentation was ineffective and failed to communicate the key points to the NASA officials. In his book, Tufte reproduces the original charts, points out the areas where the charts were deficient, and argues "had the correct scatterplot or data table been constructed, no one would have dared to risk the Challenger in such cold weather," attributing the ultimate cause as being the ineffective presentation of the evidence against launching the spacecraft.[6]

In his analysis of the problems with the engineers' charts, Tufte highlights the following point about creating visuals: "*there are right ways and wrong ways to show data; there are displays that reveal the truth and displays that do not.*"[7] As the Challenger explosion demonstrated, in technical communication, data displays that do not reveal the truth can result in devastating consequences.

IN-CLASS EXERCISE 2.1

Revising for Plain Language #1

Rewrite the following sentences to make the point clearer and more concise:

1. If the consultant delivers the manual late, the company may cancel the contract.

2. Please leave a voicemail message regarding your absence as soon as possible.

3. Return-on-investment could be calculated for proposed repairs more quickly.

4. This report recommends that the office purchase the new equipment as soon as possible, staff training can begin as soon as the equipment is installed, and every employee should get regular refresher training as new versions of the program come out.

5. Please sign and date the form and send it back to me in the envelope provided at your earliest convenience.

---

5   Edward Tufte, *Visual Explanations* (Cheshire, CT: Graphics Press, 1997), 40.

6   Tufte, *Visual Explanations*, 52.

7   Tufte, *Visual Explanations*, 45 (italics in original).

Revising for Plain Language #2

Revise these paragraphs to make them express the ideas more clearly and plainly. Your readers want to start a tenant's association, and they all rent units in non-profit apartment buildings.

HOUSING UNIT
Tenant's Handbook
What you need to know to start a tenants' association:
If you wanted to start a tenants' association in your apartment block, you will need to contact the Property Manager of your building or block who will provide you with the required assistance as well as the booklet, "City Policy on Awarding of Grants to City Non-Profit Housing Corporation Tenant Associations." This booklet gives a description of the regulations formulated by the Corporation to govern tenant association formation plus an outline of how to start an association and create an application for a supporting grant. Such associations can be eligible to receive operational funds based on the city's monthly per unit formula.

For proper initiation of the creation of an association, your group has to convene a meeting an invitation to which has been extended to all tenants. Meeting business must include the election of an executive committee, the formulation of a constitution, and the approval of a budget. The association then has an obligation to hold regularly scheduled meetings and maintenance of documentation of all operating costs.

WHAT ARE THE "RIGHT WAYS ... TO SHOW DATA"?

The important thing to know about creating visual displays is that each type of chart or graph is better suited for representing a particular type of data. If you have chosen to display a particular type of relationship among your data, you should select the display that will most clearly illustrate that relationship.

For example, a column of numbers will communicate a wealth of information to your readers, but only if they understand how to read the columns and interpret the raw numbers. Many readers are unable or unwilling to do the hard work of comprehending the various meanings embedded in the columns. In addition, there will be more information there than the particular point you intend to make, but there is no guarantee that your readers will divine your exact point from this choice of visual display. As a technical communicator, part of your job is creating a visual that highlights rather than buries the point you want to make to your readers.

How do you decide which type of visual will best display the data that you have selected? First you need to know what job each type of chart or graph can accomplish. In the section that follows there is a list of types of visual display, along with a brief summary of what they show most effectively.

SELECT THE RIGHT VISUAL FOR TELLING THAT STORY

Generally, you decide to create a visual when you find an interesting perspective in the data that you have. In other words, you find in the data a "story" that others will find intriguing as well. Never graph numbers just to include a visual: instead, make the visual accomplish a goal. It might undermine "common sense" ideas about something; it might highlight a new trend or change; it might provide motivation in a persuasive argument. Once you find that compelling story in the data, then you should decide which of the various types of charts will most effectively present this data. Each type of chart is best suited to illustrating a particular relationship between the data, so make sure that you select the method that will best convey your point.

Pie charts

Use a pie chart to show how a part or parts are related to the whole. Your data does need to be complete (add up to 100 per cent) for a pie chart to make sense.

For example, let's say that you are writing a report for the local Humane Society. You have crunched some of the numbers, and you see that three breeds of dog account for the majority of those given up for adoption last year. You decide to create a visual that will highlight the point that these breeds show up disproportionately at the shelter. Since you know that 187 dogs came into the shelter last year, and you have statistics both on breed and numbers for these dogs, you realize that a pie chart is the best choice to highlight the presence of these dogs.

To emphasize the fact that collies, shepherds, and retrievers account for nearly three-quarters of the breeds brought to the shelter, you decide to represent all three breeds using the same pattern, distinguishing between the three with background shading. This format highlights the fact that these breeds disproportionately show up at the shelter, suggesting some kind of issue with these dogs.

The pie chart format allows for comparison of the different groups as well as visually grouping and estimating percentage quantities to make a point clearly and forcefully.

Line graphs

Use a line graph to compare items over time, to show frequency or distribution, or to show correlations.

For example, you are creating a booklet on puppy care for a local veterinary clinic, a booklet the clinic can distribute to clients as part of its puppy information and care package. While you have written the informative text for the booklet, you now want to include some effective visuals that will help readers understand, among other things, the phenomenal growth curve of a healthy puppy. The office staff has given you some statistics from the clinic's records, so you decide to use Buster's records to graph his weight gain over six months. Buster is a six-month-old tri-colour Border collie that you are using as an example throughout the booklet. You have his weight history at least monthly from the age of seven weeks to six months with eight measurements in total. You decide to use a line graph to illustrate his growth curve over the six months because you want to compare his change in weight over time.

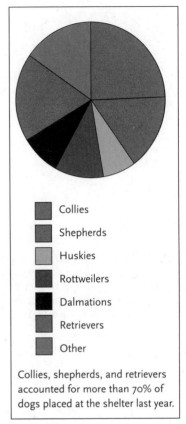

Collies, shepherds, and retrievers accounted for more than 70% of dogs placed at the shelter last year.

FIGURE 2.7
When you have data that adds up to 100 per cent, a pie chart can be an effective way to show relationships between the parts and the whole.

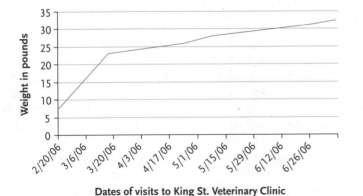

Dates of visits to King St. Veterinary Clinic

Buster's weight gain from six weeks to six months. He was born Jan. 9.

FIGURE 2.8
A line graph is a good choice of visual to illustrate a growth curve because it depicts the curve clearly and simply.

Source: King St. Veterinary Clinic medical records.

Bar charts

Use a bar chart to illustrate comparisons between items, to compare items over time, to show frequency or distribution, to show correlation.

You could also have used a bar chart to illustrate Buster's growth because a bar chart can also be an effective way to compare items over time. Figure 2.9 shows the same data presented as a bar chart. Examine the figure and assess how effective you think a bar chart is in accomplishing the goal of illustrating a growth curve.

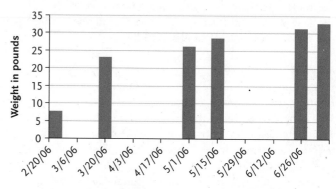

FIGURE 2.9
The bar chart is a less effective way to illustrate a growth curve because it forces readers to imagine the curve across the top of the bars.

Source: King St. Veterinary Clinic medical records.

Dates of visits to King St. Veterinary Clinic

Buster's weight gain from six weeks to six months. Buster was born Jan. 9.

A curve is present along the top of the bars, but this presentation does require readers to imagine the growth curve, making the bar chart a less clear and effective way of illustrating the comparison. On the basis of clarity, you decide the line graph is the best choice of visual in this case.

Dot charts

Use a dot chart to show correlations.

Dot charts are useful for showing clusters of data so that viewers can see relationships. For example, when you take your Irish wolfhound, Mulligan, to the King St. Veterinary Clinic, the one for which you created the puppy information booklet, your vet recommends that you protect him from heartworm disease. When you ask about the prevalence of cases in your area, the vet points to a map with all reported cases of the disease marked on it. Figure 2.10 reproduces a dot chart marking cases of heartworm in south-western Ontario. Based on the graphic representation of reported cases of heartworm, should you buy heartworm medication for Mulligan?

You see that there is a cluster of cases reported in and around your area of the country, so you decide that it is a wise precaution to protect Mulligan from heartworm.

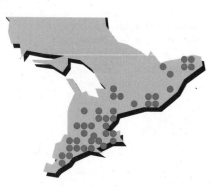

FIGURE 2.10
A dot chart clusters data to show correlation. In this case, if you lived in the Halton region, you would want to protect your dog from heartworm disease since there were numerous reported cases last year.

Tables

Use tables when the exact figures are important (e.g., measurements to two decimal places).

Figure 2.11 uses a table to present findings from a microbiology experiment. In this case, Kavita Patel selected the table because it was an effective way to summarize the important information and make it easy to check or compare the optimum pH levels for the micro-organisms listed.

Organism	Optimal pH
S. cerevisiae	5.1–6.9
E. coli	8.1 or higher
L. plantarum	3.0 or lower
S. aureus	8.1 or higher

Experimentally Determined Optimal pH of Micro-organisms

FIGURE 2.11
Effective use of a table to enable summary and comparison of findings in a microbiology lab report.

Maps

Use maps to show location or to compare two items. For example, in Figure 2.12, the clip art image shows the location of the province of British Columbia in relation to the rest of North America.

Photographs

Use photographs to render exact detail or to show something being used.

The use of a photograph in Figure 2.13 is effective because it shows the detail of both paint and carving in the totem pole illustration. In addition, the trees and hedge behind the totem pole give viewers a sense of the scale of the carving. For extra large or extra small objects, include such detail in the photograph to act as a reference point to illustrate size.

FIGURE 2.12
A map shows the location of British Columbia in relation to the larger context of North America.

Line drawings

Use a line drawing to emphasize detail or show dimensions.

While photographs are effective illustrations for showing detail, sometimes a line drawing is much clearer because it omits distracting detail to focus viewer attention on specific aspects of the item being illustrated. For example, the digital photograph in Figure 2.14 is intended to illustrate the path the water takes down the waterfall, as well as the location of the birdbath, but the pots of flowers obscure the point. The level of detail in the photograph is overwhelming and obscures the point of the illustration. Instead, a line drawing would reduce the level of detail to the principal points: the major features

FIGURE 2.13
The trees behind this totem pole illustrate the scale of the carving in downtown Victoria, BC.

FIGURE 2.14
The digital photograph does not help users locate the birdbath contained within this waterfall design.

FIGURE 2.15
The darkened areas of the sketch clarify for viewers the path of the water in the falls, as well as highlighting the location of the falls' birdbath.

of the waterfall with the birdbath area highlighted (see Figure 2.15). Usability testing showed that only 20 per cent of test users could quickly identify the location of the birdbath from the photograph. To make its location clearer, company artists created a simple line drawing from the photo that eliminated the "busy" detail and highlighted the main components. Substituting the line drawing for the photograph in this instance makes the key point in this step vivid for users. A quick follow-up test reveals that 100 per cent of users can examine the line drawing and quickly locate the birdbath on the waterfall. Not only did the visual make the detail vivid, the *right* visual reduced user confusion and error.

Gantt charts

Use a Gantt chart to indicate timelines, especially when you are writing a proposal or progress report. If you have created a Gantt chart to outline your schedule in the proposal, then recreate the chart for the progress report, noting the progress of each stage, i.e., which stages are ahead of schedule, behind schedule, or as planned. Figure 2.16 reproduces the work schedule from Jason Nguyen's proposal in Chapter 6, but it is formatted using a Gantt chart rather than the table that he used.

USE THE CONVENTIONS FOR TYPICAL VISUALS

A second component to using visuals effectively is following the conventions so that you create traditional examples of each visual. Part of the goal in using a visual is to convey a particular point clearly and efficiently; ignoring or misusing the conventions interferes with readers' or users' ability to interpret the visual quickly and easily.

Re-examine the examples in the section entitled "Select the right visual for telling that story," and try to identify some of the conventions for each type of visual. Here is a list of the conventions that are important:

1. A title

The visual should be clearly labelled with a descriptive title that identifies the point you want to convey to your readers.

2. All units labelled

Both x- and y-axes should be clearly and legibly labelled, so readers know what the units of measurement are. The items listed in the legend should also be labelled clearly and legibly, and, if you are using colour or pattern to identify the items, then the identifying boxes in the legend should be large enough for readers to distinguish one colour or pattern from another.

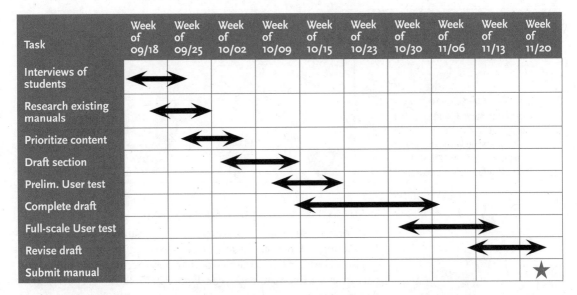

Task	Week of 09/18	Week of 09/25	Week of 10/02	Week of 10/09	Week of 10/15	Week of 10/23	Week of 10/30	Week of 11/06	Week of 11/13	Week of 11/20
Interviews of students	←→									
Research existing manuals		←→								
Prioritize content			←→							
Draft section				←→						
Prelim. User test					←→					
Complete draft						←——→				
Full-scale User test								←——→		
Revise draft									←→	
Submit manual										★

3. Source of the data

If you did not create the data yourself, you should include the source for that information, so users can evaluate its validity or follow up the source if they want to know more.

4. Source of visual

If you did not create the visual yourself, you should also include the source of the visual. If you are using the visual for commercial purposes (rather than for an educational assignment), you may need to request permission to reprint the visual before you publish your document reproducing it. Sometimes, a fee is required for reproduction; sometimes, you need only secure written permission.

FIGURE 2.16
Gantt chart mapping out work schedule for a student proposal for a technical manual.

Many more women than men are employed in teaching

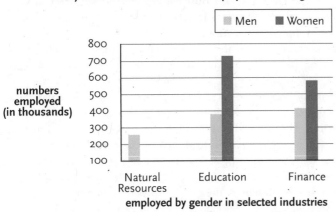

numbers employed (in thousands)

employed by gender in selected industries

FIGURE 2.17
Starting the x-axis at 100 in this graph exaggerates the number of women vs. men employed in these industries. This graph makes it appear that no women work in natural resources, which is not the case.

Source: Statistics Canada, May 2006.

FIGURE 2.18
Sales figures for Sweetest Day are increasing steadily and expected to continue to do so over the new two years; however, this graph does not represent the rate of increase effectively or accurately.

IN-CLASS EXERCISE 2.3

What Does a Gantt Chart Contribute to the Work Schedule?

Compare the work schedule in Figure 2.16, which uses a Gantt chart to outline the work schedule for a proposal, with the table used in the proposal itself, reproduced in Chapter 6 (Figure 6.8). In a small group with one or two other classmates or in a written paragraph, discuss answers to the following questions:

- Which type of visual do you think is a more effective presentation of the schedule? Why?
- What advantages do you see to using a Gantt chart?
- What advantages do you see to using a table?
- Can you think of any persuasive advantages to using the Gantt chart?

VISUALS THAT CONFUSE OR MISLEAD

Sometimes visuals are constructed to deliberately mislead viewers. For example, when an organization is writing its annual report, it might include graphs and charts that obscure the company's poor performance over the past year. Figure 2.17 shows a chart that is designed to present a misleading impression of the statistics it represents. An astute viewer will notice that the x-axis starts at 100 rather than 0, obscuring the fact that some women *do* work in natural resources. This scale also exaggerates the difference between the numbers of men who work in education and finance compared to the numbers of women in those sectors.

If you wish to use a chart that does not start at zero, then draw a break in the chart to highlight for viewers the fact that some space has been omitted between zero and the point at which the measurement starts.

Other times, in an attempt to spice up what the writer fears might be a boring visual, he or she may decide to use icons instead of numbers to represent the data being depicted. Figure 2.18 uses icons incorrectly to depict the increasing sales for greeting cards celebrating "Sweetest Day." Edward Tufte calls this use of detail to add visual interest "chartjunk" because it clutters up the clear message that the visual was intended to communicate.

The increasing sizes of the hearts reflect the increasing sales, but the size of the hearts does not proportionately represent the degree of increase. In addition, the visual does not make clear the fact that sales for 2008 were projected rather than measured. A casual glance at this visual would leave viewers thinking that card sales were exponentially higher in 2008 over 2003, but without clearer reference points, they would have no firm idea of the actual numbers. Note that the units are not represented anywhere so viewers have no idea whether the sales are measuring hundreds or hundreds of thousands of dollars: as represented, the graph shows only hundreds of dollars, a fact that makes the sales increases unimpressive at best. In this case, a better way to represent the sales would be to use hearts of a uniform size to represent a monetary unit and then reproduce as many hearts as needed to show the actual measured increase. Figure 2.19 uses icons to more accurately represent the figures.

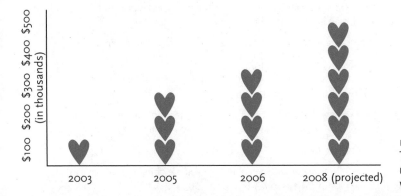

FIGURE 2.19
This icon graph more accurately represents the sales figures, so viewers can judge the increase.

EVALUATING VISUALS

Select a sample of 10 to 15 different types of visuals (preferably choosing at least one example of each type of visual described in this chapter), and analyze each one, evaluating how clear, efficient, and ethical the visual is in presenting the data to the reader. If you have access to the Internet, then use it to find online examples for this exercise.

In a memo report to your instructor, write up your analysis of the visuals, including each sample visual, as well as your assessment of it. Make sure that each of your evaluations covers the following topics for each example:

1. the type of visual
2. the completeness of its use of conventions for visuals
3. the "story" that the visual conveys
4. the clarity and ease with which you can identify the point of the visual
5. any improvements you can suggest to the visual to make it clearer or easier to understand.

LAB ASSIGNMENT 2.2

CREATING INTERESTING VISUALS

1. Visit one of these two websites:

- Bureau of Labor Statistics (US government) http://www.bls.gov/oes/home.htm
- Statistics Canada (Canadian government) http://www.statscan.ca

2. Search the site to locate data for the jobs that are projected to be most in demand for the years 2008 to 2018.

3. Create a chart or graph to display this data effectively, highlighting the types of jobs that seem to you to be the most interesting or surprising.

4. Next, identify the job category that you will apply for after graduation, and then identify the wages at the national level, in your home province or state, and in one other province or state.

5. Create a visual that compares these three levels of wages.

6. Research these statistics for three other types of jobs (if you are doing this exercise in groups, then research the jobs of each member of your group).

7. Finally, create a one to two page handout that:

- reports and synthesizes your findings for question 3,
- synthesizes and reports each group member's answers to questions 4–6, and
- integrates the visuals into your analysis and discussion.

8. Apply everything that you have learned so far this term on page layout, coherent argument, and document design to make this handout as informative and as attractive as possible.

LAB ASSIGNMENT 2.3

EVALUATING THE ETHICS OF VISUAL DISPLAY

Search online for a series of examples of visuals. Alternatively, assemble five to ten printed documents that contain visual display (e.g., annual reports, instructional documents, advertising and marketing materials, etc.) and use this sample for this exercise.

Examine each one in context at the website where you found it (or in context with the other information around it in the print document), and evaluate the effectiveness and the ethical effect of the presentation. Using the information in the previous section of the chapter, evaluate:

- whether the visual is the most effective choice for the display,
- whether it presents the data clearly and comprehensibly, and
- whether it displays the data ethically.

Write your analysis in a paragraph or two of text. Make sure your analysis covers the topics mentioned above and draws on the information and vocabulary in this chapter.

CHAPTER THREE

Researching technical subjects

Researching a subject in technical communication is often somewhat different than researching a subject in other areas. Your main
source of information may be other people rather than books, so it
may be necessary to expand your range of research skills to include
such methods as interviewing and surveying. These methods seek
out information that is not published anywhere, nor is it available in
document form. Your efforts to record the information in your technical document may be the first time this information has been com-
mitted to print. This chapter offers a concise review of three methods
of information collection: interviewing subject matter experts, effective survey design and development, and finding and evaluating traditional print and online sources.

Primary research: Interviewing

One important source of information for technical communicators
who are documenting a new product or system is often the individuals who developed it. Such information is gathered through interviewing—that is, meeting these individuals with a prepared list of
questions to discuss aspects of the product or system, so you will
be better able to write the operation or reference manual for it.
Generally the individuals who provide information about new technical products or systems are called "subject matter experts" because
they are, obviously, extremely knowledgeable about that particular
subject. Often, people who develop new products have great technical expertise but less experience in translating that knowledge into
documents that non-experts can use successfully. It may be your role,
as a technical communicator, to be the intermediary between the subject matter experts' technical expertise and the users' relative lack of
knowledge. One of the best methods for gathering the information,
then, is the interview.

There are three stages to completing a successful interview:

- Preparing for it
- Conducting it
- Writing it up.

PREPARING FOR THE INTERVIEW

Preparing yourself to conduct the interview is a crucial first step to increasing the chance that you create goodwill with the individual whom you interview and that you gather all or most of the information that you need. Prepare yourself in the following areas:

- Learn in advance everything that you can about the subject that you plan to discuss with the subject matter expert
- Learn in advance as much as you can about the subject matter expert
- Prepare a list of well-organized questions.

Learn everything you can about the subject

Read any documentation associated with the product or system that you will discuss with the subject matter expert in the interview. The greater your own technical knowledge about it, the better are your chances of understanding what it is you still need to learn, of formulating good questions that will elicit that information from your subject matter expert, and of understanding the answers from the expert in response to your questions. If you are able to discuss the new product or system using accurate terminology, you will develop credibility with the person you plan to interview because it will be clear that you do have some knowledge of the subject matter. Your own technical knowledge will give you greater confidence as you interview the expert, as well as a conceptual framework that you can expand as you learn more about the subject from him or her.

Next, discover the purpose of the product or system. Why might a user purchase the product? What will it enable her or him to do? Why is it better than other similar products? If you understand what can be done with the product or system that you are documenting, you can focus your research efforts to gather the information that will help users accomplish their goals when they come to use the device.

The next step is to determine your purpose in writing the planned document. (To persuade people? To inform them? To teach them?) If your purpose is to persuade readers to buy this product, you will want to learn about and discuss during the interview the main details regarding the advantages of your product over the competition's. If you are showing readers how to use a particular application, you need to assemble specific information about the actions required to accomplish various tasks. You should also think about the reasons or motivations someone might have for reading your document. (To make a decision? To learn? To do *x*?) If you understand their possible motivations, you can more effectively respond to them in the document that you write.

In addition to reading about the item that you plan to document, you might also attend in-house training courses (if any are available) or obtain a copy of the product or system so that you can experiment with it. Throughout all of these activities, keep notes about your experiences. Are steps missing in the existing documentation about the product? What questions does your experimentation with the product raise for you that a subject matter expert might be able to answer? Use training courses as a way to make contact with individuals who know something about the product or system. Ask them whether you can contact them later if questions arise that they might answer.

All of these strategies will help you learn about the subject of your writing. You want to use this knowledge to be as informed as possible about the subject before you begin the interview. The higher your level of knowledge the fewer basic questions you need to ask, enabling you to ferret out more easily other important information to help you accomplish your purpose in writing the document.

Learn about the subject matter expert

Before you schedule the interview, learn as much as you can about the subject matter expert. This means doing some research on her or him to find out about interests, specialties, and personality. Check out other projects he or she may have worked on. Ask co-workers about their experiences with this individual to give you some insight into what the individual is like to deal with one-on-one, but don't be influenced by other judgments, especially if they seem negative. You are collecting information to help you approach this person and motivate her or him to co-operate with you. Depending upon your attitude and approach, you may find him or her much more approachable and helpful than others report.

Prepare a list of organized questions

ORGANIZE AHEAD

Before you schedule the interview, prepare and organize your list of questions. That way, if the individual replies, "I'm not busy now; why don't you come right over?" you will be able to say, "I'm on my way."

CREATE A LEGIBLE, NUMBERED LIST

Your list of questions should be written down, either typed or in legible handwriting, and numbered. Under the stress of the moment, you don't want to be wondering what a particular word says because you scrawled it onto a scrap of paper in the middle of the night three days ago. The numbering also helps you to keep track of your questions and cross them off as they are answered. An ordered list also helps you to control and direct the interview, since your interview subject may not always want to talk about the same topics as you do. The list helps ensure that you gain the information you need about the topics that you think are important.

STRUCTURE THE QUESTIONS TO CONTROL THE INTERVIEW

Structure your questions so that there is a recognizable shape and progression to your interview. You might order them from general to more specific; you might move from discussion of basic functions of an application to more advanced features. This approach allows you to build on earlier information as well as ask impromptu questions that occur to you based on your interviewee's responses.

Organize your questions into a logical or topical progression to help you cover all necessary aspects of the subject. Ordering your questions according to the outline of your document can also help you when you begin writing, because you won't have to re-organize everything according to a different plan.

WRITE EXTRA QUESTIONS

Write more questions than you think are needed for the interview. This way, if your subject matter expert answers the questions clearly and efficiently, you won't run out of material before the interview is scheduled to end—always an embarrassing outcome.

Writing Good Questions

Good questions start with the six basic journalists' tools: who, what, where, when, why, and how. Use these to begin. As you explore the possibilities surrounding each word, more specific questions should occur to you.

Here are a few tips to help you develop questions that will give you the answers you need:

- Don't ask questions that can be answered by "yes" or "no." Ask questions that require elaboration and explanation. If you were writing an operating manual for a computer application for novice users, which question would give you the most useful information?
  1. Are the program's functions represented by icons that appear on every screen?
  2. If a new user opened the program, where would he or she find information about the functions that can be performed?

Obviously, the second version of this question is more likely to provide you with information that you don't already have (since earlier experimentation with the program—if possible—would already enable you to answer "yes").

- Ask questions that you cannot answer elsewhere.

  Once you gain access to your subject matter expert, use your time productively by asking questions that only he or she can answer. If you have conducted your research effectively into the product or system, then you should already have answered many of your own basic questions. This research should have also generated some questions and issues for you that remain unanswered at this point: use your earlier notes and observations to help you generate such questions.

- Ask about topics that you don't understand.

  Again, capitalize on the subject matter expert's knowledge by asking her or him to explain aspects of the product or system that you can't figure out.

- Include detail and background to your questions to help provide context.

  Asking a question out of the blue can confuse your interviewee. As a preamble to the question, include background information that will orient your listener to the general topic and make it faster and more efficient for her or him to formulate an answer. If it becomes clear that the background is unnecessary, you can always skip over it, as you ask the main part of the question.

- Ask what may seem to be "stupid" questions.

  Finally, don't be afraid to ask what might appear to you to be obvious or stupid questions, if you really don't know the answer. Sometimes, such questions will quickly clear up fundamental misunderstandings. Other times, these are the questions that your users might ask, were they able to, questions that no one else has considered because answers seem so obvious to individuals who are experts on the topic.

CONDUCTING THE INTERVIEW
Schedule an hour-long interview, if possible

When you have yourself well-informed and your list of questions written and organized, you should next contact the subject matter expert to schedule the interview. An appropriate length of time for the interview is usually one hour. If you schedule a longer period of time than one hour, your interviewee may baulk at the commitment of time, but you will also find that an hour is about the maximum that you can remain alert, engaged, and sharp. After the hour passes, both you and your interviewee can become too tired to make efficient

IN-CLASS EXERCISE 3.1

Prepare to Interview a Classmate

Prepare a list of questions to use in interviewing a classmate. Decide what general area of life you are interested in knowing more about and write a list of at least 10 questions that you might ask. Make sure that none of them can be answered by a simple "yes" or "no." Here are some suggestions for possible areas of inquiry:

- Plans for post-graduation?
- Grad school?
- Work?
- Travel?
- Family history?
- Biographical information?
- Hobbies and/or interests?

use of the time. Aim to work efficiently and productively. You want to avoid gaining a reputation for wasting people's time because that can make it much more difficult for you to collect the information you need to do your job effectively.

If your project requires several hours of discussion with the interviewee, then set up a series of meetings over several weeks rather than trying to complete your research in one session. But only schedule additional meetings if there is significant information that you still need to collect.

Introduce yourself and explain your project

When you call to schedule the interview, introduce yourself to the subject matter expert, explain your credentials, and describe the kind of information that you need. Explain why you believe he or she is the best source of this information, if it isn't immediately obvious.

Decide whether to tape the interview

To create a permanent record of the interviewee's responses, you will need to either tape them or take detailed written notes (using a laptop computer or pen and paper). While an audiotape or a videotape of the interview may seem obviously useful, there are a few drawbacks to this decision including the fact that you have to listen to or transcribe the tape later in real time. This can be incredibly time-consuming (plan on spending about three hours transcribing one hour of tape). It can also lead to a false sense of security during the interview, when you believe that you are capturing all of the important details, only to find out later that the recording machine has malfunctioned or the building's ventilation system drowns out the human voices. Also, some people object to having interviews that they give taped, so make sure you have your interviewee's permission before you begin to tape.

Of course, there are also advantages to taping: the interview can proceed more smoothly and naturally because the speaker doesn't have to wait for you to frantically scribble the key points before proceeding with his or her explanation. You can maintain eye contact and think about the next question or decide that a follow-up question is needed. If the information is recorded accurately, then you can review specific points the speaker made later to clarify your understanding.

Even if you do decide to tape, you should also take notes so that you can record the context of the speaker's comments as well as your impressions as the discussion continues. This way you also have a list of the major topics and points in case your recorder malfunctions, you run out of tape part way through, or the battery dies.

If you decide to take notes exclusively, then after the interview ends, you should go back over your notes as soon as you can and add details and impressions that you remember from the interview but did not have time to record.

Be an active listener

As you conduct the interview, use active listening to respond to your interviewee's answers. Active listening is the practice of checking your understanding of the speaker's comments by rephrasing them to state what you think you heard. This type of rephrasing enables the interviewee to verify that you have understood his or her point accurately and to correct any misperceptions. In addition to ensuring accuracy, this technique also communicates that you are engaged and interested in what the interviewee is saying.

Also, be conscious of the nonverbal cues that you give your speaker as he or she talks. Try to make eye contact, even if you are taking notes, and smile and nod encouragingly to show that the information is helpful. Mannerisms that indicate positive interest will motivate your speaker to continue to talk, which is your goal.

Control the interview

Sometimes you may find your subject matter expert getting bogged down in minute technical details, which he or she finds fascinating but which do not help you to accomplish the task of showing a beginner how to use the device. In this case, you need to tactfully bring the speaker back to talking about the information that you can use. For example, you might point out that, while this particular explanation is fascinating, you would appreciate it if the speaker could also explain how it might tie into the information that the user needs to know.

Working with those for whom English is a second language

Sometimes your subject matter expert will not have a good grasp of English, which makes your job a little more challenging. If he or she does not understand a question, then try rephrasing it to locate vocabulary that is familiar and will help clarify your point. You might also consider drawing pictures to illustrate the point or using the technology while the interviewee observes you and comments on your actions. These interactions require patience and ingenuity, but you can usually gather the information that you need if you accept the responsibility for making the communication work.

Closing the interview

When your information is complete or the time scheduled for your interview has passed, wrap up the discussion. If you have unanswered

Interview a Classmate

Using the questions that you developed in Exercise 3.1, interview a classmate. Your purpose in interviewing this person is to gather enough information to write a short news story or biographical sketch. Take notes as you talk so that you can refer to them later for details during the write-up.

Then, write up the results of the interview as a short news story, personal profile, or biographical sketch.

questions, you may need to schedule another interview. Thank your interviewee for talking with you, and make it clear that his or her answers have provided you with valuable information. If interviewees understand that you consider the time well spent, they will be more willing to talk with you again about later aspects of this project or another one. Also, arrange to have your subject expert answer any follow-up questions that might arise when you review your notes or convert responses into written text.

As soon as you can, following the interview, review your notes and fill in any gaps that you see with details that you can remember. Assess how well the answers you received will work to provide you with the information that you need. Schedule a follow-up interview, if you haven't already, and begin drafting your document based on the information collected from the interview.

Primary research: Conducting surveys

You have probably participated in a survey as recently as the end of your last course: student evaluations generally take the form of surveys. Your experience in filling out those forms may have given you some insight into the limitations and advantages of survey methods: do the questions sometimes direct you to answer in a certain way? Is there enough time given to express your thoughts about the course and the instructor? Are you confident that the results will be kept confidential until after the grades for the course have been turned in? Confidentiality, time limits, and loaded questions are just some of the limitations that may affect survey results. In this section of the chapter, we'll point out some ways that you can avoid these problems while benefiting from the advantages of surveys: a large number of people can be consulted, the same questions are asked of each participant, and results can be quantified and compared to those from other surveys.

Survey methodology turns up in a wide range of communication activities, everything from MuchMusic phone-in questions to election polling; you may also have been asked by telemarketers to participate in survey research projects, and some may even have offered to pay you for the time it takes to participate in the survey. Not every research project has a budget to pay participants, though, and many good projects depend on the goodwill of participants to succeed. Cancer survivors and their relatives, for example, often are more likely to contribute the time needed to answer an extensive survey for cancer research—they have an intrinsic interest in the research. If you choose to do survey research or need to do survey research as part of your writing project, one of the things you'll need to do is determine what would motivate people to participate in your survey.

Survey research can help you at two stages in your writing project: before you begin writing and as part of usability testing (revising). In the initial stages of a writing project, you could do surveys to find out what users are looking for in a manual: what are the tasks they do most often? What tasks confuse them the most? What are their most frequently used methods of solving a problem when they are using the software or device you are writing about? The answers to these kinds of questions could save you an enormous amount of time and effort if you get good information before you begin drafting your document. Not every survey has to be extensive, and not every survey needs to be formal. With a few pointers on how to get started, you should find that you can use this method to improve the quality of your writing.

ASKING GOOD QUESTIONS

Survey research is a method of generating information by asking questions of a large group of people. The quality of your survey, however, is directly related to your skill at asking good questions. There are two main types of questions to ask: closed-ended and open-ended. Closed-ended questions have the range of possible answers printed below the question itself; these questions are said to be closed because the range of answers is pre-determined.

Kind of Question	Example
Closed-ended	How often did you contact your academic advisor when you were a student? 1. Never 2. Once or twice 3. Each academic term
Open-ended	What was the best advice you got from your academic advisor while you were a student?

Figure 3.1.
Examples of open-ended and closed-ended survey questions

Let's start with open-ended questions. These questions allow respondents to answer in their own words and to give some insight into why they think the way they do. They allow for unanticipated responses—and sometimes that is the most valuable information you can obtain from a survey! For example, you could ask a respondent "Why do you take/not take public transportation to school?" The range of possible answers could be quite wide, and the unanticipated answers could lead to innovative responses that would improve services. This wide range of answers constitutes the biggest disadvantage to open-ended questions: the data is difficult to group into categories because the answers vary so much.

Closed-ended questions are more efficient for respondents: they can answer these questions quickly because the answers are right there for them:

What is the single most important reason that you avoid buying books at the campus bookstore?

1.   High prices

2.   Long lines

3.   No used copies are stocked

4.   Other (please specify) _____

FIGURE 3.2
Example of a closed-ended question

The data generated by closed-ended questions are more reliable (that is, the same question asked of the same person will almost always give the same resulting answer) and easier to code and compile into tables and statistics. These advantages may also cause problems: the pre-determined categories for the answers may force respondents to choose an answer that does not accurately reflect what they think (that is, the answers may not be valid or an accurate measure of what respondents think). There may be a combination of reasons for avoiding the campus bookstore that the question in Figure 3.2 does not capture.

One final consideration involves the time it takes to complete a survey. In general, the longer it takes for respondents to complete a survey the more likely it is that they will not finish it or return it to you. Open-ended questions take longer to answer than closed-ended ones, so limit your use of open-ended questions. Use open-ended questions to uncover the most important information you want to know.

GUIDELINES FOR ASKING GOOD QUESTIONS

Once you have decided which kinds of questions you want to ask, use the following guidelines to write the questions themselves:

- Rephrase jargon and technical language into plain language
- Ask specific questions
- Avoid loaded questions
- Break compound questions into individual questions.

Rephrase jargon and technical language into plain language
BEFORE:
Which database systems provide a variety of tools that allow specialized interfaces for tasks such as order entry and report generation to be constructed quickly?

BETTER:

Which databases provide specialized interfaces to quickly enter information and generate reports?

Ask specific questions

BEFORE:

What do you do when you cannot determine where to click?

BETTER:

When you are in the Build section of the WebCT/Vista interface, where do you click to return to the screen that shows how to enter student grades?

Avoid loaded questions

BEFORE:

Has your undergraduate advisor ever given you even a single piece of good advice?

BETTER:

How would you characterize the quality of the advice that your undergraduate advisor has provided to you?

Break compound questions into individual questions

BEFORE:

Should the undergraduate student council sponsor more social events or lower the fees that they charge you?

BETTER:

1. Should the undergraduate student council sponsor more social events?
2. Should the undergraduate student council lower the fees that they charge you?

CHOOSING APPROPRIATE RESPONSES

Asking good questions is only one half of the challenge when you write questions. The other half is creating appropriate responses. Open-ended questions, of course, do not provide a structured response by the very nature of these questions. Responses to closed-ended questions can take one of the following forms:

1. Yes/no answers
2. Rating scales
3. Comparative rating scales
4. Category scales.

YES/NO answers are, well, self-evident. Respondents can answer yes or no. The trick with these questions is to make sure that the situation you are asking about is really this black and white. Yes/no questions can also be organized into a list so that you can obtain quite a bit of information from one question:

1. Which of the following software applications have you used in the past year:
   ___ WordPerfect®
   ___ MS Word®
   ___ Excel®
   ___ Photoshop®
   ___ Dreamweaver®

RATING SCALES ask respondents to answer a question with a number that represents a response. The number they assign can vary; the following list offers some options:

- Pick one of the listed numerical responses
- Assign a number to the responses listed
- Choose among a range of numbers
- Select a number aligned with a word or phrase that describes the response each number corresponds to.

The Likert scale (named after its inventor, Rensis Likert) is one such scale, though there are many others. The traditional one uses a five-point interval, though seven and nine point intervals are also used. These intervals can be represented either as a list or more graphically along a line with numbers. Figure 3.3 shows a Likert scale using a numbered list or a numbered line.

Computer support in your workgroup is adequate:

1. STRONGLY DISAGREE
2. DISAGREE
3. NEITHER AGREE NOR DISAGREE
4. AGREE
5. STRONGLY AGREE

1	2	3	4	5
STRONGLY DISAGREE	DISAGREE	NEITHER AGREE NOR DISAGREE	AGREE	STRONGLY AGREE

FIGURE 3.3
Two examples of a Likert scale using five-point intervals. The first one provides a numbered list, the second a graphic representation with a numbered line.

COMPARATIVE RATING scales differ by asking respondents to rank each of the responses in relation to the other ones. In one survey sent with a power tool, respondents were asked this question:

Using the numbers in the above list, indicate your three most important activities:
   ___ Golf
   ___ Camping

___ Avid book reading
___ Wines
___ Wildlife
___ Gambling

Apparently, the idea was to generate a comparative ranking in an attempt to determine whether any of these activities had a connection to buying power tools.

The last kind of response you could structure establishes **categories** that respondents select. Instead of individual selections, you provide CATEGORIES or ranges for respondents. Many people, if asked, could not say how many times in the past month they used a particular software application, but they could reliably put themselves into a category that allowed them some margin of error: frequently, sometimes, or almost never are three categories that are often used to structure these answers.

PREPARING THE SURVEY FORM

Surveys can be done on paper, via the Internet, and through phone conversations. Whatever delivery method you choose, you must take care to prepare the survey form so that it is clear and easy to read; it should encourage respondents to finish. Even telephone surveys need to have clearly written and well-designed forms for the person making the call to read out to the person answering the survey. But when paper or a computer screen is all the respondent will see, the time you spend designing your form will be a crucial factor in your success or failure to obtain completed survey forms.

Follow these guidelines as you prepare the survey form:
- Put a title on the page
- Write a short introduction to motivate the respondent to complete the survey
- Order the questions: start with easy or factual answers to create a sense that the survey won't take too long to complete
- Leave plenty of space for respondents to write answers to open-ended questions
- Edit the survey; keep only the questions that you really need the answers to
- Leave lots of white space.

Reporting survey data

Once you have produced your survey, you need to distribute it. If you are doing an informal, fast survey, you will probably distribute it to a wide range of people, perhaps even leaving some forms in a public place for respondents to pick up and fill in. If you are doing more serious work, you need to decide what group of people you are surveying and how many of those people you can afford to contact. You then track how many of the people that you selected to survey actually filled in and returned the survey form: this is called the response rate (the percentage of people who responded). The higher the response rate, the stronger your data will be.

MAJOR PROJECT 3.1

CREATE A SURVEY FORM

- Create a survey form on computer lab usage to give to students who use the public labs on campus. Use the information in this section of the chapter to help you generate survey questions that tell you what you want to know about computer lab usage.
- Distribute the finished survey form, and collect your data. You should get as many responses as you can (aim for 20 to 30 completed surveys).
- Tabulate and analyze your data. Create two or three visuals from the data that you could use in a written document summarizing the results of your survey.
- Write a memo or report that summarizes the data. Direct this report or memo to the administrators at your institution who would be interested in the responses of student users of the computer labs. If your goal is to argue for improved lab service (or maintenance or equipment up-dates), use the data to make an argument as to how the administration should respond to your survey.

Your memo or report should include at least two visuals summarizing interesting points about your data. For more information on creating effective visuals, see Chapter 2, "Leading and misleading the reader."

While the quality of your data is important, it is also important to determine what type of data you've collected. Open-ended questions result in QUALITATIVE data: data that cannot be counted easily but that can describe the qualities or details of an answer well. If you get repetitive answers to an open-ended question, those answers are then seen as quantitative and reported as numbers. As you read through the words that respondents have written, look for patterns among the responses and group similar responses together. Are there any surprising responses? Qualitative data is important because it provides context for understanding the numeric patterns that emerge from quantitative data. You will use qualitative data (quotations from the open-ended questions) in your report to help explain the meaning of the numeric data. In your thinking about how to write a manual, these open-ended questions may give you key insights into how users will actually use the manual, insights that might not come up in responses to closed-ended questions.

Closed-ended questions will give you answers to count: QUANTITATIVE data. For example, in answer to the question "What year of university study are you in?" students could have responded this way:

- First year: 2
- Second year: 11
- Third year: 7
- Fourth year: 4
- Other (please explain): 1 (student at large)

You would total these results on an unfilled-out copy of the survey, but in your report based on this research you might want to present the data in a table:

Year of student	Number of responses	Percentage
First year	2	8
Second year	11	44
Third year	7	28
Fourth year	4	16
Other	1	4

FIGURE 3.4
In a report, present data in a table for easy reference for readers.

In the text of your report, you might want to combine some of these data: 72 per cent of the students in this class are second or third year students, and very few first year students enrol in it. What you are doing here is looking for patterns in the data in an attempt to generalize about what you are finding.

When collected in the initial stages of your project, survey findings can answer questions about the usefulness of the direction you plan to take. Based on the responses from your survey population, you can make adjustments early on or rest assured that your project is on track to provide the best document for your user group. When considered as part of usability testing, survey findings can reveal areas of the document that need revision, improved visuals, or clarification of a key point, or perhaps they can even highlight that the level of detail is too basic for your target user group. Direct feedback from real people can be immensely helpful as you evaluate the effectiveness of your work at different stages in its development.

Secondary research: Finding print and online sources

Depending upon what type of technical document you are writing, you may need to do some traditional library or print research on your subject. Especially if you are writing a laboratory report based on a series of experiments, you may need to investigate further research on aspects related to the topic of your experiments. If you are creating a software manual to fill a market niche, you might examine recently published existing manuals to pick up some strategies or tips about what to do or not to do. Or if you are writing a white paper on a new electronic device, you might visit the Internet to search for competitors' products that you can use as a comparison with your company's device, examples of well-written white papers about similar devices that might work as models, or consumer chat sites that evaluate and comment on similar products that might give you useful perspectives on what your readers may like or dislike about such items. A wealth of information is now available online, which facilitates thorough research efforts.

At the same time, libraries are better stocked with useful sources and information than ever before. Many schools have excellent library websites where you can conduct your search for print materials from one of the terminals in the building or through your own Internet connection at home. If you are at a larger educational institution, you may find it has more than one library. If you attend a multi-campus school, you may find that the technical communication journals and books are housed at a different location than where you attend classes. Some libraries allow you to order the books and have them shipped to your location to make it easier for you to research the subjects you are studying. In a day to two, you can visit the library nearest you and pick up your books.

Many of the technical communication journals now have their issues available online, and most educational libraries carry these subscriptions. You can search for a full-text article from your computer and download a pdf file to read on-screen or to print off a paper copy. As long as you print only one copy for your own personal and educational use, you do not have to worry about violating copyright laws.

Here is a list of the journals that publish articles and reports about research on technical communication:

- *Technostyle* (publication of Canadian Association of Teachers of Technical Writing with articles in both English and French)
- *Technical Communication Quarterly* (publication of the [American] Association of Teachers of Technical Writing)
- *Technical Communication* (publication of the Society for Technical Communication)
- *Transactions of the IEEE* (publication of the Institute of Electrical and Electronics Engineers)
- *Journal of Business and Technical Writing*

You should also identify a list of journals related to the subject area in which you are working so that you can keep current with the recent developments related to the content of your documents.

CONDUCTING AN EFFECTIVE SEARCH FOR SOURCES: LIBRARY AND INTERNET

When you have determined that you need to find some sources, either to keep yourself current on developments in your subject or because a school assignment requires citations, you want to find the sources most relevant and useful to your topic. Finding the most useful information depends largely on the keywords that you select to use in your search. If you don't use the appropriate technical terms, then your search won't locate appropriate publications.

To improve the chances that you will name your subject matter correctly in the search, generate a list of words that you associate with the topic. Then, list as many synonyms for each word as you can think of. If your list is a bit short, you could also consult web search site subject directories (e.g. Yahoo! Directory, Google Directory, or Infomine). A subject directory can help you think of subcategories related to your broader topic. You can also browse or use keyword searches at the library. Browsing allows you to search by author, title, or assigned library subject heading when you already know some of the main sources to use. Keyword searches allow you to access related information from databases. You can also mine some of the sources that your initial searches turn up for additional keywords related to your subject. Other options are to consult a specialized dictionary on your topic or the Library of Congress subject headings (for example, authorities.loc.gov), since most educational libraries use the Library of Congress Subject Headings to organize their holdings.

Once you have generated a respectable list of keywords, you will find that, if you enter just one word, the sources that you locate will be too diffuse and general for actual usefulness. To narrow your search, you may need to combine two or three key words (using AND) to focus and qualify the sources that show up on your screen. You may also be able to narrow your search by specifying what you don't want (e.g., NOT crystalline semiconductors). Some search engines simplify this process by allowing you to use a plus or minus in front of the term to indicate combining and excluding (e.g., +amorphous semiconductors –crystalline semiconductors). Others provide access to advanced search options such as this on a separate page.

When you have located several useful sources, you can also study their reference sections to locate additional information relevant to your topic. Often, a useful article will contain references to other useful articles on the same or a related subject.

If you are having difficulty finding useful sources from your own search efforts, an efficient alternative is to visit the library and get a reference librarian to help you out. Librarians can shortcut your search time by directing you to the right subject headings, and they can also point out the location of various types of sources in the building. You can get your hands on some useful material in a relatively short time.

ASSESSING THE CREDIBILITY OF YOUR SOURCES

Once you locate what look like relevant and useful books, articles, and websites, the next step is to assess the reliability and credibility of your sources. Especially for website-based information, the credibility of the source must be sound. Anyone can put up a website, and no one polices the accuracy or legitimacy of the information posted. Some websites even pretend to credibility and distinction by imitating the look of respected websites posted by well-known organizations or governments. Look closely at the URL and other details to make sure you are visiting the legitimate site.

Here is a list of the criteria that librarians use to assess printed material:

1. PUBLISHER: Who published the document? Scholarly books and journal articles are reviewed by experts in the area before they are published. If the source of the document is a scholarly one, it is likely fairly reliable: it has been screened for accuracy and reliability. If it appears in a popular magazine or book, it may be less reliable because the selection criteria in such sources are based more on interest and entertainment than accuracy or thoroughness.

2. AUTHOR: Who wrote the document? What are this person's qualifications in this area? Does the author have a professional degree or connection with the subject matter that is legitimate and sanctioned by related professional organizations?

3. CURRENCY: How recent is the document? If the topic is a hot one, such as genetic research, then it matters how recently the source was published. An article or book that is several years old may be hopelessly out of date since developments in genetic research have changed the field completely since 2000.

4. EVIDENCE: What is the basis of the information presented? Did the author conduct interviews, experiments, observations, etc. to gather the evidence he or she uses to support the claims? Does the author cite relevant and current research and provide proper documentation so you can find this material yourself? Is enough evidence presented to support the claims?

5. SLANT: Can you figure out areas where the writer seems biased in the opinions expressed? To what extent might these biases affect the information presented?

Depending upon how you answer the questions posed in the list above, you can evaluate the credibility of a particular print source as useful and relevant or biased and unsupported. Then you can decide whether to include the information in your document or continue to search for other material with more trustworthy content.

The criteria that you can use to evaluate the credibility of an Internet or website source are similar to those useful for evaluating print sources, but some of the criteria will be impossible to verify on the website. In this case, you should probably keep searching for a source that you can verify as accurate and reputable rather than use a source that may be unreliable. Here are some questions that will help you evaluate a website's credibility:

1. WEBSITE SPONSOR: What type of URL does the site use? Is it a government site (ending in .gov or .gc.ca)? Is it a commercial site (ending in .com)? Is it a non-profit site (ending in .org)? Is it a university or college-sponsored site (ending in .edu, sometimes, or sometimes just .ca in Canada)? The final tag on the website URL can give you some indication of whether or not the site is sponsored by a reputable organization. Government and educational websites tend to sponsor information that is more reliable and accurate than many commercial websites, which have as their goal selling a service or product.

2. AUTHOR: Who has written the information that you want to use? Often websites don't identify authors beyond giving their email address. Without at least a name, you may have difficulty assessing the qualifications of the writer, and therefore the validity of the opinions or information that he or she has published.

3. CURRENCY: Does the website have a date and time when the information was posted or last up-dated? Many websites do provide this detail, but others do not. If you cannot verify the currency of the posting, then you should keep searching for a source that you know is current, especially if timeliness of information is a goal.

4. EVIDENCE: Many websites do not clarify the source of their information, so you may have difficulty verifying their level of accuracy. Look for some idea of who or what organization is sponsoring the website. You can evaluate the accuracy and reliability of its content based on who is affiliated with the website. If the site does not have an obvious reputable sponsor, nor does it identify the sources for the information it presents, you should probably stay away because you cannot verify its reliability.

5. SLANT: While some websites are overtly political or slanted in their views, others cloak their bias by sounding reason-

able and scientific. They may cite statistics as evidence of their claims, but unless you can evaluate the origin of their data, you cannot really tell whether information is legitimate or fabricated.

6. ADVERTISING: Watch for sites whose main purpose is to sell you a service or product. Many sites exist solely to promote the sale of something, and any information they contain will be as reliable as any advertising.

When you have located enough reliable and useful sources, you can begin using them to develop your own document. Reputable sources and statistics can help you build a watertight case for the argument you want to make or help you feel confident about the quality of the technical information that you are presenting. The main challenge of integrating research sources into your text is ensuring that you paraphrase or cite them properly. The next section briefly reviews the difference between quoting and paraphrasing and reviews how to highlight the original source to keep your readers informed as to where you obtained the research materials that you are using.

Citing and paraphrasing researched sources

When you encounter a phrase, sentence, or paragraph written by someone else that states so perfectly what you would like to say that you want to repeat it exactly, you should quote it. Quotation means that you copy the passage word for word, and place it between quotation marks, or, if it is longer than about four lines, set it off in a block quotation, as in the example in Figure 3.5.

Note that the long passage is indented to the right and the shorter phrases are contained in quotation marks. Note also that it is important to cite your sources, to tell where a quotation came from. There are many different ways of doing this. The example left uses parenthetical documentation, which puts information about the source in parentheses. The year of the publication appears in parentheses at the end of the quotation. In the first citation, where the author is not identified, his or her name appears before the year inside the parentheses.

In the 1970s electrostatics was a field based largely on experimental evidence and requiring the understanding of three basic facts. The first fact was the "existence of electric charge itself" (Schey 1973).

H. M. Schey describes the second fact as follows:

> The second fact is called Coloumb's law, after the French physicist who discovered it. This law states that the electrostatic force between two charged particles (a) is inversely proportional to the product of their charges, (b) is inversely proportional to the square of the distance between them, and (c) acts along the line joining them. (1973)

In this passage, Schey both introduces the law and defines it for his reader, connecting the fact to the equation used to find it. He notes the third fact to be "the principle of superposition" (1973), and he goes on to define it through an equation also. More than thirty years later, the field of electrostatics has...

FIGURE 3.5
Passage from a report that illustrates how to cite direct quotations using Council of Science Editor's (CSE) style

---

In the 1970s, electrostatics was a field based largely on experimental evidence and requiring the understanding of three basic facts: 1) that electric charge exists; 2) that Coloumbic forces exist between charged particles; and 3) that the concept of "superposition" must be applied (Schey 1973). More than thirty years later, the field of electrostatics has...

FIGURE 3.6
A source paraphrased and cited correctly, using CSE style

If you find yourself quoting several passages, re-examine your work to figure out which ones you can paraphrase. If you cite too many quotations, your text tends to be taken over by your sources, and the words of your sources overshadow your own ideas. Save direct quotation for only those passages that succinctly express an idea that is critical to the point you are making. If you find yourself relying too heavily on one or two sources, you may need to create some distance between your text and the sources. Put the sources away for a day or so and try writing out what you want to say in your own words. Later you can insert quotations from the sources to support your ideas, but try not to rely overmuch on others' ideas.

If the writer of the passage in Figure 3.5 had not wanted to quote Schey's words exactly, but rather summarize them to shorten the reference, he or she would have paraphrased his words while still noting the origins of the idea. Figure 3.6 shows how to paraphrase and cite the same information.

Note that when the writer uses a technical term quoted from the source, he or she places that term (superposition) in quotation marks to highlight the fact that the original source's word is being used here. The writer has also attempted to substitute synonyms, where possible, for the exact phrasing used by Schey. In this case, paraphrasing is tricky because the passage requires a limited technical vocabulary that cannot easily be replaced while still retaining the precise meaning. For this reason, it is critical to cite the original source to clarify that you are borrowing Schey's ideas here and to avoid any appearance of plagiarism (presenting someone's ideas/words as if they were your own). When you are locating your sources, don't forget to carefully record all of the publication data so that you can cite all sources accurately and completely, should you decide to use them.

How do you know when you should cite sources? Here is a list of types of information that you should always document:

- Statements of opinion
- Claims that can be argued
- Sources for statistics
- Research findings
- Examples
- Graphs
- Charts
- Illustrations.

One type of information that you don't have to cite is facts, if they are widely known and readily available in general reference works such as an encyclopaedia. For example, you would not need to document the fact that 0 degrees C is equal to 32 degrees F.

IN-CLASS EXERCISE 3.3

Which Item Needs a Source Cited?

1. The definition of a technical term, for example, "Coloumb's law"
2. An equation to solve a physics problem
3. The year that Isaac Newton published *Opticks*
4. A sentence from Newton's *Opticks*
5. The sketch Newton used to show how he bent light to reveal the spectrum
6. The letter he sent to the Royal Society to secure his claim for primacy about his experiments with light.

IN-CLASS EXERCISE 3.4

Which Paraphrase is Legitimate and Which is Too Close to the Original?

Read the two paraphrases right. Which one is an accurate paraphrase? Explain what makes it a good paraphrase. Explain why the other passage might be considered plagiarism.

The original paragraph:

"Misogyny accounts for Pygmalion's contribution to the history of artificial intelligences. He creates Galatea in ivory because of his disgust with flesh-and-blood women; seeing his completed work, he falls in love with it—though whether what he feels is love or vanity about his own creation is hard to say. We will see that same confusion weaving endlessly through the history of men and their self-imitations (and also its opposite, as creators recoil from what they have made). In any case, Aphrodite obliges Pygmalion by breathing life into Galatea, and the two seem to have lived happily every after."

Source: P. McCorduck, Machines Who Think *(San Francisco: Freeman & Co., 1979), 5.*

Paraphrase 1:

McCorduck attributes Pygmalion's motivation for creating Galatea to misogyny. She says he was disgusted with flesh-and-blood women, so he made his own out of ivory. She questions whether he really loves Galatea or whether he is just vain about his own creation. McCorduck notes that other people in Pygmalion's position have either loved or hated their self-imitations. She concludes that after Aphrodite gave life to Galatea, she and Pygmalion lived happily ever after.

Paraphrase 2:

In her introductory chapter, McCorduck summarizes a number of historical and fictional figures who have created living beings from inanimate materials. She argues that Pygmalion, a Greek sculptor who created an ideal woman out of ivory, was motivated primarily by prejudice against women. She notes that while he fell in love with his creation, other similar individuals have repudiated their finished works. She concludes with the observation that Pygmalion and Galatea, when Venus gives her life, end up happily living out their lives together.

CHAPTER FOUR

Writing technical prose

Writing for the *National Post*, Duncan Stewart argues that "without the routine of writing at least a few pages a week, I don't think one will improve much as a writer." He offers this advice to writers: "1) readmore, 2) write more, and 3) find your voice."[1]

This chapter contains some tips and strategies for improving the quality of the technical prose that you write. Your goal as a technical communicator should be to develop a style that is clear and concise and that can be appropriately adapted to the needs of your readers or users. In other words, you want to have enough command of the language and understanding of how language works so that you can adjust your style to the demands of the genre and the audience. For example, in a proposal, you build a well-supported argument making a case for your solution to the problem. To write a well-supported argument, you need to use complete sentences, well-developed paragraphs, and coherent threads joining the paragraphs together. You also want to ignite the interest and enthusiasm of your readers so that they choose your plan as the best solution. In contrast, to write a good set of instructions or a manual, you use commands, numbering individual steps and co-ordinating visuals and text. Instructions demand their own type of coherence—a chronological movement from one step to the next with clarity being the primary goal. This chapter introduces you to some useful aspects of style that you can use to adapt your message to your goal for the document and the individuals who interact with it.

1 Duncan Stewart, "Good analysts are good writers," *National Post*, March 9, 2006.

What is style?

Style refers to three aspects of written language:

- Word choice
- Sentence composition (or make up)
- Figurative language.

WORD CHOICE

Word choice refers to your ability to select the exact word that is appropriate in a given situation so that it (and the sentence) conveys your meaning clearly and concisely.

Appropriateness

Of course, selecting the appropriate word assumes that you have a reasonably large vocabulary from which to draw words. The best way to expand the size of your vocabulary, as well as tune your ear to effective ways of using words in sentences, is through extensive reading. The more reading you do, the more words and word phrases you encounter so that you begin to recognize what words work well together to express a particular idea. Whether you are a native or non-native speaker of English, reading widely from texts in English will improve your ability to write English well. Don't limit yourself to the subjects and genres that you read: read newspapers, magazines, academic books, textbooks, non-fiction, and fiction. When you encounter unfamiliar words, look them up in a dictionary (in print or online), so you gain a better sense of how that word works in concert with the other words around it. The more you read the more you will find phrases and sentences forming in your mind when you sit down to write your own prose. You also develop a clear sense of which words work together and which words are slightly off.

Clarity

Your goal in choosing your words, especially when writing technical prose, is usually clarity. In technical communication, you address a reader or user, so your prose should communicate without ambiguity or confusion. Of course, technical concepts and jargon can be confusing and ambiguous to non-technical or non-specialist readers and users. If possible, limit your use of technical jargon when writing for non-technical readers. If particular technical terms or concepts are essential to the discussion, then define them if you believe some readers will not know what they mean. Explaining terms and concepts will also allow you to reach as broad an audience as possible, which may be appropriate to your document. Later in this chapter, we look at several techniques for defining terms and concepts, as well as for deciding the degree of detail that your readers will need in a given situation.

As to the non-technical terms that you use in technical communication, they should be "in [inter]*national* use, and in *present* use," according to Edward P. J. Corbett and Robert Connors.[2] In other words, you want to select words that are in common and widespread use today (i.e., avoiding regional dialects) so that readers will understand what you mean. For example, in one region in which we've lived, the neighbours used this expression: "That car needs washed." In another, the school children would argue that something was done "on accident." While these phrases are comprehensible, they are regional expressions that mark the speaker off as not using standard

2   Edward P. J. Corbett and Robert Connors, *Classical Rhetoric for the Modern Student*, 4th ed. (New York: Oxford University Press, 1998), 346.

edited English. In professional documents, you should avoid phrases or expressions that may distract readers from your main point.

Making judgments about the contemporary use of particular words relies on your knowledge of your readers and users.

Conciseness

In choosing your words, you want to aim for both brevity and precision—that is, the word or phrase is the quickest way to impart the idea that you have, and it imparts the idea accurately. How do you gauge accuracy? You need to develop sensitivity to the language that helps you to judge whether an expression is correct. Native speakers often recognize instinctively when a phrase or expression is awkward or "not how we say it." Non-native speakers often find these nuances the most challenging part of becoming proficient in a language. Again, reading extensively is the key here: the sheer volume of prose that you "hear" will help you eventually to identify those words that go together or that miss the mark. Of course, judging the precision of words means looking at them in context—no word is "wrong" in its own right but only in the company of the words around it.

The second component of conciseness is brevity. Although this is true of all prose, technical prose especially needs to be brief. Users and readers of technical prose consult it as a means for reaching a larger goal (for example, users consult a manual to learn how to do a mail merge to send out a widely distributed marketing document). They want the information quickly, so they can accomplish the task, and few people have patience for sentence structures that delay their learning. Include as few words as possible to accurately convey the ideas. This means that you should revise a draft looking to streamline your sentences by eliminating words or rephrasing ideas. That said, avoid pruning phrases that contribute to clarity. Sometimes writers prune so ruthlessly that they introduce confusion and ambiguity through the words they take out: aim to strike a balance between conciseness and clarity.

Connotations

The fourth area that needs your attention when you choose words is connotation. Connotation refers to what a particular word implies emotionally in addition to its main meaning. For example, compare the following two sentences:

- To prevent splattering, never jerk the hand blender out of the liquid while the blender is running.
- To prevent splattering, never remove the hand blender from the liquid while the blender is running.

IN-CLASS EXERCISE 4.2

Varying Sentence Length for Greater Impact

1. Examine Figure 4.1, focusing on the length of the sentences.

- How effective do you think the sentence lengths are in this passage, excerpted from a proposal written for a class project?
- How would you describe the style of the prose in these three sentences?
- Based on this paragraph, are you looking forward to reading the rest of the proposal? Why or why not?

2. Now examine the revision in Figure 4.2, and evaluate whether the changes make the passage easier or more difficult to read.

3. Find a paragraph from your own writing, and examine the sentence length. Then revise the paragraph changing the sentence length to create more contrast and to emphasize the key points.

4. If you don't have a paragraph from your own writing, revise the passage in Figure 4.3 to vary the sentence length and emphasize the main points.

What does the writer's use of the word "jerk" in the first sentence contribute to our understanding of the operating instruction?

The word "jerk" implies a quick, erratic removal of the hand blender from the substance being blended. It connotes speed and suddenness, perhaps even awkwardness.

Of the two versions, which do you think conveys the point more clearly? Why?

The use of "jerk" is actually less clear because it is so specific. In identifying the motion as quick and sudden, the instruction also implies the possibility that a slower removal of the kitchen tool might not create splattering. So, in this particular case, the connotation or emotional meaning of the word makes the point more ambiguous than the more neutral word "remove," which is used in the second version.

As this example illustrates, it is important to consider the nuances or connotations of the words that you select in case they introduce an emotional overtone or even a confusing possibility that you do not intend to convey.

SENTENCE COMPOSITION

Sentence composition refers to both sentence length and sentence structure. Sentence length, of course, refers to the number of words in a sentence. Longer, multi-word sentences can sometimes be more difficult to follow and read (e.g., academic prose), but sentences in a paragraph that have a similar number of words can be boring and lull the reader to inattention. Traditional advice is to vary the number of words per sentence, using some long and some short sentences. Short sentences have impact, and they are useful for emphasizing important points.

Sentence structure

Sentence structure is another useful concept that can help you improve your style, especially when you are working on a report. In a document such as a manual or a set of instructions, there is less need to vary your sentence structure, but, in a longer and more complexly written document such as a report, using different kinds of sentences can help you add inherent interest to your prose. There are four different types of sentences, based on the grammatical structure that you use:

- Simple
- Compound
- Complex
- Compound-Complex

As this travelling mural is displayed around the Chicagoland region, interested individuals have no source of information concerning details of the mural, its purpose, its artists, and its inspiration. When employees return to the display to dismantle it and move it to another location, they are often questioned by members of the public who wish to know more about the mural, but often the park employees cannot answer their questions. A brochure to accompany the mural as it is displayed at public buildings and events detailing this information would promote an appreciation of the beauty of and efforts for the project, as well as providing an advertisement for Gompers Park and an education for the public on the importance of wetlands.

FIGURE 4.1
Excerpt from a proposal in which all of the sentences are similar length.

As this travelling mural is displayed around the Chicagoland region, interested individuals have no source of information. They can't learn more about the mural's details, its purpose, artists, or inspiration. But the public wants to know more. When park employees return to move the display to another location, they are often questioned about the mural but often do not know the answers. A brochure detailing this information and accompanying the mural as it is displayed at public buildings and events would promote an appreciation of the beauty of and efforts for the project, as well as providing an advertisement for Gompers Park and an education for the public on the importance of wetlands.

FIGURE 4.2
A revision that varies sentence length. Is it more or less interesting than the original?

After deciding to become a vegan (not eat animal products of any kind) ten years ago, I was prepared to eat a variety of new foods, but what I was not prepared for was the difficulty of figuring out which of these foods and how much would keep me healthy and energized. With the demands of school and work, I never got around to educating myself, and several months later found me subsisting on a diet of peanut butter and fried tofu, not sure of what alternatives existed to meat, eggs, and cheese as good sources of protein. Every cold and flu germ that was wafting through the air seemed to find me too, even though I bought oranges and apples like they were the Holy Grail. When I started having vivid dreams of slicing and gorging on thick, juicy steaks, medium rare, I realized that I needed to educate myself on alternative foods.

FIGURE 4.3
Rewrite this passage varying the sentence length and emphasizing the main points.

SIMPLE SENTENCE

Simple sentences consist of at least a SUBJECT + VERB and often of a SUBJECT + VERB + OBJECT or a SUBJECT + LINKING VERB + COMPLEMENT. They are generally, but not always, fairly short, and they contain one main idea. Simple sentences are useful rhetorically for emphasizing a main idea because they allow you to focus reader attention on just the one point. Here are some simple sentences from some of the sample texts in this book:

- "*Serratia marcescens* grew best at 20–25°C."
- "It will briefly cover the basics and focus mainly on the flashy elements."
- "The third step will be to begin drafting the manual."

IN-CLASS EXERCISE 4.3

Practising Sentence Variety

Write a paragraph on a technical topic that you know something about, and aim to use each different kind of sentence at least once in the paragraph. Based on your experience writing this paragraph, answer the following questions (either in writing or in small group discussion).

- How hard is it to vary your sentence structure?
- Which sentence type did you find it most difficult to write?
- Why do you think that type is difficult for you?
- What do you think varying sentence structure contributes to the overall style of the paragraph?
- When do you think it might be appropriate to worry about the variety of sentences in a document?
- When do you think it might be inappropriate to vary your sentence structure in a document?

COMPOUND SENTENCES

Compound sentences are two simple sentences joined together with a co-ordinating conjunction (i.e., and, but, yet, so, nor, or, for): SUBJECT + VERB + OBJECT, & SUBJECT + VERB + OBJECT.

Compound sentences are, obviously, longer than simple ones, and they usually contain two ideas. Often the ideas are linked. Compound sentences are useful rhetorically because they allow you to make or imply relationships between the two ideas contained in the joined sentences. For example, in this sentence, "My energy levels seemed to drop, and I kept getting sick with colds and flu," the co-ordinating conjunction "and" signals to the reader that the second point adds to and intensifies the first point.

You can also use a compound sentence to introduce a conflicting view: the co-ordinating conjunctions "but" and "yet" both signal that what follows is likely an opposing point or a qualification of the first point. For example, examine this sentence: "I have two-thirds of the work to do to complete the draft, but the original schedule still seems reasonable." The first part of the sentence implies that the writer has a significant portion of the work to complete, perhaps raising doubts in the readers' minds that she can finish the project on schedule. To allay such doubts, she uses a compound sentence, introducing "but" to reassure readers that her original schedule of work was accurately forecast and she believes she can finish as scheduled, despite the apparent disproportion of work still remaining.

Compound sentences that use the co-ordinating conjunction "so" are useful for suggesting a cause-and-effect relationship between the two points in the sentence. The following example creates such a relationship: "*S. aureus* is normally a yellow colour, *so* both the colony grown at 20–25°C and the colony grown at 37°C should have been yellow."

COMPLEX SENTENCES

Complex sentences are simple sentences that have a subordinate clause added on to either the beginning or the end of the sentence: SUBORDINATE CLAUSE, + SIMPLE SENTENCE OR SIMPLE SENTENCE + SUBORDINATE CLAUSE.

When the subordinate clause appears at the beginning of a complex sentence, it can be used to introduce a qualification or clarification of the main idea expressed in the simple part of the sentence. For example, in the following sentence, the subordinate clause identifies the sources for the information before supplying the detail: "Although observations and information from the current owner confirm the roof's structural integrity, the shingles are nearly 18 years old."

In complex sentences with the subordinate clause at the end of the simple sentence, the clause can be useful for elaborating the main point made in the simple sentence. For example in the following sentence, the subordinate clause functions as elaboration: "Please remember that the personal effects of the current owner occasionally limited the scope of the inspection because the inspection team was unable to undertake extensive moving of these effects."

COMPOUND-COMPLEX SENTENCES

Compound-complex sentences are sentences that are constructed of two simple sentences joined by a co-ordinating conjunction plus a subordinate clause attached to one of the two simple sentences: e.g., SIMPLE SENTENCE, [CO-ORDINATING CONJUNCTION] SUBORDI-NATE CLAUSE, + SIMPLE SENTENCE. This type of sentence is useful for expressing complex ideas needing elaboration and qualification. In the first sample sentence—"Because she is a student at DePaul University with a major in environmental science and a minor in biology, our speaker has gained knowledge detailing ecology, function, and restoration, *and* this background will enable her to present an accurate and informative seminar tonight"—the introductory subordinate clause (the complex part of the sentence) identifies the speaker's scholastic background (environmental science and biology) before the rest of the sentence explains what this background means (knowledge of subject matter relevant to the upcoming presentation). The details about the speaker's knowledge and the significance of her credentials are both explained in the second half of the sentence (the compound clause consisting of two simple sentences joined by the conjunction "and"). In this last part of the sentence, the individual introducing the speaker notes that the student from DePaul will draw on her background to present a good seminar. From a rhetorical perspective, this sentence offers supporting evidence and an argumentative claim that many readers will find persuasive.

FIGURATIVE LANGUAGE

Many people associate figurative language (e.g., metaphors, similes, parallelism, antithesis, etc.) with the study of literature and poetry, but it is, in fact, essential to all of us in expressing ourselves. Moreover, you probably already use figurative language regularly in your day-to-day speech without always being aware of it. And that is how figurative language developed: after people had been using figures of speech for centuries, rhetoricians gave them names.

Figurative language is useful in technical communication because it provides ways for writers to make their prose clearer, more concise, and more interesting. When used effectively, it can help you connect with your readers. Specific examples and aptly chosen phrases can make the subject matter come alive, showing readers its importance and significance. You can help them feel emotionally connected to

IN-CLASS EXERCISE 4.5

Analyse the Rhetorical Effects of Sentence Variety

Identify the sentence structure in the following paragraph. Then analyse how the sentence structure contributes to the rhetorical effect of the sentence, and then the paragraph as a whole.

[1] One major cause of preventable illness and death in North America is obesity. [2] During the last ten years, the number of overweight people in industrialized countries has skyrocketed. [3] In fact, the numbers have increased so much that the World Health Organization (WHO) is calling obesity an "epidemic" in these countries. [4] For example, in the United States, one-third of the population—about 60 million people—has a weight problem. [5] In Canada, between 20 and 50 per cent of all adults are overweight, as are 10 to 25 per cent of teenagers, and even a significant proportion of children are fatter than in any previous generation. [6] An epidemic of obesity is problematic because it places large numbers of the population at much higher risk of serious medical conditions than those at a healthy weight. [7] These serious medical conditions include high blood pressure, heart attack, stroke, diabetes, gallbladder disease, and various cancers (colorectal, breast, prostate, etc.). [8] Other health risks associated with excessive weight are breathing disorders, depression, gastro-esophogeal reflux disease (GERD), and joint disease such as osteoarthritis.

your subject matter, a connection that keeps them reading and interested in the information that follows. Figurative language creates an emotional response that makes readers more receptive to both your message and your credibility as a writer.

What is figurative language?

Figurative language or *figures of speech*, as they are called in rhetoric textbooks, can be defined as an artful change to ordinary language. That is, you make a subtle change to a word or phrase with the goal of creating an effect. You can change ordinary language in two ways: through changing the word order (called a *scheme*) and through changing the meaning (called a *trope*).

SCHEMES (CHANGING WORD ORDER)

There are four ways to alter word order:

- Schemes of balance
- Schemes of unusual or inverted order
- Schemes of omission
- Schemes of repetition

SCHEMES OF BALANCE involve such elements as *parallelism* (similar structure in a series of related elements) and *antithesis* (placing contrasting ideas side-by-side in parallel structure). When you create a list of items or elements in parallel in a technical communication document, you are using this scheme of balance. For example, this passage uses parallelism:

> The introductory material in a set of instructions or a manual should accomplish four goals. It should allow users to gauge whether this document is the right one to help them answer their question(s); it should help users decide whether the instructional level is too elementary or too advanced for their current skills; it should provide a list of requirements or equipment needed to complete the procedure; and, finally, it should supply a conceptual overview of the content of the document to assist users in processing the new information.

Each element in the list uses the same sentence structure, which aids reader comprehension. From a rhetorical perspective, the parallel sentence structure imposes a sense of uniform organization on the ideas being presented. Readers will feel that the writer is informed and competent to speak on this subject matter.

SCHEMES OF UNUSUAL OR INVERTED WORD ORDER include *parenthesis* (interrupting a sentence by inserting a word or phrase midway) and *apposition* (placing two elements side-by-side whereby the second one elaborates or alters our understanding of the first one). This section uses parenthesis throughout; each scheme is defined using a parenthetical element. Parenthesis is effective for supplying a quick clarification or definition of a term or concept that readers can use if they need it or skip over if they don't. From a rhetorical perspective, parenthesis is useful for clarifying or qualifying a point quickly and concisely without sending the discussion off into an entirely different direction. Apposition works in a way similar to parenthesis, but often the information it supplies is gratuitous: "The headings, titles using hierarchical and content words to inform and describe, serve as guide posts to your users as they move through an unfamiliar process." In this sentence the appositive provides additional information about the headings. It interrupts the flow of the sentence in a way similar to parenthesis, but because it is grammatically co-ordinate with the element that it follows (both are subjects in the example), the interruption does not stand out so starkly.

SCHEMES OF OMISSION *Ellipsis* (omitting a word that can be supplied by the context) is the most well known of the schemes of omission. Ellipsis can be useful in technical communication because it aids conciseness, as you can see in this example: "A follow-up test reveals that 100 per cent of users can examine the line drawing and quickly locate the birdbath on the waterfall." Omitted words: "they can." To use ellipsis successfully, make sure that the omitted words are grammatically compatible with what is stated.

SCHEMES OF REPETITION involve repeating words or groups of words at different points in the sentence (e.g., *alliteration*—a series of words all starting with the same letter; *anaphora*—repeating the same word at the start of successive clauses; *epistrophe*—repeating the same words at the end of successive clauses). The example used to illustrate parallelism above also uses a scheme of repetition: anaphora. The four elements listed all start with the phrase "it should": "it should allow users ... ; it should help users ... ; it should provide ... ; and, finally, it should supply." The repetition of these phrases establishes a rhythm to the list that emphasizes how important it is to include all of these elements in the overview.

As you can see from these examples, artful changes to word order are common in technical communication, and they are important for adding rhetorical significance to the points being made.

TROPES (CHANGING WORD MEANING)

Tropes, or methods for changing word meaning, are another interesting and useful way to add impact and clarity to your technical

Adapting the Simile or Metaphor to the Intended Reader

- Who do you think is the intended audience for the description in Figure 4.4?
- What evidence can you point to in support of your conclusion?

Identify a different target audience, and then revise the description, changing the simile to better suit your choice.

Peristalsis is the action undertaken by your stomach to digest the food that enters it. Think of the stomach as a salad dressing pouch, the kind distributed at a fast food restaurant. The Italian dressing it contains can only exit from one end after you squeeze the pouch between your thumb and index finger. The contents move under the pressure from the sealed end of the packet down to the opening. In a similar way, food enters your stomach from the esophagus, and the muscle contractions of your stomach move the food in one direction from the entrance to the exit to the small intestines.

FIGURE 4.4

The action of peristalsis is made clearer through the use of a simile. Who is the audience for this description?

prose. While rhetoric texts identify as many as 17 different tropes, in this section, we will discuss the five that you will find most useful to incorporate into your prose in technical communication. If you find this topic interesting and would like more information, consult the sources listed under the heading "Resources on figurative language." This section defines and describes the following tropes or methods for changing word meaning:

- Metaphor (and simile)
- Metonymy
- Hyperbole
- Litotes
- Rhetorical question

Metaphor (and simile)

Most people are familiar with metaphor and simile, in which a comparison is made between two things that share something in common but are essentially different. Simile is an explicit comparison, while metaphor is implied. The function of metaphor in language has been the source of much discussion. While some people suggest that comparison plays mainly a decorative role in language, helping us to better describe our experiences, others argue that it plays a basic role in our ability to communicate and express ourselves. To support their contention that metaphor is a cognitive function that helps us organize and order our experience, George Lakoff and Mark Johnson, two cognitive linguists, point to expressions such as "I attacked Gary's argument," which only makes sense if you recognize that it draws on the metaphor that argument is war. They note other metaphors in our language that we use to conceptualize our experience. For example, in the sentence "After Patrice failed that quiz, she was really down," the speaker uses a spatial metaphor: up is good, healthy, happy, and down is bad, ill, or depressed.

Comparisons such as metaphor and simile are foundational in technical communication because they offer ways to help readers and users learn and understand complex technical ideas. Science has made extensive use of comparisons in the form of metaphor (extensively used to develop theories) and analogy (fundamental to interpreting scientific data) as an aid to understanding new phenomena. Scientists draw comparisons between the known and the unknown to gain insight into the nature and behaviour of the unknown.

As a technical communicator, you will find comparisons in the form of metaphor and simile useful for making abstract and foreign concepts more concrete and familiar to non-specialist readers. Figure 4.4 uses a simile (an explicit comparison that uses "like" or "as") to help the reader visualize the type of action and direction of movement in the concept of peristalsis.

Metonymy

Metonymy is a trope or change of meaning that substitutes an attribute or part of a thing to stand for the whole thing. For example, in the sentence "The pen is mightier than the sword," the writer has substituted "pen" for author or writer and "sword" for soldier. These substitutions of the attribute for the person make the powerful and concise argument that skilful writing can be more effective than military action. The change of meaning comes into play when the reader mentally fills in the missing parts—the professions alluded to—and comprehends the writer's point. Because readers have to participate in the discussion, drawing the connections implied by the writer, the trope of metonymy has a persuasive effect: readers who actively join the conversation feel more emotional investment in the discussion than those who passively receive another's point of view.

In technical communication, metonymy can be a useful trope because it allows you to compress a complex idea into a brief reference while also actively engaging your readers' interest. For example, scientists use metonymic substitution as a type of shorthand communication with readers. They substitute a single word or phrase for a complex theory, and their readers draw on their previous knowledge of the subject matter to fill in the gaps around the word or phrase. Of course, in this instance, the scientist's readers are also experts in the field, so the writer can rely on readers easily making these connections. If you are addressing a non-specialist or non-technical audience, then you should avoid using metonymy in this way because readers probably lack the knowledge to fill in the link between attribute and object.

However, once you have provided non-technical readers with the background they need to understand the shorthand reference, you can use metonymy to invoke the larger picture for them in a quick

---

THIS EXAMPLE DEFINES THE THEORY BEHIND THE METONYMY "ULTRAVIOLET SHIFT."

"When light falls on a semiconductor, depending on the band gap of the material, the wavelengths of light that match the band gap and larger energies are absorbed by the semiconductor and the longer wavelengths are transmitted. The visible wavelengths that are absorbed can be identified by their colour in the spectrum, whereas the infrared and ultraviolet wavelengths (which the human eye cannot see unaided) can be perceived by optical detectors. If a quantum well is created in the semiconductor, the film will absorb wavelengths up to the ultraviolet—a fact that can be measured. The shift of the optical gap toward the blue end of the spectrum—an ultraviolet shift—would provide one piece of scientific evidence that the multilayered films were forming quantum wells."

FIGURE 4.5

A brief description of the theory that becomes embodied in the phrase "ultraviolet shift," used by physicists studying amorphous silicon multilayered thin films.

Source: Heather Graves, Rhetoric in(to) Science (Cresskill, NJ: Hampton, 2005), 199.

and concise way. Figure 4.5 explains the theory behind the metonymic phrase "ultraviolet shift," used by researchers studying the properties of amorphous silicon multilayered thin films. Unless you understand the actual physics of the measurement, you cannot follow what the physicists mean by "ultraviolet shift." However, with this explanation in mind, the researchers can then assume that a reader will know what they mean when they use this phrase to describe this aspect of the film's properties. The metonymic substitution is used as a way to make a complex discussion more concise.

Hyperbole

Hyperbole refers to an expression that exaggerates the point for rhetorical effect. In the following example, Steven Krug is arguing the necessity of user testing of a website when he notes, "I could recite some of the usual awe-inspiring statistics about how many *umpteen gazillion* dollars will be left on the table this year by sites that don't mind their usability P's and Q's."[3] To make the point that poor (and untested) designs lose money, he exaggerates the amount of money that website owners will lose because they didn't test their sites to correct usability problems.

Litotes

Litotes is the opposite of hyperbole, describing an understatement, again to achieve a rhetorical effect. For example, the following warning uses understatement to inform readers of potential dangerous usages of the product it accompanies: "Using this appliance in ways incompatible with manufacturer instructions may result in unfortunate consequences including risk of fire or death." Most people consider "death" to be more significant than an "unfortunate consequence." In this case, the understatement results in emphasizing rather than downplaying the potential danger. From a psychological standpoint, readers are more likely to remember the understatement and the warning than a hysterical overstatement.

Rhetorical question

This type of question is one that is posed not because the writer or speaker expects an answer from the reader or audience but because he or she is about to elaborate an answer, usually one that pertains in some way to the point being argued. Technical manuals, especially ones conveying troubleshooting information, often use rhetorical questions by phrasing headings in the form of questions. An example is "How do I restore my hard drive to its original set of programs?" Rhetorical questions can provide a concise and accessible way to present information from the users' perspective.

3   Steven Krug, *Don't Make Me Think: A Common Sense Approach to Web Usability* (Berkeley, CA: New Riders Press, 2000), 9. (Italics were added.)

LAB ASSIGNMENT 4.1

USING RHETORICAL FIGURES IN YOUR WRITING

■ Use a paragraph from an existing assignment, or write a paragraph on the spot about a technical subject of which you have some knowledge.

■ Revise the paragraph, introducing several of these rhetorical figures into it where they can improve the clarity or rhetorical force of your prose.

■ Then write a paragraph explaining the ways in which you think the revised sentences improve or add to the style of the paragraph.

Resources on figurative language

Corbett, Edward P.J., and Robert Connors. *Classical Rhetoric for the Modern Student*. 4th ed. New York: Oxford, 1998.

Crowley, Sharon, and Debra Hawhee. *Ancient Rhetorics for Contemporary Students*. 3rd ed. New York: Longman, 2003.

Analysing prose

This section introduces you to ways of analysing the prose in different kinds of documents. You can use these tools of analysis to identify the central features of a particular genre or writing style; doing this will help you emulate it and move more quickly towards being able to write that style or genre well. After all, you may be hired in the first place based on your technical skills in accounting or engineering or information technology, but you are much more likely to keep your job and be promoted if you can speak and write effectively. As Kitty Locker notes, "Good writers earn more. Linguist Stephen Reder has found that among people with two- or four-year degrees, workers in the top 20% of writing ability earn, on average, more than three times as much as workers whose writing falls into the worst 20%."[4]

One way to move yourself into the top 20 per cent as you continue to develop and sharpen your writing abilities is to become proficient at writing a wide range of genres and styles. If you can look at a sample document and figure out how the sentences are put together and how the information is organized and presented in this kind of document, you are already one step ahead in being able to write your own version of this document. Then you can have a co-worker or supervisor review your draft to help you correct any misperceptions or misjudgements about the document. At the same time, supervisors will be impressed by your ability to learn new genres and styles quickly and relatively easily.

4   Kitty O. Locker, *Business and Administrative Communication*, 5th ed. (New York: Irwin McGraw-Hill, 2000), 4.

When you examine an unfamiliar genre for the first time, there are three different aspects that you should focus on to identify its key features:

- Style
- Structure
- Register

Style refers to such elements as sentence length, sentence kind and complexity, word choice, and the use of figurative language such as metaphors. Structure refers to the way a document or genre is organized—whether it is subdivided into sections, the general length of each section, and the type of content in each section. Register refers to the level of the language used in the document or genre. Is it casual, informal, or formal? Does the document use contractions (an indication of informality)? Does it use "I"?

In such an analysis, the goal is usually to figure out what work each paragraph is doing, starting with the introduction and then working through the paragraphs to determine what each one is accomplishing and what it contributes to the overall purpose of the document.

ANALYSING STYLE

If you are studying the prose style of a document or genre, you generally try to collect several examples of that type of genre or document to make sure that your study produces accurate conclusions. To analyse the style, you usually look closely at several stylistic features of the examples.

Analysing prose style requires some basic knowledge of grammar and some basic arithmetical skills, as you count different elements in the document that you are studying and then calculate the average of such things as sentence length, paragraph length, and type of sentence.

Once you have finished counting the stylistic features and calculating percentages, examine the numbers with the goal of making some generalizations about how these features are used in these documents. Assess the patterns that you see emerging from the similarities since these are your key features describing the style of the type of document that you want to emulate. You can use these results to help you make decisions about how to write your own version of this type of document.

Here is a list of the kinds of stylistic elements that you could examine with the goal of reaching generalized conclusions about what makes for an appropriate style in that genre or for that document:

Sentences

LENGTH

- Count the number of words in each sentence.
- Calculate the average sentence length.

What general conclusions can you reach about sentence length in this document or genre, based on your analysis?

TYPE AND VARIETY

- Identify each sentence: is it simple, compound, complex, or compound-complex?
- Count the total number of each type of sentence in the document or genre.

What is the proportion of one type of sentence used to the others?

Do you notice patterns as to where different types of sentences occur in the paragraphs? (For example, topic sentences are usually simple sentences, used at the beginning of each paragraph.)

What general conclusions can you reach, based on your analysis, about the variety of sentences use in this type of document?

PHRASES AND SUBORDINATE CLAUSES

- Count the number of phrases and subordinate clauses in the document.
- Count any phrases set off by commas.

What is the average number of phrases or dependent clauses per sentence?

What general conclusions can you reach about using phrases or dependent clauses in this document or genre?

COMBINING SIMPLE SENTENCES

- Assess how many sentences are created by combining two or more simple sentences.

What does the number of combined ideas tell you about the complexity of the ideas presented in your sample?

SUBORDINATION OF IDEAS

- Count the number of ideas that appear in subordinate clauses in the sentences in two or three paragraphs.

What does this analysis tell you about the number of ideas presented in the sentences in your sample?

How complex are the thoughts presented in your sample? (One indication of complexity comes through the number of ideas embedded in the subordinate clauses in the sentences in a paragraph).

COMPLEX SENTENCES

- Count the number of complex sentences in your sample.

What kind of work are these sentences doing in relation to the rest of the paragraph or sample?

What does the number of complex sentences in the passage tell you about the content of the information being presented?

Paragraphs

RELATIVE LENGTH

- Count the number of words in each paragraph.
- Count the number of sentences in each paragraph.

What is the average word length of paragraphs in this document?

How many sentences, on average, does the typical paragraph contain in this document?

What general conclusions can you reach about paragraph length, based on your analysis?

TOPIC SENTENCES

- Assess the use of topic sentences in this document or genre:

Does every paragraph have a topic sentence?

Where are topic sentences located in the paragraphs?

Can you reach any general conclusions about explicitness and location of topic sentences in this document or genre?

TRANSITIONAL ELEMENTS

- Locate the transitional phrases or elements that are used to move from one topic to the next.
- Count the number of transitional phrases or elements used in the document.

What is the most common method used to change topics?

What general conclusions can you reach about how transitional elements are used in this type of document or genre?

METHODS OF IDEA DEVELOPMENT

- Examine the patterns of organization used in the paragraphs.
- Count the different methods that you identify.

Based on your analysis, which is the most popular method? The least popular method?

What general conclusions can you make about how ideas are developed in the paragraphs in this document?

SUMMARY ELEMENTS

- Examine concluding sentences and paragraphs in this document.

What methods are used to conclude a point or discussion?

Count the number of times each method is used in the document.

What general conclusions can you make about how main ideas are summarized in this document or genre, based on this analysis?

Diction (word choice)

JARGON, CONVERSATION, ERUDITION

- Count the total number of nouns, pronouns, verbs, adjectives, and adverbs used in the document.
- Calculate the percentage of nouns and pronouns in relation to the total.
- Calculate the percentage of verbs in relation to the total.
- Calculate the number of adjectives and adverbs in relation to the total.

What conclusions can you reach about the weighting of these types of words in this document or genre? (For example, is the document focused on things rather than actions, based on its high usage of nouns and pronouns?)

- Count the number of words that are technical or jargon words.
- Count the number of words that are conversational or ordinary.
- Count the number of words that are academic or specialized.
- Calculate the percentage of these types of words against the total number.

What conclusions can you reach about the level of language used in this document? (Is it highly technical? Is it conversational?)

TECHNICAL JARGON (JARGON AND ETHOS)

- Examine how the technical language and jargon is used in the document or genre.

What general conclusions can you reach about when jargon is used in this type of document (e.g., to establish ethos or credibility on the subject matter; to address other specialists)?

TONE (VOICE/ETHOS OF KNOWLEDGEABLE FRIEND)—CONTRACTIONS AND DICTION

- Count the number of contractions used in the document.
- Calculate the percentage of contractions against the total number of words.

What general conclusions can you reach about the level of formality of this document, based on the use of contractions?

What other techniques (other than using contractions) did the writer use to establish and maintain the level of formality?

STYLISTIC FLOURISHES, CULTURAL CLICHÉS, AND SPECIALIST JARGON

- Count the number of unusual phrases or words that stand out in the document.
- Analyse how these phrases or words are used:

What are they supposed to add to the document, either in tone, formality, or level of sophistication?

What conclusions can you reach about the appropriateness of these types of words or phrases for this type of document or genre?

GENERATE A LIST OF THE KEY FEATURES AND CONCLUSIONS THAT YOUR ANALYSIS HAS PRODUCED THAT WILL BE MOST USEFUL FOR YOU AS YOU BEGIN TO WRITE YOUR OWN VERSION OF THIS TYPE OF DOCUMENT OR GENRE.

LAB ASSIGNMENT 4.2

ANALYSING YOUR OWN PROSE STYLE

Select 4 to 5 paragraphs (depending upon their length) from one of your recently written papers for technical communication, and apply this process of analysis to them. When you have completed analysing your prose style, write a memo reporting what you found out about your writing style. Address the memo to your instructor or to someone else whom you think would find this information interesting.

ANALYSING STRUCTURE

The next stage in this process of analysing a document with the goal of reproducing its type is to examine its structure to determine how the information is organized and presented. One place to start is with what Charles Kostelnick calls the "supratextual" elements, meaning such things as the size of the document, its orientation, the type of cover (if any), the binding, and the paper or media of presentation. After assessing the outward qualities of the document, you then explore how the information is organized and presented in the main part of the document. You are looking for such organizational markers as main and subordinate headings, chapters, the nature and location of summary information (e.g., an abstract, summary paragraphs at the end of major sections), and so on. Determine what kinds of introductory information are included in the document.

ANALYSING REGISTER

To determine the register or "form of language customarily used in particular circumstances" (*Concise Oxford Dictionary*), you should return to your earlier analysis of diction, paying special attention to the conclusions about tone, level of language, and stylistic flourishes, etc., because these are the main sources of information about the register used for this type of document. If your earlier analysis shows no use of contractions in this type of document, it suggests that the register or customary level of language for this document is toward the "formal" end of the scale.

Argumentation: Constructing a persuasive case

Another important aspect of writing effective technical prose is learning to recognize when you need to make a persuasive case for something and being able to do so. This section briefly covers the basics of writing an effective argument. Persuasion is writing that seeks to move a reader to a particular action or belief. More than 2,000 years ago, Aristotle identified three aspects of argument that can result in persuasion, when done well: *logos* (logic), or the claims and evidence that you offer in support of your position; *ethos* (credibility), or the ways that, as a writer or speaker, you demonstrate that you are trustworthy and competent to speak on your subject; and *pathos*, or the emotions that you evoke in your readers in response to what you say about your subject. These three areas work together to result in persuasion. If you ignore any of these three appeals (to logic, credibility, or emotion), you risk not achieving your goal of developing a convincing argument. If you don't convince your reader, you may find your proposal not being funded or the contract being awarded to someone else.

LOGOS

Logos, or logical appeal, refers to the internal consistency of your message. In other words, when you are writing an argument, your message should contain claims—i.e., statements that assert a position on some issue—and evidence—i.e., facts, data, or examples that support the claims and establish their validity as statements. In other words, if you assert a claim but add no evidence to back it, then that is all you have: an assertion. However, an assertion supported by evidence becomes an argument. Readers consider and evaluate the validity of your evidence (as well as your claim) and find your logic persuasive (or not). In this way, then, logical appeals target the reader's mind.

Stephen Toulmin's system of informal logic provides a useful way both to develop and to assess arguments. Figure 4.6 outlines Toulmin's informal logic, defining the basic elements and providing examples to help you understand them. Study this figure for a few minutes to familiarize yourself with the basic components of informal logic.

This type of logic was developed after Toulmin observed lawyers in courtrooms making arguments. He analysed how they constructed their arguments, that is, how and when they produced evidence to

Claim: a statement

We should update the office computers.

Stated reason: The current operating system is incompatible with new versions of software we need.

Evidence supporting stated reason (or GROUNDS): (facts, data, statistics, testimony, examples)

We need to create instructional design materials using the e-learning toolkit for Dreamweaver, but it only works with XP operating system.

Unstated assumption (or WARRANT): (draws on beliefs, values of reader)

Creating the instructional design materials is important.

Using Dreamweaver and the e-learning toolkit is the only way we can create these materials.

If we replace one computer, we should replace them all.

Evidence supporting unstated assumption (or BACKING): (facts, data, statistics, testimony, examples)

We promised state-of-the-art instructional design materials, and the e-learning toolkit is the most up-to-date program for creating these lessons.

We need everyone working on the same level of equipment.

Argument against this position (conditions of REBUTTAL):

Extra programming using JavaScript will get us a similar type of lesson without the expense of up-dating the office computers.

We can update the operating systems without replacing the computers.

Not every employee is going to use the e-learning toolkit in doing his or her job.

QUALIFIERS (hedges that should be added to a claim to make it less vulnerable to refutation)

We should update the instructional designers' office computers because they need Dreamweaver's e-learning toolkit to complete a contract, and this software is only compatible with the XP (and more recent) operating systems.

FIGURE 4.6
Toulmin's informal logic for developing and evaluating logical appeals

support claims that they made. His system uses claims, grounds, warrants, and backing to flesh out arguments that rely on assumptions, beliefs, and values potentially shared within a community. Usually, the reason stated in support of a particular claim assumes some shared ground between the speaker and listener (or the writer and reader). Listeners or readers can usually identify the assumption that underlies the arguer's point, and, if they share that assumption, then they will grant the speaker or writer's point; if they do not share that assumption, they may refute the claim or reason. Let's look at another example to give you a clearer idea of how informal logic works for developing an argument: "The Ministry of Transportation should stop using excessive salt and chemical de-icers on the roads because they are killing vegetation, including trees, along the sides of the highways."

The original claim

CLAIM: The Ministry of Transportation should stop using excessive salt and chemical de-icers on the roads.

STATED REASON: Because they [the salt and chemical de-icers] are killing vegetation, including trees, along the sides of the highways.

Adding grounds

The next step in developing this argument is to add some evidence (i.e., GROUNDS) to support the stated reason. Here are some grounds that we could use to support this statement:

- Examples of dead vegetation that can be seen along a local highway
- Statistics about vegetation death each spring
- Comparative data about vegetation death along roadsides where municipalities use more sand than salt to improve icy road conditions
- Studies showing that moderate salt use does not kill vegetation.

Warrants for this claim

In the stated reason ("because they are killing vegetation, including trees, along the sides of the highways"), what assumptions are we making about both the claim (stop using excessive salt, etc.) and the reason (the dead vegetation)? Here are some of the unstated assumptions (or WARRANTS) that underlie this statement:

- The excessive salt and chemical de-icers are the causes of the dead vegetation. (assumption)
- The dead vegetation is a problem that needs a solution. (assumption)
- It is wrong to kill trees in this way. (value)
- Other methods exist to treat the ice that do not kill the vegetation. (assumption)
- Excessive salt and other de-icer use will cause additional environmental problems.

In creating this argument, we are relying on our readers to share these assumptions or at least be willing to acknowledge them as valid assumptions (even if they contest or disagree with them). In other words, we assume that our readers share values similar to ours at least about salting icy roads.

Of the assumptions or warrants listed, do you disagree with any of them? Can you understand how other reasonable people might disagree with any of them? For example, it seems reasonable to try to think of other things that might be causing the vegetation to die: drought conditions in the fall, some disease that hasn't yet been diagnosed, etc. It also seems reasonable to ask whether the dying vegetation is really a problem. Why can't we reseed each spring? Is this really a problem that we need to solve right away? We might also ask about cost-effective alternatives to salt and chemicals.

Developing backing for the warrants

Given that we can easily think of questions about the assumptions or warrants for the original claim, we should probably develop some evidence (or BACKING) to support these warrants. What backing can we offer to support some of these assumptions?

> To support the warrant that the excessive salt and chemical de-icers cause the dead vegetation, we could do research to find studies that show how salt and chemicals kill plants.

> To back the warrant that this is a problem we should solve, we could point to the costs of removing and replanting dead trees and other vegetation along roadways (not to mention de-contaminating the soil). We might also cite research studies that show we need trees along roadways to reduce drifting and white-outs during winter storms. This backing would address the unstated assumption that, if roadside trees die, we have to replace them.

> To back the warrant that it is wrong to kill trees in this way, we could point to the costs of replacement, the value of the trees in these locations, and the role the trees have in beautifying what are essentially ugly strips of asphalt.

> Finally, to back the warrant that there are other methods of treating road ice, we might explore the alternatives (sand, sand mixed with salt, revolutionary new material that fertilizes the ground in the spring while also melting ice in winter, etc.)

With all of the evidence that we've developed through this analysis, we could easily write a paragraph that unpacks and supports the ideas originally stated in our claim. However, before we take this step, we should assess the conditions under which an unsympathetic reader might refute our claim. Once we revise our claim to qualify it somewhat, we can then write the argument.

Conditions of rebuttal

Through this analysis of the grounds, warrants, and backing of our original argumentative statement, we have come up with several places where our ideas are open to refutation, which has helped us then generate evidence to support our points more effectively.

If we now return to the original claim, and think hard about the weaknesses that we have not considered, we can identify some of its conditions of rebuttal: "The Ministry of Transportation should stop using excessive salt and chemical de-icers on the roads because they are killing vegetation, including trees, along the sides of the highways." Here are some of the potential problems we can see with this claim:

> We call for abandoning the use of excessive salt on *all* roadways. Opponents to this position might point to certain roads where the use of salt to reduce accidents and preserve human life might outweigh the cost of replacing vegetation and trees.

> Not all chemical de-icers kill vegetation, so by lumping salt and all chemical de-icers together in the original version, we undermine the validity of our whole claim.

> In addition, we might question the definition of "excessive": what quantity is excessive?

Qualifying our original claim

At this point, we should probably re-state our original claim, adding qualifiers to make it less easily open to refutation:

> The Ministry of Transportation should stop using salt on some roadways because it kills or significantly weakens the trees planted alongside the roads.

FIGURE 4.7
We have used some of the points from our analysis earlier to develop the revised claim into a well-supported claim, which is part of a larger argument.

The Ministry of Transportation should stop using salt on some roadways because it kills or significantly weakens the trees planted alongside the roads. The Salt Institute (http://www.saltinstitute.org) points out that excessive use of salt for road de-icing can kill vegetation because of its corrosive and toxic properties. One has only to drive along Highway 401 to see the brown pine and spruce trees that died last winter when ploughs shot roadside snow encrusted with salt twenty feet across the shoulder into the conifer forests that border the highway in many places. This dead vegetation is unattractive to drivers, and it may also constitute a road hazard when these dead trees begin falling after a few years. Branches and tree trunks along the roadside will have to be cleared away to stop them from being obstacles during accidents on the shoulders. Trees that were originally planted as windbreaks will have to be replaced or white-out and drifting hazards will increase along these stretches of road. These increased costs are directly related to the use of salt on our roadways in winter.

Figure 4.7 offers one way that our qualified claim could be developed into a well-supported paragraph that effectively argues our point. Usually the paragraph would be part of a larger argument (perhaps appearing in an environmental engineer's technical report on damage caused by roadways), in this case, arguing the environmental dangers of overusing road salt.

ETHOS

Ethos refers to the writer's credibility and trustworthiness. An ethical appeal is not directly related to "ethics" the way it is discussed in Chapter 2, but it is indirectly related in that, if the reader does not judge you to be an ethical speaker, based on the words that you use to present your viewpoint, he or she will likely not be persuaded by your argument. The goal in creating an ethical appeal is to present yourself as a knowledgeable, competent, and trustworthy person. While the logical appeal targets the readers' minds, the ethical appeal targets both their hearts and their minds. As they assess the persuasiveness of your arguments, readers are judging you as an authority on your topic. If you appear knowledgeable and thoughtful as you write, they will decide that you are a decent person and they should continue to read what you have written. If you contradict yourself or overlook an important point in the discussion, then readers will grow more sceptical of you as a credible voice on this subject. If readers judge you as incompetent or mean-spirited in your argument, they will not be persuaded by your ideas no matter how brilliant and logical they may be.

Here are three ways to create an ethical appeal in writing:

- Appear knowledgeable about your subject matter
- Respond fairly to opposing viewpoints
- Establish common ground with your readers.

Appear knowledgeable

In technical communication, there are several ways to demonstrate your knowledge of your subject matter. First, use technical language accurately when it is appropriate. That is, show that you know the key terms and concepts of the field by using them in context. At the same time, supply readers with definitions and explanations when they may not share your expertise in the area. Even if they are not entirely expert in the field, they will want to know that you are competent and well-informed since they are hiring you to complete a contract or project for them.

Second, provide a thorough and detailed discussion of the issues relevant to the topic. Another way to show your knowledge is to include a comprehensive discussion to demonstrate that you are familiar with the major issues and problems associated with the

---

IN-CLASS EXERCISE 4.7

Developing Evidence to Support a Claim

Expand each claim into a paragraph that provides support for the assumptions that underlie the claim and reason.

1. You should replace your worn asphalt shingles with a stainless steel roof because it will save you money.

2. Pesticides should be banned on residential lawns because they pollute the groundwater.

3. People who don't shovel their sidewalks within 24 hours of a winter storm should be fined because unshovelled walkways can cause injury to pedestrians.

4. The municipal government should identify several possible back-up dumpsites because the current landfill site is filling up faster than engineers predicted.

5. Wind turbines are a better source of electricity than nuclear power because they are safer and cleaner.

IN-CLASS EXERCISE 4.8

Demonstrating Credibility

Select a controversial issue in your field about which you have some knowledge, and write a one-paragraph argument in which you demonstrate that you are qualified to speak about the topic as you develop your perspective about the issue. Use the three methods discussed earlier to show your trustworthiness as a speaker on this topic.

topic. Of course, by suggesting you be comprehensive, we don't mean to also condone a wordy discussion—hit the important points, but also aim for clarity and conciseness, when these are appropriate.

Respond fairly to opposing viewpoints

When you are outlining a problem and arguing for a particular solution, you can enhance your credibility by acknowledging alternative solutions to the problem. Not only does this show your wide knowledge of the problem, but it also shows that you have considered alternatives other than the one you are recommending. The fact that you think about other possibilities will strengthen your argument for the solution that you do propose, especially from the perspective of building a strong ethical appeal.

Establish common ground

You can strengthen your relationship with your readers by demonstrating that you share some of their beliefs, values, and assumptions. These shared values and assumptions generally come out in the way that you talk about your subject matter. If you are going to have a sense of the beliefs, values, and assumptions of your readers, you must first have a clear sense of who your readers are. Some of the audience analysis techniques discussed in Chapter 1 will help you gain insight into your readers so that you can better anticipate their views on the subjects that you address in your technical prose. For example, if you are preparing a manual for novice users of a computer program, your knowledge of this user group may tell you that they are intimidated by learning complex functions. If you acknowledge this attitude briefly and then attempt to accommodate it by showing how the apparently complex function is really a series of relatively simple steps, a number of which they already know, you can create a strong ethical appeal through demonstrating that you understand and can respond to their concerns.

If you are writing a proposal to bid on a contract and you realize from the request for bids that the organization values the quality of the solution equally with the price, you can account for these values in the way that you underscore the high quality of your solution as well as its cost-effectiveness. Showing that you understand clients' needs can go a long way to demonstrating your shared values and your credibility as a potential contract worker.

PATHOS (EMOTIONAL APPEAL)

Pathos is a Greek word referring to the way that you invoke your readers' emotions to help them feel personally connected to your subject matter. It refers to the legitimate use of your readers' emotions or feelings to engage their minds on the topic. By legitimate, we mean valid emotion evoked by an understanding of the issues and their importance. Most people are familiar with advertisements that target your emotions to try to get you to purchase a product. For example, print and television ads try to convince you that you will be cool and hip if you drink their beverage; conversely, they try to make you anxious that others will perceive you as a loser if you don't drink this beverage. Since these appeals rely primarily on emotion, conjured up separately from reason or logic (does anyone *really* believe that drinking one brand of liquid over another can change a person's basic character?), they are illegitimate appeals to emotion. In argument, ethical use of emotion seeks to help readers become engaged in the topic by showing them its importance and helping them to feel a personal stake in the issues. If you are arguing for something that *is* important, then helping readers "feel" that importance is a critical step in persuading them to act. In fact, people can listen to a logical argument and believe that the speaker is a trustworthy person, but they will not change their behaviour unless they also feel some investment in the issue. In this way, a good emotional appeal targets the heart. At the same time, a powerful emotional appeal without either well-reasoned logic or an apparently trustworthy speaker will result in propaganda, which is not the kind of persuasion we are trying to achieve.

Here are two ways to create an effective emotional appeal:

- Use concrete examples and illustrations
- Use appropriate word choice, metaphors, and analogies.

Use examples

Creating an effective emotional appeal relies on bringing the subject matter alive for your readers. Concrete examples do this by adding specific detail that aids the imagination in painting a vivid picture. When readers can "see" the problem or point, they begin to care more about potential solutions or at least they want to hear more. Sometimes you can paint the picture in words; other times a visual might be more appropriate.

Use word choice, metaphors, and analogies

Another effective way to engage the emotions of your readers is through choosing the appropriate word to help them understand more clearly. For example, if a co-worker invites you to contribute your expertise to a project that he or she is working on, would you be more interested in participating if the project is described as a project, increased workload, a challenge, or an intriguing opportunity? Each word choice focuses on a different aspect of the experience:

- "Project" is neutral;
- "Increased workload" is negative, reminding you that you will get paid the same whether you participate or not;
- "Challenge" highlights the intellectual or innovative aspects of the work;
- "Intriguing opportunity" casts the work as positive and intellectually rewarding.

Now, of course, if the phrase chosen doesn't actually describe the work accurately (it is neither intriguing nor challenging) then such "shaping" tends to call attention to itself, perhaps generating cynicism and ridicule rather than participation. But the point is that the word chosen to describe the work can affect how you might react and respond to the invitation, whether you would be interested in the additional work because of what you might learn or accomplish from it or whether you would refuse the work because you are already over-subscribed.

If the concept or term is something that may be unfamiliar or uninteresting to readers, a comparison (metaphor or simile) can help them understand or see the similarities between the new idea and something that is familiar. If you can help your reader see the concept in terms of something familiar or important, you can kindle their interest in the topic, because they recognize its importance. For example, if you were writing an opinion piece on alternative sources of energy and you were discussing the tar sand deposits as a lucrative source of energy in Canada, you might point out to readers that reclaiming the oil from the tar sands has real costs in terms of the fresh water needed to extract the oil: "Let's not forget that refining the oil from the Canadian tar sands requires enormous quantities of fresh water that become too contaminated by the end of the process to reclaim. When we have removed the oil from the tar sands, we could risk ending up *like the archetypal castaway on the desert island* who moans, 'Water, water everywhere, but not a drop to drink!'" The comparison of Canadians to the castaway on the desert island who has no usable water is effective in focusing reader attention on a possible outcome of fully tapping the oil sand deposits. Readers who may not have been interested will likely have a sudden interest in knowing more about the refiners' plans to clean up this water or learn more about alternative energy sources to the tar sands. In this case, an apt comparison can educate your readers as to the important implications of the subject that you are discussing.

LAB ASSIGNMENT 4.3

CONSTRUCTING A PERSUASIVE ARGUMENT

Write a one-page argument on a subject with which you are familiar. Use the information in this section on creating logical, ethical, and emotional appeals to make your argument as well developed and convincing as you can.

Defining, describing, and explaining

As a technical communicator, you may find yourself frequently adjusting your writing to readers who have varying levels of knowledge of your subject matter. In one document, you may address readers who have sophisticated technical knowledge of a related field but an incomplete knowledge of the subject you are discussing, for example, health care workers who are learning a new treatment procedure. Such a situation requires some background explanation but not nearly as much as you would need for a lay audience or a novice. The health care workers would likely already know how to perform related procedures, so you could build on their existing knowledge. If you are writing primarily for novice users, you may define technical terms that would be unfamiliar to them and explain related technical concepts in a general way. The general description of concepts will help readers form a basic idea of the subject but not overwhelm them with details that they cannot process until they have additional knowledge and experience. If you are writing an operation manual for a new product, for example, a new type of magnetic resonance imaging machine (MRI), you may decide to include an illustration and description of the key features of the new design before you begin the instructions for use. These scenarios identify two techniques that technical communicators use to produce top quality documents: definition and description.

Definition and description are useful tools for a technical communicator. In technical communication, definitions are used to explain important subject matter related to concepts or terms. If readers are unfamiliar with a term, a well-placed definition can educate them exactly when they need it. Sometimes a term may have different meanings in different contexts so you define it to clarify how you are using it in your document. A clear definition removes potential confusion and ambiguity. A description is a verbal portrait of something—an object or an event.

DEFINITION

Definitions come in three kinds:

- Brief
- Formal or categorical
- Extended.

Brief definition

A brief definition is the practice of clarifying the meaning of a word by substituting a more familiar synonym (i.e., a parenthetical definition) or restating a word in different terms to make its meaning clear. For example, in an introduction to Middle Eastern cuisine, the writer uses parenthetical definitions to define clearly and concisely the two terms in the sentence that may be unfamiliar to cooks new to this cuisine: "Tahini (sesame seed paste) is a central ingredient of hummus (chick pea dip), as well as several other popular dishes."

Use a brief definition when your readers do not need detailed information. In the example above, the parenthetical inserts clarify the potentially unfamiliar terms, and readers who understand the terms without help can easily skip over these definitions. The following example is also a brief definition, although it is longer than the parenthetical version:

> The Archimedean screw is a wooden pump that was developed two millennia ago. The screw is encased in a cylinder, and water is lifted up by the screw when the handle is turned. When the water reaches the top of the screw, it pours out, into a pitcher or basin placed to catch it.

This definition explains how the Archimedean screw raises water from a river or well to ground level or higher. Two sentences provide you with the main components of the device as well as a brief description of how it works. Unless you are explaining how to build one, this explanation is probably sufficient for most readers.

TERM	CLASS	FEATURES
LED	Semiconductor	■ Light bulb without a filament ■ Doesn't get hot
Saturated fat	Fats from animals	■ Solid at room temperature ■ Liquid when heated
Wind turbines	Power generators	■ Create electricity from the power of the wind

TABLE 4.1
Parts of a formal or categorical definition.

Formal or categorical definition

A formal or categorical definition dates back to Aristotle's time in ancient Greece (500 BCE), and it consists of three parts:

- The term
- The class
- The features.

Here are several examples of categorical definitions (i.e., they "categorize" the term):

- An LED (light-emitting diode) [*the term*] is the simplest type of semiconductor [*the class*] that is a small light bulb without a filament and that doesn't get hot [*the features*].
- Saturated fats [*the term*] are fats produced from animals [*the class*] that are solid at room temperature and liquid when heated [*the features*].
- Wind turbines [*the term*] are power generators [*the class*] that create electricity from the power of the wind [*the features*].

The challenge to writing an accurate categorical definition is to use the three parts to progressively specialize the description so that the features listed pertain only to the term that you are defining. That is, the term lists an unfamiliar concept for readers (wind turbines); the class groups the concept into a larger group that shares some characteristics (power generators—methods of generating electricity from such things as water, nuclear fission, etc.); and then the features describe the concept further by distinguishing it from the larger group (uses wind power). Notice that the progression here is from the specific term to the more general category to the more specific details, so that by the time you are describing the features, they should be aspects that apply only to the small group and not to the larger group.

Extended definition

The third type of definition that you will use when writing technical prose is the extended definition, which, as it suggests, refers to a longer and more detailed characterization than the previous two. Use them when readers need more detail. The length of your extended definition should be based on both your readers' needs and your purpose in writing it: it may be as short as a paragraph or as long as several pages.

While your choices for creating a brief, parenthetical definition or even a formal/categorical definition are limited, your options for expanding a definition are several. Here is a list of strategies for developing extended definitions and descriptions:

- Operational definition
- Negative definition

IN-CLASS EXERCISE 4.9

Writing Categorical Definitions

Choose three technical terms from one of your areas of expertise, and write categorical definitions for each, being sure that the features you use to describe the term differentiate it from other members of the larger class.

HOW AN ATOMIC CLOCK WORKS

An atomic clock is a precise timekeeper based on measuring the electrical oscillation of an atom, such as cesium 133. An atomic clock keeps time by exciting a series of atoms, passing them through magnetic and microwave fields to alter their energy states, and, from their oscillation frequency, calculating the exact interval of one second.

An atomic clock works by heating cesium in a vacuum tube until the atoms boil. As they boil off, they move down the tube and pass through a magnetic field (the first of two that they will move through). This field collects cesium atoms of the correct energy state, which then pass through a microwave field generated by a crystal oscillator. At some point in each cycle, the microwave field crosses the frequency of 9,192,631,770 Hertz (cycles per second). The cesium atoms change their energy state when they come in contact with this frequency.

A second magnetic field at the far end of the vacuum tube collects those atoms that have changed their energy state. A detector measures the output of changed atoms striking it, and when the output peaks, the peak is used to correct the crystal oscillator and bring the microwave field to the exact frequency. The exact frequency is then divided by 9,192,631,770, which gives one pulse per second, the basic unit of time on our terrestrial clocks.

FIGURE 4.8
Operational definition of an atomic clock.

Source: Information adapted from howstuffworks.com.

IN-CLASS EXERCISE 4.10

Distinguish an Operational Definition from a Set of Instructions

- Which of the two passages in Figure 4.9 is the definition and which is the set of instructions? How can you tell?
- If you tried to make a biscuit joint using only the extended definition, how successful do you think your joint would be? Why or why not?

Write down a list of the notable characteristics that distinguish an operational definition from a set of instructions.

- Description of parts
- History/background
- Etymology
- Examples
- Cause and effect
- Analogy/comparison.

OPERATIONAL DEFINITION

An operational definition explains how something works to define what it is. Organize and develop an operational definition using these three steps:

1. Describe the whole device—that is, give an overview to orient your reader.
2. Explain in detail how the parts work together.
3. Conclude with an explanation of the way the parts work together to get their particular jobs done.

Figure 4.8 uses this organizational pattern to explain how an atomic clock works. It begins with a brief definition, noting the two basic aspects of this type of clock: how it works and what it's made of. The second part of the overview summarizes the components that comprise an atomic clock.

The second paragraph of the operational definition identifies the different parts of the clock and explains how they work together. The third paragraph shows how the parts interact to correct one another to measure accurately the one-second interval.

A. HOW A BISCUIT JOINER WORKS

A biscuit joiner is a small hand-held tool that cuts thin, half-moon-shaped slices of wood from the vertical sides of planed boards so that they can form a strong joint when they are glued together. Think of your tabletop, which is usually fashioned from a series of planks joined side-by-side. Small, oval wafers of wood coated with glue are then inserted into the half-moon-shaped incisions in the planks and clamped together until the glue dries. A series of skilfully cut biscuit joints will result in a perfectly flat, almost seamless looking tabletop that is both sturdy and beautiful.

B. HOW TO MAKE A BISCUIT JOINT

To make a biscuit joint, you will need the following:

Two planks of equal thickness

Waterproof wood glue

Three or four 5 cm. biscuit wafers

Two or three pipe clamps

Biscuit joiner

1. Calculate how many joints you will need (space them 8 to 12 inches apart).

2. Mark their locations on the right side of one plank and the left side of the other (i.e., the two surfaces that you will be joining together).

3. Hold the joiner parallel to the edge where you plan to make the joints.

4. Following your placement marks, depress trigger and form first joint.

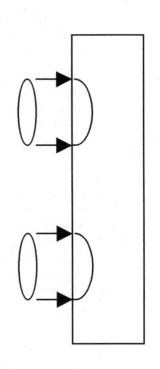

HOW IS AN OPERATIONAL DEFINITION DIFFERENT FROM A SET OF INSTRUCTIONS? Some students are initially confused about the difference between a set of instructions and an operational definition, especially when they attempt to define a process operationally. Examine Figure 4.9, and write a paragraph noting the ways in which the definition treats the subject matter as compared to how the instructions treat it.

FIGURE 4.9
An operational definition and a set of instructions.

NEGATIVE DEFINITION

Another strategy for developing an extended definition or description is to use a negative definition. That is, describe what the term or concept is *not* in order to highlight what it *is*. Figure 4.10 uses a negative definition to clarify the difference between a mummy and a fossil.

DESCRIPTION OF PARTS

A third technique for developing an extended definition is a description of the term or concept's parts. You can use a labelled visual

WHAT IS A MUMMY?

A mummy is the body of a person or animal in which some of the soft tissue, such as the organs or skin, does not decay. In the case of a mummy, the actual body of the corpse is preserved, either through natural or human processes. In this way, a mummy is different from a skeleton or fossil. A skeleton is just the bones from the body without any soft tissue. A fossil preserves the shape of the body (or plant) but the body then changes and hardens into rock.

FIGURE 4.10
An example of a negative definition.

FIGURE 4.11
This figure uses both a labelled visual and a description to educate readers on the parts of a sewing machine.

to depict the parts, or you can use a prose description, or both, as illustrated in Figure 4.11. The visual labels the major parts of a sewing machine that are mentioned in the prose description. The prose adds information about how the parts work together. Between the two media, readers gain an understanding of the machine as a whole and how it works.

HISTORY OR BACKGROUND

A fourth technique for extending a definition is to provide some history or background of the term or concept. For example, you might describe who invented the device or machine and when (if this information is appropriate). For example, "*Nanotechnology* first entered the scientific lexicon back in 1959 in a talk given by Nobel Prize-winning physicist Richard Feynman, when he proposed a new kind of manufacturing that would start with atoms and build up, in contrast to traditional manufacturing which starts with a large quantity of material and cuts away until it creates the finished product."

Another tactic is to elaborate the problem that the device or concept was intended to solve. Figure 4.12 is an example of an extended definition that elaborates the problem that beta-blocker medication was intended to solve.

A third strategy is to highlight key moments through history to show different nuances in the development of the idea or concept. Here is an example:

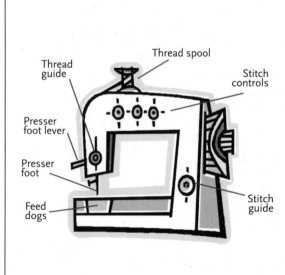

A sewing machine consists of several moving and stationary parts. A post on the top holds the spool of thread, while the loose end of the thread is inserted into THREAD GUIDES down the front of the machine, through the PRESSER FOOT thread guide, to the hole in the needle. On the front side of the machine, you will see three separate sets of knobs: three across the top, one on the left-hand side, and one on the right-hand side. The three knobs at the top (STITCH CONTROLS) allow you to select different types of stitches, as well as controlling the width of the stitches. The knob on the right upright (STITCH GAUGE) allows you to control the length of the stitch. The knob on the left-hand side (THREAD GUIDE) controls the thread tension, as well as acting as a guide to hold the thread in place while the machine is running. Under the needle, you will see a series of serrated plates: these are called the FEED DOGS, and they move the fabric under the needle as you sew a seam.

The idea of cold fusion has motivated scientific research since the nineteenth century when the ability of palladium to absorb hydrogen was first recognized. In the early twentieth century, several scientists claimed to have fused hydrogen into helium using palladium electrodes. In 1989, two chemists, Stanley Pons and Martin Fleischmann, announced a series of experiments in which they had produced excess heat that appeared to be due to a nuclear reaction. The term "cold fusion," originally invented in 1986 by Paul Palmer for his work with "geo-fusion," was appropriated for the work by Pons and Fleischmann in 1989.

Source: Information adapted from howstuffworks.com.

ETYMOLOGY

Explaining the etymology of a word is sometimes a useful tactic for elaborating an extended definition. By exploring the origin of the meaning of the term, you can help readers to understand its nuances. Here is an example from the *Concise Oxford Dictionary*: "Hydration is the noun form based on the verb 'hydrate,' which means 'to combine chemically with water; cause to absorb water' and it comes from the Greek word for water, *hudōr*."

WHAT ARE BETA-BLOCKER MEDICATIONS?

Beta-blockers are medications used to treat various types of heart disease including atrial fibrillation.

Atrial fibrillation (or congestive heart failure) refers to an irregular heartbeat caused by the contraction of the heart chambers in a disorganized way. In a healthy heart, the different chambers of the heart contract in a specific pattern. As electrical impulses travel through the heart chambers, they set off contractions, signalling to the right and left atria to contract. When they contract, the atria pump blood to the ventricles. In the ventricles, the electric impulse stimulates the right ventricle to pump blood to the lungs, while the left ventricle gets a message to pump blood to the rest of the body.

In a person who has atrial fibrillation, this normal rhythm does not happen. Instead the electrical impulses travel randomly through the heart chambers, triggering disorganized contractions that cause a variety of problems and symptoms, resulting in shortness of breath, chest pain, and possibly stroke.

Beta-blockers, used to treat patients with stable atrial fibrillation, work by slowing the heart rate....

FIGURE 4.12
This example elaborates one of the medical problems that the medication being defined (beta-blocker) is used to treat.

Groundwater pollution takes place when a number of critical factors are in place. These factors include the type of chemical, the type of soil around the chemical, the proximity of the groundwater at the site, and the decisions of humans at the site. For example, the method used to apply pesticides to a field, as well as the amount used and the timing of the application, can all determine whether the pesticide will reach groundwater reservoirs. If the pesticide is incorporated into the soil, the likelihood that it leaches through the soil will be much higher than if it were applied to foliage or surfaces. Again, if the pesticide is applied immediately before irrigation or a heavy rain, the chances are much higher that it will leach into the soil rather than serving as an effective barrier to crop infestations.

FIGURE 4.13
This example uses both cause and effect (how the pesticide is applied, the likely outcome) and example (human decisions).

WHAT IS A POTENTIAL ENERGY WELL?

A potential energy well is a one-dimensional well (imagine the furrows in a ploughed field where the individual furrow extends indefinitely in either direction but is bounded on either side by the adjacent furrows) in which a particle or electron is trapped in the well with infinite boundaries (the length of the furrow) and infinite barriers (the adjacent furrows). The particle (or electron) can move along the plane of the well, but it cannot move through the barrier. After the particle becomes trapped in the well, however, its energy can become "quantized." If the barrier has a finite height and width, then the quantized particle can "tunnel" or move through the barrier, rendering it essentially transparent.

FIGURE 4.14
In this passage the writer draws an analogy between a potential energy well (in quantum physics) and the furrows in a ploughed field to make clear the significant characteristics of a potential energy well.

Source: Heather Graves, Rhetoric in(to) Science *(Cresskill, NJ: Hampton, 2005).*

EXAMPLES

Giving one or a series of examples is another way to make a concept or term clearer to readers. For example, the various figures in this section of the chapter are intended to help you to see some of the possibilities of these various ways of defining or describing technical phenomena, so as to assist you in your own work. As you can see, an example fills in the details and answers questions that a brief statement may raise. It can also spark an inspiration for a good way to complete a task.

CAUSE AND EFFECT

Another way to describe or define a term or concept is to use cause and effect to explain a process or procedure. For example, Figure 4.13 is part of a longer discussion on groundwater pollution. In defining the factors that contribute to groundwater pollution, the writer elaborates what is meant by "human decisions" by providing an example of how farmers may use pesticides. The decision to apply

a pesticide into the soil around plants can lead to the increased likelihood of it leaching through the soil to the groundwater. In addition,
deciding to apply the pesticide immediately before irrigating the field
or before a downpour is another *cause* that can lead to the pesticide
being washed off the field and into drainage ditches (*effect*) and eventually into groundwater supplies.

ANALOGY/COMPARISON

Another effective way to explain or describe a complex concept is
to use a comparison or an analogy—that is, compare the new and
unfamiliar idea to an ordinary or well-known concept or thing. The
areas of similarity between the two entities can help readers begin
to understand the key features of the unfamiliar concept and move
more quickly towards comprehension. Figure 4.14 uses an analogy
to bring readers up to speed quickly on a sophisticated scientific idea,
the quantum or potential energy well.

LAB ASSIGNMENT 4.4

IDENTIFYING METHODS OF DEFINING, DESCRIBING, AND EXPLAINING

Using the Internet, find three or four good examples of extended definitions (howstuffworks.
com is a good place to start). Analyse each example to determine which strategies the writer
has used to develop the expanded definition or description.

Write a memo reporting the results of your analysis of the three or four examples:

■ Which strategies seemed most popular? Useful? (Quote the text critical to your analysis as
  evidence for your conclusions.)
■ Did you identify any strategies that were not mentioned in this section? If so, include them
  in your report.
■ Then write a paragraph explaining the ways in which you think the revised sentences
  improve or add to the style of the paragraph.

LAB ASSIGNMENT 4.5

DEFINING OR DESCRIBING A TECHNICAL CONCEPT OR DEVICE

Select a technical concept or device and write a definition or description of it using as many of
the strategies from this section of Chapter 4 as you can.

■ Select a specific audience for your definition/description (*not* a general audience, but one
  with a certain level of knowledge of the subject matter).
■ Length depends on the complexity of the topic and the needs of your audience.

CHAPTER FIVE

Designing documents and page layout

What is document design?

The term "document design" refers to the page layout of a document, that is, where the visuals and information are placed on a page and the visual connection or relationship between these elements on one page and other pages in a multi-page document (for example, a user manual or a technical report). While the placement of illustrations, text, and headings might seem like an insignificant matter, the way that the information on a page is organized and laid out can have a critical impact on users and their experience with the text. Many of us have had the experience of buying a product that needs assembly and then wrestling with the instructions because the order of presentation of information is not logical or easy to understand. Sometimes the information is presented from an educational rather than an action perspective. For example, the instructions might first advertise other, related products or highlight various features of your purchase rather than giving you a brief overview of how the assembly information is organized and what equipment you need to use during the assembly process, and then proceeding directly to the first step that moves you toward your goal: using the item.

The introductory explanation and the order in which information is presented directly affect your experience as a user of the product, and a thoughtful (i.e., presented from the perspective of the user) or useful presentation can mean the difference between quick assembly and several hours of frustration and anger as you try various configurations, none of which seem to work. The result can be your decision to return the item and demand a refund because you could not assemble it successfully. This outcome is really the worst possible one because it results not only in products returned to the manufacturer but also in the long-term generation of ill will on the part of consumers toward a company's products. Research has shown that people who are pleased with a product will tell three or four people

FIGURE 5.1
A user guide
that pays no
attention to
document
design.

Thanks for buying "Easy Guide to HTML." Also check out our other great products: "Easy Guide to NotePad" and "Easy Guide to Internet Searching," available at your favourite electronics store. "Easy Guide to HTML" gives you a quick introduction to the web-design language, HTML, or "hyper-text-markup-language," which will assist you in creating your own web pages without having to spend a lot of money on one of those fancy WYSYWYG (what you see is what you get) web design programs, such as FrontPage, Dreamweaver, etc. To get started creating your own web page, you need to open the Notepad program on your computer, which is usually available through the start button, then scroll up to programs, then click on Notepad. When the new page opens, you can begin right away by typing some of the basic HTML commands listed below.

about it, while people who are dissatisfied will tell seventeen people about their bad experience. Very many of these bad experiences can negatively affect a company's profits.

What is the difference between a well-designed document and one that isn't? Examine and compare the way information is laid out in Figures 5.1 and 5.2.

The writer of the user guide in Figure 5.1 has paid no attention to document design. Instead, this writer has structured the information in paragraph form, used a non-proportioned type face (courier) that is hard to read, and omitted headings, illustrations, and other aids that would help users to recognize the overall organization and find

EASY GUIDE TO HTML

Overview
This guide should get you started with the basics of HTML. It lists system requirements, as well as basic to advanced codes for creating a web page using HTML. Instructions are marked according to the user's background experience.

System Requirements
- Notepad program
- Internet connection
- Server space for posting your files
- Web browser for previewing your files

Figure 1.1. Opening Notepad.

A. Opening Notepad (for beginners)
1. Click on the "start" icon in the bottom left corner of your screen.
2. Scroll up to "all programs," and "click."
3. Scroll up to "accessories," and "click."
4. Scroll down the column of choices, and click on "Notepad."

See Figure 1.1.
The program will open, and you will see a blank file.

B. Creating your first file (Index.htm)

FIGURE 5.2
Principles of
document
design applied
to a users'
manual

the key points they need quickly. Without such signposts to provide a context for the information, users have to start reading at the first line and proceed through all of the text, whether or not they are actually interested in this information, hoping to find a relevant sentence or two on how to get started. Some users will persevere; others will not. Some will proceed without instructions, playing around with the possibilities, hoping to stumble on something useful; others will jump ahead looking for a paragraph that seems as if it might be relevant. Now compare the page layout in Figure 5.2 on the previous page. In this version of the user's guide, the extraneous information has been separated from the actual instructions on how to begin using HTML. Headings divide the sections and cue readers as to where to look for the specific steps they would like to perform. If readers are not beginners, then they can easily skip over the first step, which contains information they already know. An illustration complements the text in Step A.

In Figure 5.2 the writer has paid attention to both organization and presentation by breaking up the information into manageable sections that are easy to distinguish. Figures 5.1 and 5.2 highlight how attention to page layout can facilitate or hinder users in their quest to accomplish a goal. This chapter sets out some specific strategies that should be useful in helping you to think about how to organize and present your information. In addition, it outlines several design principles that will also help you judge whether or not your layout is effective and useful.

TO BUILD YOUR SKILLS: You should start to critically examine the layout and design of other documents that you encounter in your life. Decide how effective their design is, and assess how the principles from this chapter might be applied to improve the design. Also collect effective design ideas that you might incorporate into your own projects.

Exercise 5.1 should give you some insight into the primary competing demands in document design: aesthetics versus usability. Technical communicators must always negotiate the competing demands of attractiveness (aesthetics) and ease of use (usability) when they create technical documents. If attractiveness gets the upper hand, users may enthusiastically open the manual but be confused about how to begin; on the other hand, a completely functional design can sap users' interest before they even open the cover. Who hasn't unfolded the 8 ½" x 14" black and white instructions that come with any new gadget, looked at the poorly reproduced line drawings, and felt that sinking feeling that comes from being unsure where to begin? Your goal as a technical communicator is to balance the attractiveness and the usefulness of your page layout.

IN-CLASS EXERCISE 5.1

Evaluating Quality in Document Design

Gather together a sample of technical documents, perhaps including owners' manuals, assembly instructions, reference guides, and maybe an insurance policy or annual report. You need a selection of pieces that present technical information for a lay audience. When you have five or six different examples, study the page layout of each one and compare the way the information is presented.

Consider such elements as
- the typeface choices;
- the use and function of headings;
- the length of paragraphs;
- the number of paragraphs in each section;
- the type, location, and function of any visuals;
- the labelling of figures or tables;
- the formatting and presentation of any instructions;
- the formatting of notes, cautions, or warnings; and
- any other design choices that contribute to how the information is laid out on the page or pages.

Use the questions below to help you compare the quality of the design displayed in your selection of sample documents:
- Which layout seems more attractive to you? Easier to follow?

continued...

- What relationship do you see between how eye-catching the layout is and how easy it is to locate a particular piece of information?
- Can you find sections that seem out of order or that relate to the other sections in a confusing way?
- What techniques have the designers used to guide you through the page content?
- Which samples appear to have the most logical presentation of information?
- How appropriate are any visuals to the purpose of the document?
- Can you find any samples that don't have illustrations but probably should have?
- What kinds of visuals do you think would improve the presentation of information?
- How easy is it to locate the section headings?
- How easy is it to understand the relationship between one section and the others?

Based on your analysis of the different samples, which one do you think is most attractively designed? Which one do you think would be the easiest to use? If you chose a different sample to answer the two questions above, decide which elements make the one more useful and the other more attractive? Which one do you think is better designed?

What are the elements of document design?

Table 5.1 below lists the different components of document design about which you should make conscious decisions as you prepare a technical document.

Components	Definition and Usage Conventions
Typefaces and fonts	"Typeface" refers to the print version of text; "font" refers to the on-screen version of text. There is a wide array of possibilities. Choose something that complements your subject matter and that is easy to read.
White space	The space on the page not inhabited by text or visuals is called white space. Use it to organize and highlight your information.
Layout	This refers to how the information appears on the page: - How the information is grouped - What kinds of headings are used to identify groups - Where headings are aligned on the page - Where visuals are placed.
Boxes (and shaded backgrounds in boxes)	These include text or icons placed within a rectangular or oval frame. Boxes are useful for emphasizing material: - Cautions or warnings - Design elements repeated to establish coherence across a page or several pages.
Lines	Lines are useful in ways similar to boxes. Use them to - Direct your user's attention - Separate elements on a page - Emphasize information.
Illustrations (tables, charts, graphs, diagrams)	Illustrations provide visual support for written text. Select the visual or illustration that best presents the information that you wish to convey. (See Chapter 8 for more information about selecting visuals).
Icons	These are images or pictures that represent links between steps or ideas. Use icons (or symbols) to unite sections of a page or document or to highlight associations between related steps or ideas.
Lists: bullets/numbers	Any time you have a series of linked ideas or steps, format them as a bulleted list. If there is a chronological or important order to the steps, then use numbers to emphasize the sequence.
Arrows	Use arrows to draw the reader's attention to important details in a visual.

TABLE 5.1
The components of document design.

TYPEFACES AND FONTS

Select a paragraph of text that you've written and format it in various typefaces. Note that some selections are much easier to read than others, depending upon the style chosen. For example, decorative fonts such as papyrus or old English text are difficult to read when they are used for more than a word or two in a document. Similarly, fonts that are not proportioned, such as courier new, are slower to read because your eye has to move longer distances to understand the text. Also compare the experience of reading a serif font (such as Times New Roman or Garamond) versus reading a sans-serif font (such as Arial or Tahoma).

For example, decorative fonts such as this one, in Edwardian Script, are difficult to read when they are used for more than a word or two in a

FIGURE 5.3
Edwardian Script is an unreadable font.

Should I use a serif or sans-serif font?

There is some controversy about whether a writer should use serif or sans-serif typefaces for the body text of a document (from a usability rather than an aesthetic perspective). In the 1990s, Colin Wheildon conducted several studies comparing the level of understanding that readers had of the same text printed in a serif font (Times New Roman) and a sans-serif font (Arial). He found that, out of one million readers, 670,000 read and thoroughly comprehended the message when it was presented in a serif font. In comparison, only 120,000 readers thoroughly comprehended the same message printed in a sans-serif font. This research seems to suggest that a serif font is a better choice for the body text of your document.

Some people interpret the results of this study to mean that you should then use a serif font for *everything* in your document. The main drawback to a "use Garamond everywhere" approach is that your text becomes uniform and conservative looking—it doesn't draw the reader in by creating a visually inviting display. One solution to this dilemma is to use a more readable, serif font for your body text and then use a contrasting sans-serif font for your headings. The visual contrast in typefaces adds interest without sacrificing readability.

Of course, Wheildon's research was done with printed text. If you are displaying your work on screen, then make exactly the *reverse* font choices: use serif fonts sparingly and only for title or heading choices because they are difficult to read on screen. Use sans-serif fonts for the main body of your online text because they are the least taxing to the eyes when read on screen. Check it out for yourself: the serif fonts waver and shimmer onscreen, making your eyes water after a while. The sans-serif fonts stay put, and you can more easily read and interpret the information that you need.

Another study suggests that readers respond differently to serif and sans-serif typefaces. A document design expert at Carnegie-Mellon University, Karen Schriver, studied users' responses to techni-

FIGURE 5.4
Take the serif/sans-
serif challenge.

Take the typeface challenge yourself. Which typeface do you find easier to read and understand: serif or sans-serif? The thinking is that the serifs (or lines at the base and tops of the thick and thin strokes on the letters) make the edges of each letter easier for your brain to recognize and process, thereby allowing it to turn your effort into understanding and knowledge quickly and effectively.

cal information depending upon whether it was printed in a serif or a sans-serif typeface. She found that the majority of her test users preferred technical documents when they were formatted in a sans-serif font. They felt the documents using sans-serif fonts (one was a set of instructions on assembling an appliance and the other one was on filling out a tax form) were "less intimidating" and more "user friendly." These same users preferred a short story printed in a serif font rather than a sans-serif font. Now, of course, there is a difference between "user preference" and "user comprehension." As a technical communicator, you need to consider both users' responses to the information when they first encounter it and their experiences interacting with it.

FIGURE 5.5
Is text in a sans-serif font
harder to understand?

On the other hand, a sans-serif font gives you neat, clean edges and a sleek look to the page. Your document will look stylish and contemporary. At the same time, however, the sleek edges make it less clear where the letters end, slightly slowing down the reader's progress through the text. The synapses in your cerebral cortex fire infinitesimally slower, delaying efficient processing of the Latinate words in this linguistic construction and resulting in your inhibited understanding of the kernel of this idea. In other words, Wheildon's research also suggests that, when the content of a text is complex technical information, you will be less likely to understand it when it's printed in a sans-serif typeface. Do you notice that you are reading this text more slowly than you did the Times Roman font in Figure 5.4?

But what does this research mean for you, as a technical communicator, when you reflect on a fitting font choice for your assembly instructions? We believe that it means that you need to pay attention to the typefaces that you select for your technical documents. Whether you choose a serif or sans-serif typeface may affect the usability of your text. How will you know? Test your typeface choices out with your target user group. (See Chapter 9 for more information about usability testing.) As part of your usability test, format test documents in serif fonts for one group and sans-serif fonts for another. If you are using a small test group, then try formatting different sections of the test document in a serif and sans-serif typeface and ask the users at the end of the test which section of the document they found easiest to read. Your target user group is always the best source of information to guide your final choices on decisions about document design such as font choices.

WHITE SPACE

White space refers to the areas on a page that have no text. These include the space between lines, in the margins, around visuals, between the visual and its caption, and around titles and headings. The white space is the background, and the text and visuals are the foreground or figure that stands out against the background. Gestalt theory is helpful for thinking about white space and how to use it because it explains how people distinguish one entity from another. They tend to look at a page and initially see general shapes. For example, the shapes of the paragraphs of text signal information about the nature and extent of the information being presented. Headings, according to their size and boldness, will also stand out, forecasting separate sections of the page. Images will separate themselves from the paragraphs of text and signal relationships between themselves and the text, depending upon their placement on the page.

Review Figure 5.1 and 5.2 from the perspective of the shapes that the information forms on the page. In Figure 5.1, the main impression of white space comes from four shorter lines of text, as well as the bottom of the paragraph. These areas jump off the page because of the uniform sea of text on the rest of the page. But they don't contribute anything from the perspective of helping the user interpret the meaning on the page. In this way, the white space in Figure 5.1 is wasted: it doesn't communicate with the reader or user. In contrast, in Figure 5.2, the formatting of the sections creates geometrical grey shapes against the white background. The white space beside the "System Requirements" serves to frame the text in that section. Figure 5.6 above sketches out the basic shapes created by the formatting of the text and visuals in Figure 5.2. This shaping is useful in three ways:

- it creates visual interest on the page,
- it frames important pieces of information, and
- it directs the user's eye to parts of the page that it might otherwise overlook (such as the system requirements, which, if formatted as a paragraph, might be skipped over entirely by many users).

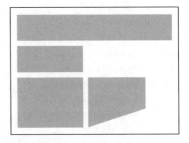

FIGURE 5.6
Shapes (or figures) formed by the text and visuals against the white background.

IN-CLASS EXERCISE 5.2

Assessing Your Use of White Space

Using one of the assignments you've written for this class, sketch out the shapes or ground images created by the text and visuals against the white space. Now evaluate your use of fore-ground and background in this document, basing your criteria on the previous discussion in this chapter.

- What changes would you make now to your page lay-out to create a more effective use of white space?
- Is there an area of text that you could better emphasize by its placement on the page?
- Would re-organizing the information improve its presentation?
- How might you re-organize it to better display and empha-size the main points that your reader or user will be looking for?

Write a one or two paragraph summary of your analysis.

Then re-sketch a revised organi-zation for one page of the as-signment to present its content more effectively.

The lesson here is to use your white space to signal relationships between the elements on your page, to add emphasis by the space around an important item, and to direct your user through the text. At the same time, be careful that the contrast between the white space (or background) and the text/visuals (or figure) is clear and dramatic enough that users can quickly and easily identify the impor-tant information. For example, many inexperienced web designers will create a web page that uses a dark background and lighter text. If the text is not dramatically lighter than the background, the letters will dissolve into the background and make the text illegible. (For example, think purple background and light yellow text—practically blinding onscreen. A better choice would be a white background with black lettering).

SHOULD MARGINS BE JUSTIFIED OR RAGGED?

Ragged right is generally easier to read. Why?

- Ragged right preserves the normal spacing between letters.
- Ragged right can add the unexpected (i.e., more interesting visually).
- Ragged borders can be used to attach captions to photos.

SHOULD YOU USE CAPITALS OR LOWER CASE?

By nature, capital letters are used to call attention to features of words. Their overuse defeats the purpose. This point is important because we read by word groups, not individual letters: all-caps words don't have the variation in the edges that we need to identify the pattern. We must decipher each letter individually and then put them together. When we read upper and lower case, the ascenders and descenders help us to recognize words by the irregular silhou-ettes, not by deciphering individual letters and assembling them. Obviously, all caps slow us down as readers. In addition, uppercase takes up much more space on the page than upper and lower com-bined (30%).

When to use all caps:

- Seldom: only when you really must
- In small amounts, restricted to a few words
- To achieve what they are suited for: startling, getting attention
- For text that must simulate screen captures.

Strategic solutions: Four design principles

In *The Non-Designer's Design Book*, Robin Williams, a graphic designer (not the actor), has developed four design principles that are fairly easily adopted by non-designers to help them develop and improve their design skills. Her four principles are exceedingly useful for technical communicators, helping them make decisions about how to lay out pages that look attractive and professional. These principles are helpful whether you have to design your own documents or just interact with a graphic designer because they supply some design vocabulary to aid discussion (and credibility).

These principles are:

- Proximity
- Alignment
- Repetition
- Contrast.

PROXIMITY

Proximity refers to the grouping of related items together. When you group items together, usually you are implying some kind of relationship between them. In contrast, unrelated items are usually separated from one another. For example, in Figure 5.7 (upper), the equal amount of space between each line in the first title page suggests that you have six different items, all unrelated to one another. If you group the elements of the title together, the authors' names, and the publisher, then, even without being able to understand English, you can tell that the top three lines are related in some way, as are the three items towards the bottom of the page. The placement of these items towards the bottom indicates that they are not part of the title, simply because of the distance between them and the title.

How do I create proximity?

Here are some ways to use proximity effectively in your placement of page elements:

- Decide how many visual elements are on the page by counting when your eye stops.
- See which items might be grouped together to form one visual unit.
- Aim for 3 to 5 items on one page.

In the business card design in Figure 5.8, the first text box shows the items that will appear on the page; the lower text box shows the related items grouped together. For example, the names of the organization and the individual form a visual unit at the top of the card, as does the contact information towards the bottom of the card.

Here are some strategies to avoid when using proximity:

- Putting too many separate elements on a page
- Sticking things in the corners and centre of the page (as in Figure 5.8, upper)

A Strategic Guide to Technical Communication
Heather Graves
Roger Graves
Broadview Press

A Strategic Guide to Technical Communication

Heather Graves
Roger Graves

Broadview Press

FIGURE 5.7
A title page where the elements seem unrelated (above), and one (below) where the spacing (or proximity) signals that the title lines are related in some way, as are the authors' and publisher's names.

Little Bo Peep (773) 325-7000
Lincoln Park Sheep Farm
715 W. Lincoln St. Chicago, IL

Lincoln Park Sheep Farm
Little Bo Peep
715 W. Lincoln St.
Chicago, IL
(773) 325-7000

FIGURE 5.8
The business card design above uses proximity badly; the lower design groups the names as one visual unit and the contact information as another.

- Putting equal white space between unrelated elements
- Creating relationships between unrelated elements by grouping them together.

As you saw in Figure 5.8, putting the elements in the corners and centre of the business card results in a less than professional looking card. Even just grouping the related elements together is an improvement.

ALIGNMENT

The second design principle is alignment, which refers to the lining up of elements on the page. For example, this textbook often uses left alignment: most headings, paragraph edges, and figure and table edges are placed along a vertical line towards the left side of the page. Alignment is useful to help you make decisions about where to place items on a page so that their placement is not arbitrary. It is also a way to create visual connections among the items on a page.

You have three choices of alignment: left, centred, and right. See Figure 5.9 for examples of each. As noted in the caption, if you select a centred alignment, then your items will be lined up along the centre point of the page. Left alignment will create a consistent margin on the left edge of your document and distribute text and graphics in relation to this margin and towards the left side of the page, while a right alignment will place the right edge of these items in relation to a consistent margin to the right of the page.

Many writers with no knowledge of page design automatically centre all titles and left-align paragraphs and headings (see Figure 5.10).

Left alignment
will place text here.

Centred alignment
will place text here.

Right alignment
will place text here.

FIGURE 5.9
Centring places all text down the centre of the page. Left alignment places text towards the left of the page, and right alignment places the right edge of the item towards the right side of the page.

FIGURE 5.10
Default mix of centring and left alignment that signals unprofessional document design.

I.B. ENGINEERING
Recommendations

Extensive study and testing of the interior wall of the basement shows significant water damage, apparently due to flooding. The following recommendations should alleviate the dampness problem in the client's basement:

1. Add 1 metre extension to downspout on west corner of structure.
2. Landscape yard on west corner of structure to elevate soil levels 30 to 40 cm. higher than they are currently to prevent rainwater from pooling at the edge of the foundation.

This default choice is easy, but it also signals the writers' lack of knowledge of effective document design, creating an amateurish rather than professional impression.

Centring is the alignment that most beginners choose because it's safe, familiar, traditional, but it can also be DULL. If you are looking for a conservative or formal design, then centring is a good choice. For example, wedding invitations are generally centred, but that's because weddings are serious, formal, and traditional occasions—exactly the impression you create by selecting this design. On the other hand, if you know that centring is traditional, you might choose to signal your departure from tradition by using a left or right alignment for your invitation design. The essential point here is that you select the alignment *consciously*, based on the impression that you wish to create.

Here is the main strategy that you want to avoid: more than one alignment on the page (i.e., avoid Figure 5.10 which uses both centring and left alignment). Instead format all of your text flush left, flush right, or centred. Now, especially with left and right alignment, this does *not* mean that every item is placed along a vertical line the same number of centimetres from the left or right margin. Rather it means that you may have several points of alignment on the page, but they are all towards the left or the right. (See Figure 5.2 where the instructions are left-aligned along the right side of the visual that accompanies them rather than flush along the left margin.)

On the title page in Figure 5.11, the right alignment forms a visual link between the title and the author's name, even though they are separated on the page. The alignment suggests a link, despite the proximity. Also notice that the right alignment creates a more sophisticated and dramatic impression than does a centred alignment.

Rhetoric in(to) Science
Style as Invention in Inquiry

Heather Graves

FIGURE 5.11
Right alignment creates a dramatic impression that centring does not.

USING NOTEPAD: THE BASICS

Finding Word Wrap
After you open the Notepad program, set Word Wrap by following the instructions below.

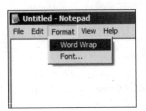

Figure A: Setting Word Wrap

1. Using the cursor, scroll across the menu at the top of the file to **Format**.
2. Click on Format, scroll down to **Word Wrap**.
3. Click on **Word Wrap**.
4. Begin typing your document.

FIGURE 5.12
Note how the instructions are left-aligned against the right side of the illustration. Effective left alignment does not require that every item on the page be placed flush against the left margin.

Alignment is useful for accomplishing two goals:

- To organize your page and unify the various elements
- To create an artistic impression for your document.

Basic strategies for creating alignment

Just as good technical writers use proximity effectively, you should make conscious choices about where you place the items on your page. To use alignment effectively, always find something else on the page to align an element with, even if the two items are physically distant from one another. For example, in Figure 5.12, the right side of the visual is used as a point of alignment along which other items are placed.

Repetition

The third useful design principle is repetition, which consists of taking some aspect of the design and incorporating it throughout the entire document. These aspects can include your choice of typefaces, lines, bullets, or even an element that you add simply for aesthetic effect. Especially in multi-page documents, repetition is critical for creating unity among the pages—that is, as you flip from page to page, you can tell from the design that you are examining one complete document rather than a series of discrete pages.

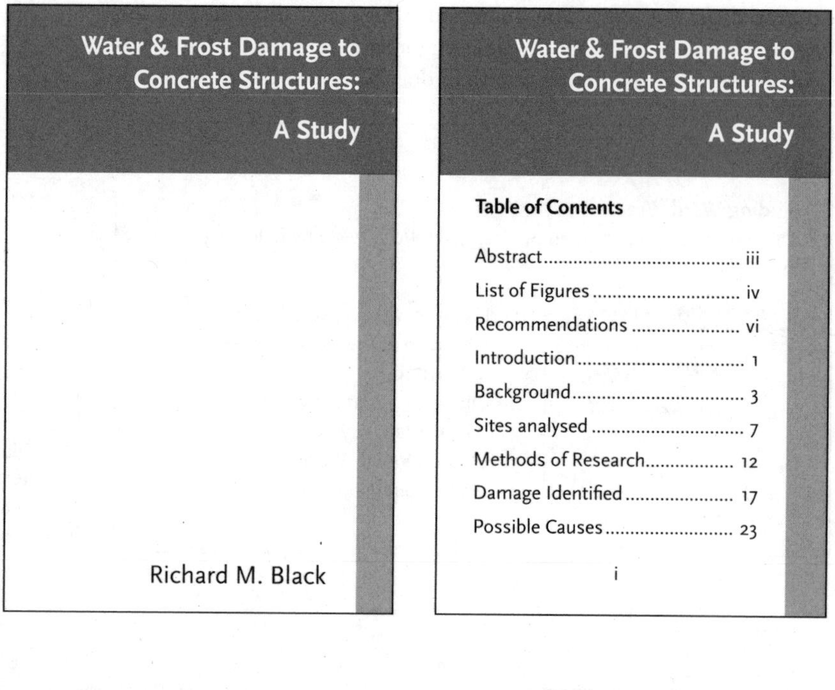

FIGURE 5.13
This technical report uses reverse text boxes to create a design element that will carry across the whole document.

Water & Frost Damage to
Concrete Structures:

A Study

Richard M. Black

Water & Frost Damage to
Concrete Structures:

A Study

Table of Contents

i

Repetition is useful to achieve the following goals:

- To unify the pages
- To add visual interest
- To increase the likelihood that your pages will be read.

Strategies for using repetition effectively:

- Take elements of design—for example, typefaces—and use them consciously, that is, use the same typeface for all of your headings but vary the size, depending upon whether it is a major or minor section heading.
- Turn some elements of the document into conscious parts of the design. For example, you might decide to put a 4 pt. rule under your headings to emphasize them, as well as add style to the page.
- You might also decide to add elements to the design expressly to create repetition. For example, in your résumé, you might decide to use a script font for your name and headings, perhaps *Vladimir Script* rather than Arial Narrow, because it adds a tone of elegance and sophistication. Or in a technical report, you might decide to put all of your headings in black text boxes with white lettering to carry the white on black theme from your report title page.

While repetition can be a powerful tool for unifying your pages and signalling to your user the overall organization of the document, it can also become a problem if you overuse it to the point that the repeated element(s) become excessive. If you aren't sure whether you are overusing a particular design item, then ask some of your co-workers or even work it into a usability test to find out what others think. They don't have to be trained in design to be able to say whether they find the repetition irritating.

CONTRAST

The fourth and final design principle that you will find useful is contrast. The primary rule of contrast is that you either make two items identical or make them look obviously different.

Use contrast to achieve these goals:

- To make clear the purpose and organization of the document
- To create visual interest on the page.

Effective use of contrast can make the difference between your users enthusiastically consulting your work or putting it aside to try to figure out the device or program on their own. Here is a list of design elements that you can contrast to add visual appeal to your pages:

Planting your tulips

When you receive your shipment of tulips in the late fall, plant them as soon as you can.

Requirements for planting
Bulb growth formula
Small planting shovel
Large spade
Moist earth
Light gardening gloves

Preparing the soil
1. Using the large spade, dig up the area to a depth of 8 to 10 in. where you plan to plant the bulbs.

FIGURE 5.14
In these planting instructions, the designer has contrasted a 1 pt. line with a 1 ½ pt. line. It looks more like an error than a contrast in line weights, doesn't it?

Planting your tulips

When you receive your shipment of tulips in the late fall, plant them as soon as you can.

Requirements for planting
Bulb growth formula
Small planting shovel
Large spade
Moist earth
Light gardening gloves

Preparing the soil
1. Using the large spade, dig up the area to a depth of 8 to 10 in. where you plan to plant the bulbs.

FIGURE 5.15
Using a 12 pt. font for the title adds emphasis. The ¼ pt. rule under the title contrasts well with the 3 pt. rule further down.

- Size—contrast large type with small type
- Typefaces—contrast a serif font with a sans-serif, script, or decorative font
- Lines—contrast a thin ¼ pt. line with a 4 ½ pt. line
- Colours—contrast cool colours (e.g., green) with warm ones (e.g., yellow)
- Textures—juxtapose a smooth texture with a rough one
- Horizontal and vertical—contrast a horizontal element (e.g. a long line of text) with a vertical element (e.g., a narrow column of text).

While adding contrast seems fairly straightforward, there is one critical way in which you can make an error: contrasting a narrow line with a slightly wider line. These lines are so similar that there is no contrast; it just looks like you made a mistake. For example, in "Planting your tulips" in Figure 5.14, the writer has contrasted a 1 pt. rule with a 1½ pt. rule. Rather than contrasting, it looks like a mistake. Similarly, the title is formatted in 10 pt. Arial narrow, while the headings are 9 pt.: the small difference in size looks like a formatting error rather than a contrast. The rule of thumb, then, is that if two items are not exactly the same, then make them *very different*. Figure 5.15 corrects these problems by adding more dramatic contrast between the elements.

The title is now clearly larger than the headings. The rule under the title is much lighter than the rule between the introductory infor-

RHG Medical Labs

X-RAY SPECIALISTS
BLOOD TECHNICIANS
DIAGNOSTIC & EXPLORATORY
MAMMOGRAPHY
ULTRASOUND ❧ MRI ❧ CAT SCAN
BLOOD ANALYSIS ❧ URINANALYSIS
COLONOSCOPY ❧ SIGMOIDOSCOPY
BY APPOINTMENT
DOCTOR'S REFERRAL REQUIRED
BRING REFERRAL TO APPOINTMENT

1257 KING ST. W
LEEDS, MB
❧
205-123-4567
SCHEDULING@ RHGLABS.COM

LAB ASSIGNMENT 5.1

CRITIQUING AN EXISTING DESIGN

Examine the advertisement left from the perspective of Williams' four design principles.

- Which principles are used effectively?
- Which principles are used ineffectively?
- What changes would you make to improve the overall design?

When you have identified the main aspects that need change, redesign the ad so that it uses all four design principles effectively.

LAB ASSIGNMENT 5.2

REVISING A POOR DESIGN

The flyer to the right is adapted from one that a colleague found on his windshield a few years ago in a university parking lot, advertising a taxi service in the city. The prospects for revision are so broad that it's an interesting exercise to try to design an attractive and readable advertising flyer.

MAJOR PROJECT 5.1

REDESIGNING A BROCHURE

Find an existing brochure that is poorly designed, or that you think you could design better, and redesign it using the document design principles covered in this chapter (e.g., proximity, alignment, contrast, repetition, contrasting choice of typefaces, arrangement, emphasis, figure/ground). (You may also choose to re-present information currently structured as a handout in an effectively designed tri-fold brochure.)
- Design both sides of the page
- Fold the brochure whichever way you feel is appropriate (i.e. accordion fold or into the centre panel)
- Add images (e.g., clip art or photos) to the brochure.

ANDY (days) 312-123-4567	OASIS CAB COMPANY D.B.A. United Cab Association # 1234	GREG (nights) 312-123-5678

- ARE YOU A PERSON WHO GOES TO THE AIRPORT OFTEN ON BUSINESS OR PLEASURE IN A CAB?
- TIRED OF DIRTY CABS OR HAVING TO WONDER HOW LONG YOUR DRIVER'S BEEN IN CHICAGO?
- TIRED OF HAVING CALLED THE CAB CO. FOR A 5 A.M. PICKUP AND THE CAB FINALLY PULLS UP AROUND 6 A.M.?
WELL—LOOK NO FURTHER!!!!

I'D LIKE TO TAKE THIS OPPORTUNITY TO SERVE ALL YOUR AIRPORT NEEDS AND OFFER YOU A CLEAN & COMFORTABLE RIDE, A DRIVER WHO IS A NATIVE OF CHICAGO, ALONG WITH COURTEOUS AND VERY RELIABLE SERVICE, PLUS A FEW EXTRAS SUCH AS:
- MORNING NEWSPAPER
- MAGAZINES
- T.V. AND STEREO

. . . TO MAKE YOUR TRIP TO THE AIRPORT A LITTLE BIT MORE PLEASURABLE (and yes I shower every day!).
FOR BEST RESULTS CALL BUSINESS # 12 HOURS PRIOR TO PICKUP. (SHORT NOTICE MAY BE POSSIBLE BY CALLING BEEPER #'S 1 HR. PRIOR TO PICKUP)

OHARE $25.00 to $ 28.00 CHARTERS . . . . . $30.00 per hr. (2 hr. min.) SUBURBS. . . reasonable rates CORPORATION ACCOUNTS WELCOMED (Interest free!)	MIDWAY $23.00 TO $26.00 _____Cut along here & save_____ Oasis Cab Company D.B.A. UNITED CAB ASSOCIATION BUSINESS: 708-123-6789 BEEPER # 312-123-4566 BEEPER# 312-123-5678

MAJOR PROJECT 5.2

DESIGNING A NEWSLETTER

The idea for this assignment is to create a newsletter design that reflects good document design practice (based on the information in this chapter), that is appropriate to the organization, and that suitably targets the audience for the newsletter.

Choose from among these options:
1. If you are affiliated with a business or organization that would like you to design a format for its newsletter, you can do this task for the assignment. Just hand in a copy of the original design with your new layout.
2. If you have connections that can provide the content for a newsletter (for example, your extended family sends around a newsletter listing everyone's activities and accomplishments over the past year, as well as giving details about the upcoming family reunion), you are welcome to adapt this assignment to your situation.
3. Find a newsletter that you think could be better designed and redesign it, using the principles covered in this chapter. Hand in the original design along with your revised version.
4. Finally, if you have designed newsletters before and the thought of doing yet another one doesn't really thrill you, propose something different that does make you feel interested.

mation and the actual instructions. In what other ways does this example use contrast?

- Typeface choices (sans-serif & serif)
- Image vs. text
- Vertical column of text vs. horizontal column of text
- Bullets vs. numbers.

What other functions do you see these elements of contrast playing in the usability (rather than the attractiveness) of the instructions?

For example, the 3 pt. rule draws your eye to the bottom of the page, where you see the actual planting instructions. How do the other elements contribute to helping you follow the subject matter?

Designing a layout grid

A layout grid refers to the overall plan you develop for organizing the information on a single page or over many pages. If you plan a basic grid structure that presents various types of information in similar ways from page to page, you can greatly aid your user in being able to quickly view and understand the information presented. For example, if you designate a particular area of the page as a place for visuals, your user will quickly recognize and anticipate visuals on that part of the page. Similarly, headings that appear in the same location from page to page make it much easier to find specific passages. By planning out where to place similar information on a page, you can increase its impact on the user or reader.

FIGURE 5.16
In this example, the text and the image form two squares, which together form the rectangle that encapsulates and presents step two of the roof insulation process.

INSTALL FIBREGLASS BATS

STEP

2

1. Unroll the bat of insulation between the rafters. (10 cm. fibreglass is recommended).

2. Butt it against the walls and cut it to length with a utility knife.

3. Cover all available space between rafters.

4. Cover entire installation area.

HOW DO YOU USE THE SPACE ON YOUR PAGE TO CREATE IMPACT?

Think of your page in terms of strong figures—rectangles, squares, circles, or triangles—as principles of organization. Decide how you will use both the vertical and horizontal space on the page. For example, Figure 5.16 uses two squares to create a strong rectangular figure that organizes the instructions in step two. Having followed step one, users then anticipate that the step number will appear on the left third, the instructions in the centre third, and the illustration on the right third. In this instance, three areas of vertical space are aligned to create a varied but functional horizontal space.

To organize a layout grid for your work, plan how you will use the vertical and horizontal space on your pages. Vertical space refers to the top-to-bottom perpendicular distance between the elements on the page—the distance between consecutive lines of text, the space between paragraphs, between the edges of pictures and their captions, and between subheadings and text. Vertical space also refers to the length down the page of text boxes, visuals, and tables, in other words, to the top and bottom margins of your document. Horizontal space refers to the left-to-right measurement of visual or verbal elements—line lengths, areas of blank space between elements—the space between elements on a page, and the width of objects and how far apart they are.

HOW DO YOU VARY THE HORIZONTAL OR VERTICAL SPACE ON A PAGE?

In Figure 5.17a, the vertical space between the elements is roughly the same; in Figure 5.17b, the writer uses check bullets to indent the points and highlight the important information.

The check bullets in the example right serve as spatial markers to draw reader attention to the important information and to provide clues as to the structure of the document. If you plan the architecture of your pages, you can add such spatial cues to the design that help your readers quickly understand your intended structure. The grid is one way that you can signal the structure of your document.

WHAT IS A GRID?

A grid subdivides a page (or mirror pages) into columns (vertical) and rows (horizontal). As the columns and rows intersect, they form standardized units of space that you can use as compartments for placing verbal and visual elements. If you standardize the units of space, you create consistent-sized areas in which to locate text and images. The grid also enables you to separate elements (e.g., headings) with vertical and horizontal space between columns and rows.

Shingling roof gutters

Contemporary roofers now line roof and dormer seams with copper flashing and overlap the shingle edge by 5 cm. (2 in.) onto the flashing.

There are three main reasons to switch to flashing rather than shingling through the gutter:

Ice dams in the winter cannot penetrate the metal flashing or cause leaking.

Installation is 30% faster.

The flashing and shingle combination is more aesthetically appealing.

a.

Shingling roof gutters

Contemporary roofers now line roof and dormer seams with copper flashing and overlap the shingle edge by 5 cm. (2 in.) onto the flashing.

There are three main reasons to switch to flashing rather than shingling through the gutter:

✓ Ice dams in the winter cannot penetrate the metal flashing or cause leaking.

✓ Installation is 30% faster.

✓ The flashing and shingle combination is more aesthetically appealing.

b.

FIGURE 5.17
Version b uses bullet points to emphasize important information.

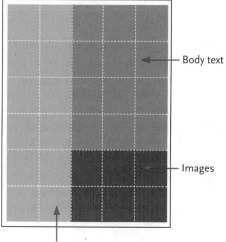

Body text

Images

Sidebar/notes

FIGURE 5.18
The page was divided into a 5x6 grid. The 2x6 grid on the left will hold sidebar information. The top 3x4 grid will contain body text. The bottom 3x2 grid will hold visuals.

Headings

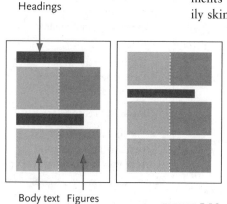

Body text   Figures

FIGURE 5.19
Grid design for procedures. The left page features a 2x2 grid; the right a 2x3 grid.

In Figure 5.18, the writer has divided the page into a 5x6 grid for a newsletter. The 2x6 grid on the left will contain sidebar information, such as the table of contents, quotations, and important notes. The 3x4 grid on the top will contain body text, such as articles, interviews, and notices. The 3x2 grid on the bottom will contain visuals— photographs, charts, and drawings.

HOW DO I DESIGN A GRID FOR MY PROJECT?

The first step is to create an inventory of all of the text elements that you will use in the document. This list should include such elements as headings, subheadings, body text, footnotes, pictures, tables, figures, charts, graphs, references, lists, numbered lists, sidebars, table of contents, page numbers, any headers or footers, and picture or chart captions. When you have identified all of the elements that you need, organize them into related groups. For example, the pictures or charts and captions go together; the headers or footnotes and page numbers work together. In a set of instructions, the steps and illustrating figures form a group. Generally, the headings or subheadings are grouped with the body text to which they refer.

The third step in creating a grid is to sketch a variety of different arrangements. This is your opportunity to experiment with how you might arrange the elements of each group to highlight how the parts are related to one another. Your goal in experimenting with possible grid structures is to invent a visually interesting layout that also shows how the parts of the document are related to each other rhetorically. You want to focus on how you can arrange your elements vertically and horizontally so that readers or users can easily skim through and understand the content. Play around with the arrangements to devise an order that makes sense to your reader, one that helps readers understand and process your content. If your document is poorly design, your groupings may strike the reader as inconsistent or illogical.

Figure 5.19 presents a sample grid for a set of procedures that highlights the rhetorical relationship among the elements. The headings signal the change of topic from one group of steps to another. The body text or the instructions on the left are illustrated by the visuals on the right. This layout reinforces the rhetorical relationship between the three key elements that make up the groupings.

Figure 5.19 shows a basic grid arrangement. The next step is to figure out what the actual size of your page will be and then calculate how long and wide you will have your columns of text. Use millimetres, inches, or points to decide on the scale of your pages. Also decide whether a landscape (horizontal) or portrait (vertical) orientation best suits the presentation of your information. When you are calculating the size of your various rhetorical groupings, don't forget that you may also need margins and space for binding the pages. All of these spatial constraints should figure into your grid design.

Divide your page into columns and rows. Most designs use the same number of columns as rows (between one and six). When you lay out your content, you can use the individual columns or group them into larger units (e.g., Figure 5.18). The two pages in Figure 5.19 use a 2x2 grid on the left side and a 2x3 grid on the right side. Whichever side the writer uses for a specific page will depend on the length of a particular stage of the procedures (one, two, three, or more steps).

After selecting the number of columns and rows, you decide on a simple ratio to organize the main elements. For example, you could divide the page into two groups: items that need the most space vs. items that require the least space. In a six-column grid, you choose from among the following ratios: 6:1, 4:2, 1:2:3 or 3:3.

Once you have selected a possible ratio, experiment with the groupings that you organized earlier to see which placements provide the best visual emphasis for the most important elements. Those items of less importance should be located in subordinate visual positions. Decide whether the layout should be predominantly vertical, horizontal, or a combination of the two. Sketch out several grid designs to be sure that your final selection is the best one from both a usability and an aesthetic point of view. Don't be afraid to tweak your design until you come up with one that properly highlights the important information on the page while also subordinating the supporting information. Options include using the same grid for the whole document, using a mirror grid, or developing two different but complementary grids.

The final step, after you feel that you cannot improve your design grid any further, is to test it with members of your target user group. If your design does not help your audience to find and use the content in useful and efficient ways, you need to revise the grid, perhaps even to the point of starting over. If you find that, for the most part, your design works well, focus next on making final minor adjustments that enhance your content and the usefulness of your design.

WHAT ABOUT USING A TEMPLATE FOR MY GRID DESIGN?

Unless the template was designed specially for a given project, then avoid using a template because the visual uniformity of every page will make your document look dull and uninviting (as will using a

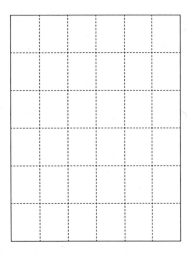

FIGURE 5.20
A page divided into 6 columns and 6 rows (a 6x6 grid), which can be further subdivided into an organized but flexible page layout.

FIGURE 5.21
This layout uses a 1:3:2 ratio of vertical columns. Sidebar information will go in the 1 column, body text in the 3 column, and visuals in the 2 column.

template for your résumé). Creating your own grid to suit the information that you want to present can transform your content into something users are excited to use. For example, a student in one of our classes used a series of arrows and geometric designs to present to her co-workers in the medical profession information on drawing blood, and they loved how attractive and interesting the information (which they already knew) looked when presented imaginatively. Everything they needed was on the page, with the most important information highlighted by the page design. They felt that they were much more likely to notice points they might otherwise skip because of the visually stimulating page layout. If you can generate this kind of excitement and interest in your technical documents, you will go a long way toward providing the kind of high quality documentation that society needs.

MAJOR PROJECT 5.3

CREATE YOUR OWN PROJECT

Choose your own document to design. It should be a genre different from what you've done before, unless you have a compelling argument as to why you want to create, say, a second brochure.

The first stage of this project is to write a two or three paragraph description of the project that you'd like to create. In your description, explain the following:
- what is the project,
- what is its purpose,
- who is its audience, and
- how will this project enhance your design skills?

If possible, choose a project that is directly relevant to someone's needs: it can be a project for work, a design for someone you know (a friend or family member), or a document that will benefit just you.

CHAPTER SIX

Writing winning proposals

Why write proposals?

Proposal writing is a skill that you will find immensely useful if you become good at it. Much of the work in industry and in business advances through proposals. Companies respond to "requests for proposals" (RFPs) to obtain contracts that provide the income which keeps their employees on the payroll. These RFPs arise from a problem that an organization has identified, and the proposals that are submitted in response present potential solutions to that problem. The requesting organization selects the proposal that seems to provide the best solution, and a contract is won. Even if you are self-employed as a contractor (say, a computer programmer or a technical communicator), you will find that you must respond to RFPs to obtain projects that generate income. You may also find yourself writing prospecting proposals—proposals that attempt to create business by identifying how your company or service could help a potential customer. In mid-size to large companies, proposals form part of the administrative tracking that must go on to organize and approve of how employees spend their time and to ensure that the activities of individual employees contribute to the organization's overall goals and objectives.

Several elements distinguish a winning proposal from an unsuccessful one. First, winning proposals come from content that is carefully and thoughtfully analysed. They also arise from efficient and effective design—a winning proposal presents the main ideas clearly and concisely using a layout that readers can quickly and easily understand. Third, winning proposals display "sales moxie." That is, they display courage and daring to sell the solution they propose. They make plain the benefits of this solution over the other possibilities. Finally, winning proposals build a persuasive case for the desirability of their solution and the team that will implement it.

> **OTHER NAMES FOR RFPs:**
> - Telephone buy (T-buy)
> - Request for Quotation (RFQ)
> - Invitation to Tender (ITT)
> - Request for Standing Offer (RFSO)
> - Request for Supply Arrangement (RFSA)

What kinds of proposals are there?

There are several different types of proposals: internal, solicited, unsolicited, and sole-source contracts. Internal proposals are usually written by a division within a company to persuade management to approve an idea or project. While they are generally intended for internal use, they also follow the standard format for other types of proposals. Solicited proposals are submitted in response to published "requests for proposals" (RFPs) or "specs" (specifications). These specify certain requirements that need to be included in the solution, but they also leave a lot of room for various approaches to the solution. Organizations generally use RFPs to ensure that many providers have the opportunity to compete for a contract. Figure 6.1 illustrates a sample RFP.

SCIENCE/TECHNOLOGY

Posted: July 5, 2002
Deadline: August 15 and January 5, annually

LEAKEY FOUNDATION OFFERS FUNDING FOR RESEARCH INTO HUMAN ORIGINS
The Leakey Foundation was formed to further research into human origins. Recent priorities include research into the environments, archaeology, and human palaeontology of the Miocene, Pliocene, and Pleistocene; into the behavior, morphology, and ecology of the great apes and other primate species; and into the behavioral ecology of contemporary hunter-gatherers.

The foundation's General Research Grants are awarded twice annually. Priority for funding is given to the exploratory phases of promising new research projects that meet the stated purpose of the foundation.

Advanced doctoral students as well as established scientists are eligible to apply. Applicants must either hold a Ph.D. or equivalent qualification in anthropology or a related discipline or be enrolled in a doctoral program with all degree requirements fulfilled other than the dissertation. There are no citizenship restrictions. Qualified individuals are eligible without regard to nationality.

The majority of the foundation's general research grants to doctoral students are in the $3,000–$12,000 range; the limit of funding for a single proposal submitted by a post-doctoral applicant or a senior scientist is $20,000. Small grants cover research expenses directly related and essential to the project (i.e., travel, living expenses during fieldwork, supplies, research assistance, and other relevant expenditures).

For complete program guidelines, see the foundation's Web site.

FIGURE 6.1
Here is a sample RFP from the Leakey Foundation to fund research into human origins.

Figure 6.1 requests proposals describing "the exploratory phases of promising new research projects that meet the stated purpose of the [Leakey] foundation." For details on whether the reader's research project might fit, he or she would need to visit the foundation's website for additional information. However, the initial posting on the website of the *Philanthropy News Digest: The Foundation Center* (http://foundationcenter.org/pnd/) allows readers to decide whether they would fit the criteria well enough to pursue further this avenue of funding.

If you are interested in bidding on projects advertised by the Government of Canada, information is available on the Contracts Canada website (http://contractscanada.gc.ca/en/biddin-e.htm). Figure 6.2 is an example of a request for proposal (RFP) pulled from the Contracts Canada website (October 23, 2006). Just the "description" part of the request is reproduced here as an example of the kind of text you might expect. From here, you would review the information about submitting proposals posted on the Contracts Canada website to be sure you include the details that they require. You would also incorporate the requirements mentioned in the request itself.

Unsolicited proposals generally come from an individual or company that has identified a problem and devised a solution that the proposal presents. This type of proposal has as its primary goal convincing the reader that the problem exists and is serious enough to warrant a solution. The unsolicited proposal must make a strong case for the benefits of the solution being proposed because the reader may be unaware of the problem and sceptical of proceeding with a solution. Writing this type of proposal carries with it a high degree of risk; the time invested in creating the proposal may not pay off if you are unable to convince the company to change its traditional way of doing something. Generally, organizations do not pursue unsolicited or prospecting proposals unless they have conducted extensive market research that suggests the move is likely to be successful.

Sole-source proposals indicate that an organization intends to engage only one company to supply a product or service, usually because prior experience has established a strong relationship between the supplier and the client. Generally, this type of proposal is written to meet regulations rather than because there is any competition for the contract. If an apparently "open" contract RFP is actually targeted to a specific organization, then your company will be unlikely to be awarded the contract. You may be wasting your time preparing a proposal for an RFP that that is a sole-source contract in disguise.

What is a proposal?

Robert Hamper and Sue Baugh, authors of the *Handbook for Writing Proposals*, define proposals as "primarily a sophisticated sales piece that seeks to define a client's problem and/or opportunities and to sell the client on your company's ability to provide solutions and

---

> **RFP: CUSTOMER SATISFACTION SURVEY**
>
> **DESCRIPTION:**
> Request for Proposal on behalf of Service New Brunswick who is seeking vendor with a demonstrated track record to administer all telephone surveys on its behalf and present us with the raw findings as per the attached RFP Document.
>
> The purpose of conducting a customer satisfaction survey for all three main service delivery channels is to allow SNB to benchmark against themselves and other similar business providers. As well, we want to learn about our strengths and areas for improvement to ensure we remain ahead on issues relating to customer service delivery.
>
> Chappelle, Ariadne
> Central Tendering Branch
> Section Centrale des Appels D'Offres
> P O Box 8000 – C.P. 8000
> Fredericton, NB
> E3B 5H6
> 1 (506) 123-4567

FIGURE 6.2

An RFP (request for proposal) by the government of New Brunswick inviting proposals to conduct a customer satisfaction survey for Service New Brunswick customers. Proposals would be submitted outlining the expertise and ability of the proposing organization to provide the services described in the request.

1   Robert J. Hamper and L. Sue Baugh, *Handbook for Writing Proposals* (Chicago: NTC Contemporary Publishing Group, 1995), 3.

2   Adapted from Robert J. Hamper and L. Sue Baugh, *Handbook for Writing Proposals* (Chicago: NTC Contemporary Publishing Group, 1995), 12.

strategies."[1] The main focus is not so much displaying what your organization can do generally but showing how the services or products that you provide can help to solve the client's problem. In other words, you tailor the proposal to the specific needs of the client and demonstrate how your organization is uniquely positioned to meet those needs effectively. To be able to make a strong argument for your unique qualifications, you want to select carefully the contracts that you bid on. If you select those opportunities, which most closely match your areas of expertise, you can make the most convincing argument for choosing your organization over others that may bid. This means that you don't apply for every job even remotely related to your firm's areas of expertise: instead you analyse the RFPs to select only the ones that you are most likely to have a chance of winning.

When should you decline to write a proposal?

Hamper and Baugh advise against submitting a proposal if one or more of the following situations are present:

- The timeframe for submitting the proposal is too short for you to do a good job;
- The RFP announces follow-up work to a larger project (which means that you will compete against the organizations that have completed earlier stages);
- You are not equipped to produce the technical or other specifications listed, but your competitors are;
- The contract is outside your field of expertise;
- You have no real competitive edge over the competition;
- You lack staff and resources to prepare the best proposal you can write; and
- Your chances of winning the proposal are less that 50 per cent.[2]

How do proposals get evaluated?

If you decide that your organization can produce a compelling proposal, the next step is to decide what information will be most effectively included in it. To help you decide on a persuasive appeal, it is important to understand what type of criteria a client will use to compare and judge the proposals. Here is a list of the main questions that you will want your proposal to answer:

- Do you fully understand the client's needs and problems?
- Do you know how to satisfy the needs or solve the problems?

- Do you offer a suitable plan, strategy, or program that will reach the desired goal?
- Are you well qualified by virtue of experience and resources—including qualified personnel—to carry out the proposed plan or program?
- Has your organization completed other similar projects in a timely and satisfactory way?
- What makes your organization superior to the others who are also bidding?
- From a presentation perspective, is this proposal attractive and professional looking?

One common mistake made by newcomers to the field is to write proposals showing that their organizations can do a job well but not showing how they can do it *better* than the competition. By highlighting the strengths of your solution, you can build a compelling argument as to why you should get the contract. While it is clear that proposals must present information, describe the details of the solution, communicate the solution's merits, and provide examples, they must more than anything persuade. An excellent plan does not sell itself; your job as a proposal writer is to sell your ideas, not just present them.

Research shows that price is not the primary criterion of selection; rather it is the technical or professional competence and the prior record of accomplishment of the individual or team who proposes to create the solution. With this knowledge in mind, you want to prepare a proposal with a great solution, but you also want to sell the experience and prior successes of the individuals who will do the work. In this way, a proposal is primarily a persuasive document.

Who is the audience for a proposal?

There are various answers to this question, depending on what kind of proposal you are writing. An internal proposal, in which you perhaps suggest a change of procedure that will save your organization money, should be directed to the individuals who have the power to implement your recommendations. The same with an unsolicited proposal: it should reach the individuals who will be interested in your solution and can make a decision about implementing it. For an internal proposal, you have fairly easy access to the information you need.

If you are responding to an RFP, there are several possible sources of information:

- The RFP itself should be analysed carefully and thoroughly.

- Organizational materials available in the public domain, such as annual reports, newsletters, and press releases, will provide insight into the culture, financial stability, and management style of the client, among other things.
- Client conversations—if these are permitted by the bidding process—are useful as a follow-up to the close analysis of the RFP.
- Your own expertise as a professional in the field will help you take an innovative and unique perspective on the problem described by the client.

In your study of the RFP, learn everything you can about the problem, as stated, and then look for dimensions of the problem that are not explicitly stated but still relevant. Your goal in this analysis is to ensure that you understand the problem thoroughly. If you miss some crucial component, the solution that you propose will be irrelevant, no matter how well the proposal is written.

Some bidding situations allow you to contact the organization for additional information. If client contact is permitted, then schedule an appointment only after you have thoroughly studied the RFP. Use this contact to explore any unclear aspects or to gain background information about the problem. Hamper and Baugh recommend that you speak to individuals at different levels within the company, if possible, because the people at each level—from line workers to upper management—will have their own perspectives on the problem that can give you additional valuable insight.

How do you analyse a RFP?

Near the end of this chapter, a major project asking you to write a proposal is described. This description is really a request for a proposal. It outlines the proposal assignment for a technical communications course and represents the first stage of the final project in the course. To help you understand what we mean by analysing an RFP as the first step in creating a proposal, we work through the relevant points of the assignment to illustrate the process. First read the "Request for a proposal to write a manual" (see Major Project 6.1), and then examine the analysis that follows.

Sample RFP analysis

WHAT KIND OF PROPOSAL IS REQUESTED?

The first thing to determine is what kind of proposal is being requested in the RFP. Since the writer of the above RFP (the instructor of the course) is asking for proposals, your ideas are being "solicited." This means that you do not have to work to persuade your reader to read the proposal. In addition, the selection process does not appear to be competitive. That is, it seems likely that the instructor will approve all proposals that are reasonable and feasible rather than choosing just the best one and having only one person or group in the class produce a final project. So the judgment of quality will focus not on "best" but on questions such as these:

- Is it feasible that this topic can be completed in the number of weeks left in the term?
- Does the writer have the resources and expertise to complete the topic he or she proposes?
- Are the costs of this project reasonable for a student budget?

WHAT ARE THE PRIMARY CRITERIA LISTED IN THE RFP?

Criteria are listed in the order of importance (presumably) in this request. First, "Create an instructional manual that does not currently exist." So we can't merely revise an existing manual to improve it. We need to document some kind of system or process that is not currently documented. The next part of the sentence explains further how the instructor is defining "does not currently exist": "identify a process or procedure that has not been documented for a particular audience." This qualifies the first criterion in that the topic does not have to be completely brand new, so you could use a process that has been documented but create an original set of instructions tailored to a new and specific audience. For example, most software how-to manuals attempt to reach the largest possible audience, so the coverage is broad and detailed. By choosing a more targeted audience—for example, senior citizens who want to have an email account but do not know how to sign up for or use one—you could identify just the functions that audience members need to know how to do and create a manual targeted to their specific level of understanding and experience with electronic mail.

A second qualifier or suggestion for sources of possible topics follows the first: document procedures at your place of employment that have not previously been documented. At many workplaces, especially smaller businesses, there are a number of procedures that employees have to follow that have never been written down. Choosing a topic that would benefit your employer would give you an applicable and useful document to create, as well as building goodwill with your boss and your present and future co-workers, who will have an easy source of information about how to do the processes that you cover in your manual.

The second set of criteria to evaluate the proposal is presented in the first set of bullet points: Your proposal will need to do the following:

1. Explain the subject matter of your project. (In other words, you must give enough background so that your instructor can evaluate the usefulness and necessity of the manual you propose.)
2. Outline the research you need to do to write your manual and your plans for illustrating the procedures.
3. Make a persuasive case that a need for this particular manual exists.

From this set of criteria, we can identify information that **must** be contained in the proposal: background information, why your audience needs the manual that you propose, and how you will research and illustrate the steps that you include in the manual.

Next, the RFP describes the range of topics to choose from, listing the kinds of things that students have done in the past. Embedded in this list of suggestions is also information about suitable topics, appropriate audiences, and the proper length for the project. For example, many manuals exist on how to use PowerPoint, but none of them are tailored to the needs of postsecondary students who must create oral presentations for class. There is one source of ideas for topics. There is also a range of topics listed in the RFP from how to use particular devices to procedures and information that are specific to a particular environment or organization. This range of topics is intended to provide insight and inspiration as you contemplate topics for your own project.

The third set of criteria by which the proposal will be evaluated appears in the second list of bullet points. Here you have the various headings to include in the proposal and, presumably, the information that you will discuss under each. In this particular content outline, the instructor is requesting not only the problem statement but also a section that explains your expected purpose in producing the type of manual that you propose. The third heading, "Topics to Investigate," indicates that you are supposed to consider the parts of the topic about which your knowledge is incomplete. You might list several sources (books, websites, individuals) that you can consult to fill the gaps so as to ensure that your manual is complete and well researched, to the extent that this is appropriate. The fourth heading,

"Audience," suggests that you should also do some analysis of your target audience:

- What is their level of expertise in this area?
- What are their attitudes towards the information that you will be presenting?
- Do they have special needs or working conditions that would affect the best method of presenting the information to them?

The section on "Methods and Procedures" asks you to think through your plan for creating the manual and to articulate the various main stages that you anticipate will be necessary to complete it. "Qualifications and Resources" asks you to explain the source of your expertise in the subject matter you propose and any connections or special resources you have that make you a better candidate than someone else to produce the manual that you propose. The seventh heading, "Work Schedule," indicates that you need to work out a clear and detailed plan of the steps that you can anticipate to complete the project. Often, this section is presented as a table or chart that efficiently displays the main stages necessary for completing the project. The heading "Budget" contains a qualifier, "if appropriate," suggesting that you may not need to include this section in your proposal if you find that the cost of producing this manual will be quite low. It also suggests that you do need to consider the appropriateness of including a budget and perhaps some argument in support of being compensated for negligible costs. The final section of the proposal, the "Call to Action," is not standard for some proposals: often they just end after a budget table. However, in this case, the instructor is requesting some kind of concluding paragraph or two. Generally, a "Call to Action" includes a brief summary of the main point of the proposal, along with a clear statement of what the writer expects the reader to do next (e.g., approve this proposal so he/she can get started) and a positive, forward-looking statement that expresses interest and enthusiasm in the project.

Once you thoroughly understand the requirements of the RFP, you can begin to plan your own project ideas and then consider how to explain the project within the categories given for discussion. Above all, you want to highlight why the project is necessary and explain its value to the intended audience, as well as emphasize your own expertise to complete this project. To accomplish these three goals, you want to build a persuasive argument for your ideas and your qualifications, an argument that will result in reader action—that is, in your proposal being approved.

IN-CLASS EXERCISE 6.1

Analyse an Assignment as an RFP

Select a "major project" assignment from one of the chapters in this textbook and treat it like an RFP, analysing it in detail to determine the requirements of the assignment. Use the previous analysis as a model for dissecting the parts of the assignment, and summarize your findings. You can list them as a series of bullet points or write out a coherent paragraph, depending upon what your instructor requests.

What is persuasion?

Persuasion is writing that seeks to move readers to a particular action. It is an argument that makes use of logical, ethical, and emotional appeals to convince readers of the validity of the position stated. For example, Orlando Gonzalez states the goal of his proposed procedure manual to be as follows: "My goal is to create an easy-to-follow, quick reference guide that will allow even the novice to use the valuable two MB of space allotted to all North Central [University] students." In this sentence, Gonzalez sets out the terms of his project in a way that makes it difficult for a reader to disagree—that is, who might readily object to him creating an easy-to-use guide that will allow new users (who lack the background) to easily create a web page to store on the university server? His suggestion seems both logical and innovative. Of course, one sentence doesn't make a logical argument; Gonzalez also needs to elaborate and add evidence (for example, evidence that such a guide is needed and does not currently exist).

WHAT ARE THE COMPONENTS OF AN ARGUMENT?

Arguments consist of three components:

- logic,
- credibility (or ethical appeal), and
- *pathos* (or emotion).

LOGIC (in Aristotelian terms, *logos* or the logical appeal) refers to the internal consistency of a writer's message. The message is composed of claims that the reader makes, which are supported by evidence. The claims develop the main points that the writer wishes to cover so as to discuss the subject matter coherently and completely. The evidence that supports the claims is shaped to convince the reader that the writer can develop and deliver the appropriate solution.

In a proposal, the main claims that the writer would make include identifying and elaborating the problem, giving a clear and convincing description of the solution being proposed, identifying the tangible outcome that the writer proposes to create, discussing the writer's qualifications for creating this solution, clarifying the superior points of this solution in relation to other possible solutions, and outlining a proposed schedule for producing the solution. The logic of an argument generally targets the reader's mind: it anticipates and responds to questions that readers may have as they move through the argument.

HOW DO YOU CREATE A STRONG LOGICAL APPEAL?

Here are three ways to create a strong logical appeal in a proposal:

- Show the need for a solution to the problem that you identify.
- Show how your solution will be superior to the other proposed solutions to the problem.
- Explain the benefits of your approach.

In his problem statement, Gonzalez shows that North Central University students would benefit from some kind of quick reference guide to help them make use of the free server space given by the university. He outlines the situation that he feels creates a need for the guide he proposes:

> To encourage innovative use of technology and individual expression, North Central University currently allots 2 megabytes of server space to every one of its students. However, resources to guide the user in creating a web page are scarce. Those that are available are technical and confusing to the average user. Existing manuals are geared to the computer literate and the experienced user. Most are for the moderate to advanced user. If you are not computer savvy, a computer science student, or know someone who is, the potential for such individual expression goes untapped.

He addresses most of the questions that might arise for the reader in connection with his proposed project:

- What's wrong with current manuals? (Too technical for beginners; they assume existing experience which Gonzalez's audience lacks).
- Why try to reach student users? (Encourage comfort with technology; outlet for creativity and innovation).

What Gonzalez does not do in his problem statement (that would make it better) is to identify some existing manuals or guides and briefly analyse their organization and level of complexity. His argument currently asserts that the manuals are too complex for his audience without actually providing evidence to back up this claim.

In the following example, Sylvie Bélanger proposes to create a similar reference guide (in the same technical communication course). She provides different evidence in her problem statement to back up her claim that the quick reference guide is needed:

> Although quick reference guides on HTML and web design currently exist, none are tailored to specifically meet the needs of college [and university] students who have little to no computer science background but wish to create their own websites. This quick reference manual will help those students who want to create

a website as quickly and easily as possible but have no idea where to begin.

She notes that existing guides have a broader audience than just college or university students and so will not provide the quick and easy introduction that these students need. The emphasis on quick and easy logically fits her target audience because students don't have much time for learning new skills outside of the classes they are taking. A short guide will meet their needs; the weighty manuals in existence will not get student users quickly designing web pages. Again, if she had identified two or three existing manuals and listed their disadvantages for her target audience, she would have strengthened her argument by including compelling evidence that existing manuals are inadequate. As it is, readers have to trust that what she is saying is, in fact, true.

CREDIBILITY or *ethos* (the trustworthiness of the writer) is another essential component of the argument in a proposal, and it refers to the extent to which readers respect you and trust what you say as a writer. If readers have never met you before, how will they know whether to trust you? The answer to this question is especially important in proposal writing because, in addition to selling your solution, you are also selling yourself and your ability (and that of your team, if it's a collaborative effort) to implement the solution. While the logical appeal targeted mainly the mind of your reader (convincing him or her of the reasonableness of your proposal), the ethical appeal aims to win over the heart as well as the mind of the reader. If readers feel you know what you are talking about and they trust you, then they will grant you credibility as a writer.

There are several effective ways of demonstrating your trustworthiness as a writer when writing a proposal:

- By appearing knowledgeable about your subject matter
- By submitting a realistic and detailed work schedule.

HOW DO YOU APPEAR KNOWLEDGEABLE ABOUT YOUR TOPIC?

There are three ways to show that you know what you are talking about:

- Provide a thorough and detailed discussion of the issues relevant to the topic.
- Use appropriate technical language.
- Include details about your qualifications and resources.

Discuss details of the topic:

To execute the first strategy successfully, you need to do your groundwork before beginning to write the proposal. Conduct any research that needs to be done, sketch out a comprehensive plan, not only for the solution that you propose but also for the argument that you need to develop in the proposal itself. As we mentioned before, a great solution is only part of the proposal; the argument that reveals the solution is also critical. In the cases of Gonzalez and Bélanger, both the logic of their argument and their credibility would have been strengthened by a short visit to the bookstore to check out the competition, to look for guides that provide a quick introduction to HTML for the college or university student. Citing the authors and titles of published guides and critiquing their shortcomings would have shown the reader of their proposals that Gonzalez and Bélanger had done their homework prior to drafting these proposals. If you were the customer, would you prefer to pay for production of a manual that you *knew* had a market or one that you only *hoped* had a market? An important part of establishing your credibility with your reader in a proposal, then, is your ability to demonstrate that you spent sufficient time developing the solution before you began to write.

For example, Melissa Roberts was proposing to create a brochure that would accompany a mural that had been created to display at public buildings and events around Illinois:

> As this travelling mural is displayed around the Chicagoland region, interested individuals have no source of information concerning details of the mural, its purpose, its artists, and its inspiration. A brochure to accompany the mural as it is displayed at public buildings and events detailing this information would promote an appreciation of the beauty of and efforts for the project, as well as providing an advertisement for Gompers Park and an education for the public on the importance of wetlands.

In this section, Roberts inspires trust both by detailing the problem that the lack of explanation creates for viewers and by noting the benefits of a brochure. This level of detail demonstrates that she has thought about the situation beyond an initial surface consideration. The brochure, she notes, in addition to solving the immediate problem of a lack of information about the mural (short-term consequence of the brochure), may also inspire some viewers to visit the park that the mural celebrates (long-term consequence of the brochure) and raise general awareness of the positive contributions of wetlands (extended positive consequences). Roberts has framed the issue here in a way that emphasizes the short- and long-term importance of the brochure, so it becomes clear to the reader that she understands the problem and has come up with a solution that has multiple positive effects. We are left with the impression that she has a great idea, and we are receptive to the plan that she will unfold to create the brochure. This is how an ethical appeal works in a proposal.

Use technical language.

You can also demonstrate your expertise in the area by using the correct language where it is appropriate. Although many technical communicators pride themselves on being able to translate complex technical information into terms that lay readers can follow, a proposal is not the place to do this. Your ability to discuss the key issues using the same vocabulary as the reader (or other experts in the field) will signal that you have the background knowledge you need to complete the project that you propose. Even if your reader has less knowledge of the subject matter than you do (which could easily be the case), you still want to use the technical terms where appropriate to underscore your knowledge and competence.

For example, in the qualifications and resources section of her proposal, Roberts states her educational qualifications as well as her prior experience to instil confidence that she has the expertise required for the project: "As a student at North Central University with a major in environmental science and a minor in biology, I have gained knowledge detailing ecology, function, and restoration that will enable me to include accurate and informative descriptions in the brochure." As readers, we understand that her coursework in environmental science and biology provides her with the scientific knowledge she would need to create effective content for the brochure; Roberts demonstrates this through her technically accurate use of "ecology, function, and restoration" in connection with wetland management. Again, we feel confident that she has sufficient subject area expertise to create such a brochure.

Discuss details about qualifications and resources.

Avoid misplaced modesty when you discuss your qualifications for a particular project in a proposal. You want to include everything that is relevant and in sufficient detail that readers will fully understand what makes you a better choice for solving their problem than others. In the project discussed earlier, Roberts noted in a sentence following the one quoted above that prior internship experience at Gompers Park has provided her with additional background on the specific situation that will enable her to include accurate information about the artists and inspiration for the mural. Obviously, other individuals who might propose to do a similar project would lack this hands-on experience, making her, clearly, the best choice for this project. These are the kinds of details, then, that achieve the point identified earlier as central to a winning proposal: showing how you can solve the problem *better* than the competition.

Why submit a realistic and detailed work schedule?

The final aspect of demonstrating your trustworthiness for a project comes through creating and submitting a realistic and detailed work schedule. If your work schedule accurately identifies the various tasks that must be completed to produce the project and, with equal accuracy, predicts the amount of time each stage will take, your credibility is greatly strengthened. If your work schedule omits important steps or underestimates the amount of time that steps will take, you can seriously undercut the credibility that you've worked so hard to establish in the earlier sections of your proposal. Planning, then, is essential so that you can accurately predict and meet the deadlines that the proposal sets out because, if your proposal is accepted, it becomes a contract between you and the customer. You will be held to the deadlines that you previously established. If you miss those deadlines, your credibility, not only as a writer but also as a practitioner in the field, will be undermined.

As instructors of technical communication, we have found that students take the work schedule least seriously of the various sections of a proposal, but it turns out that, as readers, we have learned to anticipate which individuals will have difficulty completing their projects to deadline based on missing steps and underestimates of time in the work schedule. Use your work schedule as one way to demonstrate the thought and care that you've put into your project, whether it is at school or on the job.

Task	Time Required	Completion Date
Research health issues	2 hours	Feb. 10
Research and prepare conversion chart	2 hours	Feb. 16
Decide recipes to include	4 hours	Feb. 17
Prepare draft copy	6 hours	Feb. 24
Revise draft copy	3 hours	Feb. 25
Submit final draft	1 hour	Feb. 27

TABLE 6.1
In the work schedule left, the writer has omitted a key step—user testing her draft before she revises. Should the reader conclude from this that she doesn't plan to test her draft? Also, what kind of credibility does she build by suggesting that she plans to spend parts of 6 days (18 hours total) on this (major) project?

THE EMOTIONAL APPEAL (*pathos*) refers to the *legitimate* use of readers' emotions and feelings to engage their minds. By legitimate, we mean including truthful and clear evidence to support your claims so that readers can understand the importance of the situation that you describe. Persuasion cannot happen if readers find your arguments merely trustworthy and logical. They may accept your point, but they will not take action on your information unless they feel a personal connection with the subject. A successful emotional appeal, then, aims to make the subject matter come alive for readers, to make the topic appeal to their imaginations and become significant and important. In the case of your proposal, you want readers to be convinced that your solution is clearly superior and that yours is the best team to undertake this project. You want them to feel motivated enough by your discussion to select your proposal and award you or your group the contract. This final clinching of the deal comes primarily from the emotional appeal but only if your other appeals are also well done: your plan must be solid and your credibility strong. A strong emotional appeal cannot compensate for weaknesses in the other two appeals.

There is, of course, a thin line between legitimate and illegitimate emotional appeals. You are, no doubt, familiar with the *illegitimate* use of emotion, the kind that advertising uses to make you feel anxious about your personal hygiene or your lack of an expensive car. In these cases, the advertisers seek to create emotional responses based on spurious arguments or nonsensical imagery because there are few logical arguments to be made in favour of spending a year's salary on a vehicle that in twenty years will be scrap metal. When a *legitimate* emotional appeal is added to sound logic and clear thinking, however, the effect will engage the reader in a more powerful way than can clear logic alone. An effective emotional appeal adds force to your argument by evoking readers' feelings.

HOW DO YOU CREATE AN EFFECTIVE EMOTIONAL APPEAL?

To create an emotional appeal in your writing, you need to pay attention to elements of style in your writing. Here are three ways to build emotional appeal:

- Use concrete examples.
- Use examples and illustrations.
- Use suitable word choice, metaphors, and analogies.

Avoid generalizations when you write your proposal. Instead, bring in specific examples that will paint a picture before your readers' eyes, so they can imagine and feel the scope of the problem. For example, compare Rachel Blanchard's proposal to produce a vegan recipe book in the following excerpt with the basic statement in Figure 6.3. Blanchard uses all three strategies as she tries to create sympathy and understanding in readers (who are unlikely to be vegan themselves) by describing her own experience:

After deciding to become a vegan (not eat animal products of any kind) ten years ago, I was prepared to eat a variety of new foods

---

When I decided to become a vegan ten years ago, I didn't anticipate how difficult it would be to find substitutions for the foods that I was used to eating. Instead of substituting, I just cut out the forbidden foods. My energy levels seemed to drop, and I kept getting sick with colds and flu. When I realized that I would have to learn more about alternative foods, I didn't find existing resources very helpful. So I was forced to develop my own recipes. I propose to write a cookbook that will help people who want to become vegan avoid the ill health that I experienced when I first switched my diet.

FIGURE 6.3
This problem statement baldly states the argument, but it lacks a compelling emotional appeal. While readers can follow the argument, they won't easily identify with Blanchard's experience.

but what I was not prepared for was the difficulty of figuring out which of these foods and how much would keep me healthy and energized. With the demands of school and work, I never got around to educating myself and several months later found me subsisting on a diet of peanut butter and fried tofu, not sure of what alternatives existed to meat, eggs, and cheese as good sources of protein. Every cold and flu germ that was wafting through the air seemed to find me too, even though I bought oranges and apples as if they were the Holy Grail. When I started having vivid dreams of slicing and gorging on thick, juicy steaks, medium rare, I realized that I needed to educate myself on alternative foods. I found many recipe books that used exotic and hard-to-locate ingredients (sometimes impossible, in the small town I was living in) like brewer's yeast and textured soy protein that, when made up, did not appeal to me very much no matter how much ketchup was slathered on. That was when it occurred to me to develop my own recipes, using ingredients that weren't strange or odd tasting, and I also began to experiment with food groups like nuts and legumes to develop cheap, easy-to-prepare vegan meals that left me feeling energetic and satisfied. I propose to share this experience with other students considering a vegan diet by preparing a cookbook of not only recipes but also information that will help them understand the nutritional needs of their bodies and how to substitute non-animal-based products in traditional North American dishes.

Use concrete examples.

In the problem statement above, Blanchard includes a number of specific examples such as "textured soy protein" and "brewer's yeast" to illustrate the kinds of ingredients she saw as "exotic." She also describes hiding the flavour of these exotic dishes with ketchup, something that many of her readers will also have done to make objectionable foods more palatable. She describes her early diet as consisting of "peanut butter and fried tofu" to help the reader identify with the obvious alternatives to animal-based protein. Readers who have not thought about vegan diets before would likely fall back on the same strategies that Blanchard describes and respond in similar ways to eating alternative foods.

Use examples and illustrations.

Through listing the elements that she has in mind, Blanchard builds an emotional connection with her readers who are more likely to share or identify, even just in imagination, with her experience. The specific examples also help to heighten the argument that this solution is needed to help other postsecondary students in a similar position. She could have further strengthened her emotional appeal (as well as her logical appeal) by adding a statistic about the percentage of young adults who decide to change their diets to vegetarian or vegan during their postsecondary education. This evidence would support her contention that a growing audience exists for this type of guide, so it is an important project.

Use suitable word choice, metaphors, and analogies.
Blanchard uses one comparison here, "I bought oranges and apples as if they were the Holy Grail," which underscores the cost and value she placed on eating fresh fruit as an attempt to avoid illness. The simile exaggerates the zealousness with which she bought and ate the fruit to show the reader that these excessive efforts were in vain. This strategy also helps to set up the argument that follows: she needed help, as will many others like her who decide, without adequate preparation, to radically change their basic diets.

Note that using metaphors and analogies effectively can enhance your emotional appeal, but it can also improve your ethical appeal. Selecting a metaphor that is appropriate to your subject area can also signal to readers your knowledge of and membership in that area of expertise. At the same time, a wildly inappropriate choice of metaphor or analogy can also undermine your ethical appeal, so give some thought to the suitability of the metaphors and analogies that you might choose to include. For example, in an earlier draft of Blanchard's problem statement, she wrote that she "ate bananas and oranges like a caged gorilla." Given her vegan lifestyle, the simile seems inappropriate because it implies at least a neutral stance toward, if not an acceptance of, zoos and caging wild animals. This stated moral vision undercuts the one implied by her vegan lifestyle. A writer's credibility stands on a foundation of coherent stated and implied beliefs and values, expressed through word choice, examples, and comparisons.

An effective emotional appeal in a proposal can mean the difference between readers being convinced that the situation and solution are exactly as you say and merely acknowledging that in your proposal you make a good point. Creating a good argument will not get you the job but creating the best argument will.

How do you organize a proposal?

The proposal genre has a number of requirements. It uses a standard sequence of sections; different parts of the project are discussed in each section. Generally, the sections are laid out for you in the RFP: use the headings as listed in the original request and answer the questions as posed in each section. If the RFP seems to assume your prior familiarity with its expected format, you can either contact the

LAB ASSIGNMENT 6.1

CREATING EFFECTIVE EMOTIONAL APPEALS

1. Review an existing problem statement that you've written, or draft one for a technical communication project that you have the knowledge and ability to create. Revise the problem statement enhancing the emotional appeal where appropriate using the strategies outline above: concrete examples; example and illustrations; suitable word choice, metaphors, and analogies.

2. Experiment with the metaphors and analogies that you develop for your problem statement. Create ones that are appropriate and ones that are not, and then analyse the implications of each one. Which ones signal your expertise in the area? Which ones suggest possible lack of understanding? Which ones undercut your ethos as a professional in this area? Which ones imply beliefs or values contradictory to those that underlie your argument?

3. Have a classmate or colleague read your revised problem statement. Ask him or her to respond to the different aspects of the statement including his or her emotional response to the subject matter, view of you as a credible writer about that subject, and judgement concerning whether your discussion and solution are credible.

listed reference person for more specific information, or you can use a standard generic format.

WHAT IS THE STANDARD GENERIC FORMAT FOR A PROPOSAL?

To some extent, it depends on the type of proposal. However, most proposals cover the following areas in this order using some variation on these headings:

- Problem statement/Background
- Methods/Procedures
- Qualifications/Resources
- Work Schedule
- Budget

You can use the headings as a heuristic or brainstorming exercise to help you decide what to include in each section. There should be a minimum of overlap in your discussion from section to section. Each section, read in sequence, should reveal your detailed and complete plan to develop the product or project that the proposal describes.

Another way to generate ideas about the content for your proposal is as a series of paragraph answers to a series of single questions. As you work your way through answering the questions in the order in which they are posed, you will find that the general organization of your argument emerges. At the same time, as readers move through your proposal, they should end up with a clear and coherent idea of the project that you are proposing. As you review the following list of questions that the proposal must answer, think about the role that persuasion plays in answering these questions, especially in answering questions 4 and 5.

Questions a proposal must answer

1. What problem are you going to solve?
   Usually answered in the problem statement section.
2. How are you going to solve the problem?
   Answered in the problem statement and the methods section.
3. What exactly will you provide for us?
   Answered in the problem statement.
4. Can you deliver what you promise?
   Answered through the information presented in the methods, qualifications, and work schedule sections.
5. What benefits can you offer?
   Answered through the information presented in the problem statement and the qualifications sections.
6. When will you complete the work?
   Revealed in the work schedule.
7. How much will it cost?
   Revealed in the budget statement.

HOW DO YOU INCORPORATE PERSUASION INTO THE FORMAT TO CREATE A WINNING PROPOSAL?

In Chapter 4, "Writing technical prose," we outline Stephen Toulmin's system of informal logic as a helpful way for you to develop strong and well-supported claims about the problem you are describing. This method of developing arguments is especially useful in writing proposals because it helps you build persuasive arguments based on the assumptions that you and your readers share. Toulmin's informal logic is most helpful as a way to develop your claims and then ensure that they are effectively supported by evidence. Any statement that lacks supporting evidence is just an assertion and not an argument. You can use this system to help you identify the assumptions you are making about your claim and to assess whether your readers will share these assumptions.

While the three rhetorical appeals function throughout each section of the proposal, sometimes one or two of the appeals takes precedence in a particular section. For example, in the problem statement, your logical discussion of the issues regarding the problem kick-starts your ethical appeal by showing your sensitive and sophisticated grasp of the problem. In convincing readers of the seriousness of the problem and the excellence of your proposed solution, you also employ elements of an emotional appeal. The invoking of emotion helps readers to become engaged with your ideas and perspective, increasing the chances that they will approve your proposal. But the central goal, after you secure your readers' trust, is to lay out a coherent and convincing statement of the problem and overview of the solution (i.e., your logical appeal).

To show you how, we have included Jason Nguyen's problem statement for a proposal in Figure 6.4. He proposes to develop a 20-page reference guide for postsecondary students introducing them to the basics of PowerPoint to help them create class presentations. As a third-year engineering student, he sees his classmates as a primary audience for this project. Nguyen's proposal was written in response to the RFP described earlier in this chapter, which you might review (including the analysis) to refresh your memory on the details of the assignment.

A QUICK START GUIDE TO POWERPOINT FOR COLLEGE AND UNIVERSITY STUDENTS

Problem Statement

An important part of an engineer's education is the public presentation of various class projects. While a few students were fortunate enough to learn the basics of presentation programs such as PowerPoint in high school, many were not. Professors expect them to be familiar with such a program because they assign numerous public presentations on student class projects. These assignments mean that students who are not familiar with PowerPoint must quickly learn it, on top of getting used to their new lives at the university, the challenging subject matter in their classes, and the homework load. Most students want to be able to generate a creative and professional presentation because it will boost their GPA. However, most first term engineers don't have spare time during which they can struggle with the basics of the program. Existing manuals, such as Finkelstein's *How to do Everything with PowerPoint*, (400+ pages, 1.6 lbs., lists at $25.00 USD), Lowe's *PowerPoint 2003 for Dummies* (300+ pages, 1.2 lbs., lists at $20.00 USD), or Wempen's *PowerPoint 2003 Bible* (800+ pages, 2.9 lbs., lists at $40.00 USD), are too large, too heavy, and too expensive for the average college student. Imagine the panic that most students must feel upon opening Wempen's 800+ page tome at 2 a.m. to figure out how to insert a data chart for their presentation scheduled for 8:30 later that morning! What these students need is a short (20 pages max.) guide that lists only the functions they need for their presentations in class.

I propose to create this quick-start guide especially tailored to first-year undergraduates in engineering, as well as other majors who have little time to learn new computer programs. It will briefly cover the basics (assuming most students know how to open and save files, etc.) and focus mainly on the flashy elements that make a student presentation memorable.

FIGURE 6.4
A well-developed logical argument for the problem statement of one student proposal.

In Figure 6.4, there are two claims stated in the form described in the discussion of informal logic: claim + because + stated reason. The first claim is "Professors expect them to be familiar with such a program because they assign numerous public presentations on student class projects." In support of this claim, the writer notes that professors assign various presentations, but they don't go over the basics of the program that would help students get started. Professors expect students to teach themselves or already know. The second claim builds on the situation set up in the first. Students want to learn PowerPoint quickly so they can create good presentations: "Most students want to be able to generate a creative and professional presentation because it will boost their GPA." The implication here is that creative and professional means knowing how to use more than just the basic functions of PowerPoint.

A third claim is stated with supporting evidence rather than using a "because" clause: "Existing manuals are ... too large, too heavy, and too expensive for the average college student." This claim is supported by parenthetical information that lists the page count, the weight, and the list price of each manual, assuming that readers will agree that the cost, weight, and size are all too much for students. The final persuasive point made in the problem statement of this proposal is the proposed content for the manual: "It will briefly cover the basics ... and focus mainly on the flashy elements that make a student presentation memorable." Following up the point made earlier that students want to produce creative and professional presentations, Nguyen claims that, logically, these students will benefit from a manual that teaches them how to use the more impressive features of the program.

Claims that the writer does not bother to support include the stresses encountered by first-year engineering students: "getting used to their new lives at the university, the challenging subject matter in their classes, and the homework load." Few readers will dispute that most first-year students find their new situation challenging and the workload heavy. The points that *do* need support are those claims that either are open to rebuttal or form the framework for justifying the solution that you propose. The sample problem statement in Figure 6.4 supports the key points in the argument: 1) that students need the manual because they don't have another easy source for this information and 2) that they want to know the more impressive functions so they can create memorable presentations. The evidence supplied in the argument is mainly intended to support these two points because, if readers accept the truth of these arguments, they will also agree that the manual should be written.

In Figure 6.5 and 6.6, you will find the next sections of Nguyen's proposal draft. The following analysis should highlight for you the ways in which he has tried to create a strong logical, ethical, and emotional appeal under each heading to explain the need for this project and demonstrate his ability to complete it.

THREE SECTIONS OF JASON NGUYEN'S PROPOSAL DRAFT

Purpose
The main purpose of the Quick Start Guide is to provide a fast entry for busy college and university students into some of the more complex functions of PowerPoint. They need and want to be able to add the more impressive features of the program (such as dissolving text, custom animations, and so on) to their class presentations to ensure that they are memorable as well as informative. A secondary purpose is to introduce the basics quickly and briefly, with the main focus of the manual being on the more sophisticated functions.

Topics to Investigate
While already expert at using PowerPoint, I want to build my knowledge further to be sure my instructions are as complete and up to date as possible. So I plan to study existing PowerPoint manuals for useful tips and tricks that I can include in my student-targeted version. I also plan to interview three or four of my classmates in my general engineering class to get feedback on their perspectives concerning which aspects of PowerPoint are most useful to know. I will also talk to three or four students in other majors to gather broader feedback about the needs of students other than engineers as well.

Audience
My primary audience for this manual is comprised of first-year engineering students with a basic knowledge of the program (e.g., how to add points to a slide) but who want to learn the more advanced capabilities quickly. My secondary audience will be students in programs outside of engineering who also want to know more about PowerPoint to improve the quality of their class presentations. I expect that communications and journalism majors will be especially interested in this manual because they have to do a lot of oral presentations as part of their coursework too. The initial audience will, of course, be Professor Patel, the instructor for this course.

FIGURE 6.5
Three sections of Jason Nguyen's proposal draft.

If Nguyen has made a strong enough logical appeal in his problem statement, then readers will pass without comment through his purpose statement because they will have already agreed on the need for the manual. However, a sharply focused restatement of the main goals of the manual helps readers to recall and remember the problem statement because of the repetition.

In "Topics to Investigate," Nguyen notes that he is already an expert user of the program, perhaps a point that would tempt him to avoid including this section of the proposal at all because he knows everything. However, he actually strengthens his ethical appeal in this situation by expressing an interest in improving his current level of expertise. He acknowledges that there may be some new aspects of the program that he is not completely familiar with and states that, to ensure the accuracy of his manual, he will do additional research. He will also consult members of his target user group to collect their input to help him include the relevant information in the order they would find most useful.

The fourth heading, "Audience," identifies three levels of users that he considers most central to his project. The fact that he considers users beyond the basic primary level also strengthens his credibility by demonstrating his knowledge of the technical communication course material (discussions of audience from Chapter 1). His reader (the instructor) will continue to review his discussion as indicating a competent, responsible member of the class.

METHODS AND PROCEDURES

The first stage of this project will be to interview the students, as mentioned earlier, to get feedback about what the target audience sees as its primary needs in such a manual. Since I will have to fit these in around my full schedule of classes, I expect it will take about a week to complete these. An additional step will be to examine the existing published manuals for PowerPoint to get some insight into their specific shortcomings that my manual will address, as well as tips and tricks that might be new to me but useful to include in my manual.

When I feel that my research has given me enough supplementary information, then I will decide which functions will be most useful to my users. I will draft an outline of the functions, with estimations of the approximate length of each section. These functions I will order from most to least importance to my audience, so I can omit the less important ones if the manual seems that it might become too long. This stage should take only a day or two because it is mainly organizational.

The third step will be to begin drafting the manual. I plan to use screen shots to illustrate the steps. After I complete the first function, I will have several of my classmates look over the instructions to see if they are clear, complete, and easy to follow. Using their feedback, I will continue to develop the rest of the functions according to my priorities established in stage two. This will be the most time-consuming stage of the process, probably taking two to three weeks.

The fourth stage will be to user test the draft manual with two or three first-year students who fit the user profile described above. I will try to get at least one student outside of engineering, but, since my primary audience is first-year engineers, I will definitely have at least two of my test users from this group. This stage will take about one and one-half to two weeks.

Following the user tests, I will revise my draft instructions, making whatever changes are necessary to be sure I have created the best possible set of instructions for my target user group. These final revisions will likely take two or three days.

FIGURE 6.6
The methods section of Jason Nguyen's proposal.

The "Methods and Procedure" section (Figure 6.6) sketches out in some detail the plan Nguyen has put together to finish the manual. He uses this section to extend both his logical and his ethical appeal. The level of detail that he sketches out about his plan shows that he has thought through the process of creating the manual. His plan is internally consistent, sufficiently detailed, and sounds reasonable and manageable. He also includes an estimate of the time he expects each stage to take, given his heavy regular course load. The reasonable estimates contribute to his credibility as a writer—he seems to have considered this aspect carefully, so readers will be disposed to believe the other claims he makes as well. The clarity of this plan also supports his claims in the following section for expertise in this area. He demonstrates that he knows what he's doing in the methods section; he likely also knows what he's doing in relation to the content aspects of the manual.

QUALIFICATIONS AND RESOURCES

As a five-year user of PowerPoint not only in school settings but also at an organization where it was the primary word processing program available (no kidding!), I am uniquely qualified to create this manual. Given the constraints of my employment situation from 2002–2004, I figured out how to do things with PowerPoint that no one else can do (e.g., create an animation starting with a basic clip art drawing). I am also a second-year engineering student who has helped countless classmates learn the secrets of the program so that they can improve the quality of their presentations, so I have a good idea of the needs and background of this group of students. My expertise is legendary; people seek me out to help them who aren't even engineers because friends give them my name. Third, I have several friends who are journalism and communications majors that I can interview for additional perspectives on the needs of my target users.

Work Schedule

Task	Estimated Time	Completion Date
Interview students	One week	September 22
Examine existing manuals	One week	September 29
Establish content priorities	Three days	October 3
Draft one function and receive classmate feedback	One week	October 10
Complete draft	Three weeks	November 1
Usability testing	Two weeks	November 15
Revisions based on testing	One week	November 22
Submit completed manual	Up to two hours travel time to campus	November 23

FIGURE 6.7
The qualifications and work schedule sections of Jason Nguyen's proposal.

Figure 6.7 details Nguyen's qualifications and work schedule for the proposed project. He notes that he has five years' experience working with PowerPoint, and he supports his claim for expert status by pointing out that, when he worked for a previous employer, PowerPoint was the only word processing program in the office, so employees had to make it work for every document they needed to create. He points out that his expertise is so extensive he can even create custom animations using PowerPoint and clip art. This detail makes his claims for background knowledge more convincing.

He also supports his claim for being able to teach PowerPoint by pointing out his prior experience doing just that with fellow students. He underscores this area of expertise by telling us about students from other fields who seek him out to answer their questions about obscure parts of the program. Both of these pieces of evidence suggest that he can teach well one-to-one. He wants us to extend our trust in his teaching ability to cover teaching through text, and, because of the details that he gives us and his demonstration of carefully thinking through the project, we are inclined as readers to do so.

The "Work Schedule" section further strengthens both Nguyen's logical and ethical appeals by laying out times and dates in a readable format (a table). Readers can quickly scan the columns of the table, check dates, and see that his work schedule is consistent with his discussion in the "Methods and Procedures" section (i.e., internal consistency of message). In addition, the reasonable timeframe for each section strengthens his credibility further because it adds evidence that he understands the work involved in the proposed project.

The final two sections of the proposal, the "Budget" and the "Call to Action," appear in Figure 6.8. Although there are no significant costs to this project, Nguyen still included a discussion of the budget to reinforce the competence of his project plan. He includes eventualities such as purchasing a new colour ink cartridge, although he won't necessarily need to replace his current one. This statement demonstrates that he's trying to anticipate even remotely possible costs associated with the project. The fact that he's also thought about how to bind the manual, both for the user test and the final project, indicates that he plans to incorporate ideas about format into his own project.

Finally, the "Call to Action" provides a neat summary, repeating the importance of the project (by pointing out the potential audience for this manual) and also including an emotional appeal designed to encourage the reader to approve the project and do so quickly so that he can get started. The combination of need, importance, and Nguyen's expressed enthusiasm should work to spur the reader to action, the final step in the persuasive process.

Budget

There are no significant costs associated with this project. I plan to go to the local bookstore and examine existing manuals from the shelves. Since I buy my textbooks there, the managers should have no problem with me using their facilities to study the books for an hour or two. Of course, there will be some printing costs associated with this project, but only slightly more than the average costs for a class. There are also binding costs for the draft and final copy of the manual, but those will be between $10 and $15 dollars. If I decide to print the illustrations in colour, I may need to purchase a new ink cartridge for my printer, and that will cost about $100.00. But I will need to replace the ink cartridge at some point anyway, whether I create this brochure or not. The total possible cost for creating this manual will be between $15 and $115.00 (worst case scenario).

Call to Action

With nearly 1500 new first-year students on campus this term, there is a potentially wide audience for this manual on this campus alone. Once I complete this project, hundreds of first-year students will find their first year of study just that much easier because they will have access to a brief guide tailored specifically to their needs. And several professors will notice the quality of the oral presentations in their classes improve as students are able to present their ideas in exciting and innovative ways. Please approve this project as quickly as you can, so I can begin the first stage of research as soon as possible.

FIGURE 6.8
Final two sections of Jason Nguyen's proposal.

As you write your own proposal, use the discussion in this chapter to help you think about ways to develop your persuasive appeals in the different sections of the proposal. Use what you learned about analysing your reader in Chapter 1 to help you tailor your logic, credibility, and emotional impact to maximize the effect of the case you build for the importance and usefulness of your project.

LAB ASSIGNMENT 6.2

PRACTISING RHETORICAL APPEALS

Identify a process or procedure that you are familiar with and that you could document. Then draft a problem statement that lays out an argument for why this set of instructions should exist. Use the information on Toulmin's informal logic to help you develop evidence in support of your argument that these instructions will solve an existing problem.

MAJOR PROJECT 6.1

WRITING A PROPOSAL

1. Option to write a manual:

Write a proposal to create an instructional manual that *does not currently exist*: that is, you need to identify a process or procedure that has not been documented for a particular audience but that you would be qualified to create.

If there are procedures that could be documented at your place of employment but are not, you may propose to create a manual that could be used at your work place.

In the proposal, do the following:

- Explain the subject matter for the manual that you propose to create.
- Explain your plan to assemble the reference material you need to write and illustrate the procedures that a particular audience has need of but that are not currently available.
- Include an argument showing that the manual that you propose does not currently exist but that there is a need for it.

The topic of your proposal is open, which is disconcerting at the start. However, the best work is generally that which genuinely seeks to solve real-life, real-time problems. To help you get started, here is a list of topics that other students have worked on in the past.

- Manual for college students on how to use PowerPoint to create oral presentations
- Quick reference guide to using the advanced functions of a Nokia flip phone
- Orientation manual for new employees
- Manual for creating a website for a student using HTML
- Reception desk manual
- Guide for college students for converting to vegetarianism
- Guide to using clipart to create original animations in PowerPoint
- A children's colour-based guide to solving the Rubik's cube

Use the outline below to structure your proposal, and draw on the rhetorical appeals discussed in this chapter to develop and explain your project idea:

- Problem Statement
- Purpose
- Topics to Investigate
- Audience
- Methods and Procedure
- Qualifications and Resources
- Work Schedule
- Budget (if appropriate)
- Call to Action

2. Option to write a recommendation report:

Identify a problem for which you are qualified to find a solution, and then write a proposal in which you make a case for the seriousness of the problem, your ideas about a solution, and your plan for arriving at the best solution. If there is a problem at work for which your supervisor or employee would appreciate a solution, consider using this topic as the subject of your report.

In the proposal, do the following:

- Explain the problem that you will solve in the report that you propose to create.
- Explain your plan to research the problem, to assemble whatever reference material you might need, and to decide on the most appropriate solution for the problem that you've identified.
- Include an argument showing that the problem that you have identified needs to be solved and that you are well qualified to solve it.

The topic of your proposal is open, which is disconcerting at the start. However, the best work is generally that which genuinely seeks to solve real-life, real-time problems.

Use the outline below to structure your proposal, and draw on the rhetorical appeals discussed in this chapter to develop and explain your project idea:

- Problem Statement
- Purpose
- Topics to Investigate
- Audience
- Methods and Procedure
- Qualifications and Resources
- Work Schedule
- Budget (if appropriate)
- Call to Action

CHAPTER SEVEN

Reporting technical information

Generally, reports are characterized by two qualities: they contain a "systematic record of a particular technical study" and they are usually written for others to read.[1] Like so many of the activities discussed in this book, reporting technical information means keeping in mind the needs of your readers. You are usually presenting complex technical information for readers who *may* but likely *do not* share the same level of knowledge of specialized subject matter that you do. For this reason, you should consider whether to define technical terms or concepts to help readers navigate through your discussion. You should also consider including adequate background information to quickly educate novice readers about what they need to know to follow and evaluate the information presented in the report. Readers who don't need this background can skip over it, while readers who do will appreciate the grounding. And you will appreciate your readers being able to give their full attention and judgement to the final product of your extensive research efforts.

This chapter focuses on four different types of reports:

- the status or progress report
- the information report or white paper
- the laboratory report
- the recommendation report.

In it, you will find information about what you are trying to accomplish in writing these reports, how to format the different genres, and useful strategies for responding effectively to the rhetorical challenges presented by these types of reports.

Status or progress reports

Status reports are also known as progress or activity reports, depending upon the focus of the report. Activity reports are generally used as a way for employees to update supervisors on how they have spent

1   Hans F. Ebel, Claus Bliefert, and William E. Russey, *The Art of Scientific Writing: From Student Reports to Professional Publications in Chemistry and Related Fields*, 2nd ed. (Weinheim, Germany: Wiley-VCH, 2004), 7.

their workweek, noting accomplishments on various assigned tasks or alerting managers to potential or real problems that may be looming. Status or progress reports generally focus on the progress of a particular project. In some organizations, all three terms may be used interchangeably to refer to the same type of document.

PURPOSE OF STATUS REPORTS

Writing a status report fulfils several functions in an organization:

- To update team members and managers on the progress and status of projects within an organization,
- To show an organization's or individual's competence in pursuing and completing a task, and
- To help those doing the work to assess it and plan future work.

Status reports document the progress of work at an organization. They provide concise, coherent, and clear summaries of what work has been completed and what remains still to be done. Many organizations have employees write brief, one-page status reports each week to account for how they have spent their time. Supervisors scan these reports to ensure that employees are productively engaged and projects are moving ahead. Any potentially serious problems come to supervisors' attention early, and solutions can be proposed or developed to head off delay or disaster.

Status reports also perform a rhetorical function by giving writers the opportunity to demonstrate either their own or their company's competence and ability. For example, if you reach the goals set out in the original project proposal each week, you can highlight this fact in the status report. If you encounter an obstacle to reaching the goal but also develop a solution that quickly gets the project back on track, you can emphasize your successful problem-solving abilities in the status report. This document enables you to impress your supervisors favourably with regular updates of accomplishments.

Think of the status report as an opportunity for not only supervisors but also you and your team members to reflect on how well the project is going. You can measure your progress against the dates originally predicted in the (proposal) work schedule to assess how accurate you were in forecasting the actual time required to complete each stage. If you miscalculated, either by under- or over-estimating the time or costs, you can suggest adjustments in the status report, as well as improve your knowledge base to help you judge more accurately in subsequent projects.

You should also anticipate the next stages of the work. Given what you have accomplished so far, should you alter the plan in any way to accommodate the next major task? You can also use this report as an opportunity to reflect on whether preparatory work needs to begin to ensure that later stages will proceed without delay.

CONTENT OF STATUS REPORT

Usually the status report contains information about the status of all current projects:

- It summarizes what has been accomplished.
- It supplies information about any problems.
- It describes the actions taken to resolve problems.
- It outlines the writer's plans for the coming weeks.

Figure 7.1 lists a generic outline for a status report. If your organization doesn't have its own format, then adapt this one to your particular situation.

STRUCTURE OF A STATUS REPORT

Beginning:

INTRODUCTION OR PROJECT DESCRIPTION

This section should refresh your reader's memory on your project and briefly summarize its central points.

Middle:

WORK COMPLETED

- Task 1
- Task 2

This section details the work that you have completed, task by task. If you encountered any problems with these tasks, you also describe the actions that you took to resolve the difficulties.

WORK REMAINING

- Task 3
- Task 4

This section describes the tasks that still remain before you complete the project. It lists the tasks that remain, but with limited elaboration. Any potential obstacles that you anticipate may be mentioned here, as well as solutions that you propose.

COST

Report on how much budget has been used to this point and how much remains. Explain any discrepancies between the plan and reality.

End:

OVERALL ASSESSMENT OF PROGRESS TO DATE

CONCLUSIONS AND RECOMMENDATIONS

Conclude the status report by appraising your progress to this point for your supervisor. Assess whether you believe the project will be completed as anticipated in the proposal. If you have any recommendations about changes to the plan or schedule, include those here.

FIGURE 7.1
A generic structure for a status report. Adapt this structure to suit your rhetorical situation.

WRITING THE STATUS REPORT: RHETORICAL CONSIDERATIONS

Remember that a status report is a persuasive document. What are you hoping to persuade your reader of? At least two things, in fact: the ongoing progress toward success of your project and your competence and ability as an employee.

Since the status report is a persuasive document, you should assess what you are writing and how you are writing it. Present the information on your progress as clearly and accurately as you can. Provide the level of detail necessary to convey your progress unambiguously, but also recognize that your reader has many other responsibilities, so be concise.

You also want to demonstrate your competence. Include details that show your commitment and expertise. If you are going to make generalizations about your progress, support them with detailed factual accomplishments. In other words, if you want to say that the project is proceeding splendidly, then include several statements that support this judgment by outlining the tasks that have been completed and the timelines that you have met.

If you have encountered problems that have slowed your progress, present those problems honestly, and, if possible, emphasize positive solutions to those problems. For example, if the web design team has learned that the original layout needs to be revised based on usability feedback (i.e., test users did not recognize the navigational bar because it used images instead of legible text), then explain the changes that the team thinks will make the navigational bar more prominent (e.g., fade out the saturation of the images and add contrasting, underlined text), and note that additional informal testing suggests that this revision eliminates the problem without introducing new ones.

Do not skip over problems that have delayed progress. It will *not* be easier to break the bad news later that the project will miss its deadline. Supervisors appreciate knowing early that the project is behind schedule. If they are not told promptly about delays, they will assume that everything is going well—until the product is not ready the day before its release. *Not* a good career move!

Figure 7.2 and Figure 7.3 provide an example of a student-written status report prepared in response to Major Project 7.1. In this memo, Rebecca McGregor reports on the progress of her proposal to create a training manual for computer engineering students who arrive for a work term at SportSystems Unlimited, a company that manufactures dasher boards for hockey and indoor soccer arenas.

MEMO

To: Professor Chang
From: Rebecca McGregor
Subject: Status report on training manual for co-op students at
             SportSystems Unlimited
Date: October 7, 2007

Project description

SportSystems Unlimited is a small manufacturing firm that produces arena boards for inline skating pads, hockey rinks, and indoor soccer fields. Recently, they have hired several mechatronics engineering co-op students to help write programming code for a robot they have installed that will increase productivity as well as product quality. So far, the company lacks any orientation or training information that would help newly arrived co-op students quickly learn the basics about the business. I am writing a manual that documents the basic information and procedures that new students need to know about SportSystems Unlimited when they arrive. This manual will be a quick reference to answer basic questions that students may have about the products that SportSystems sells and the procedures that they need to know as they get started on their assigned projects. The manual covers the following topics:

- An overview of SportSystems' products and specialties
- A brief description of the key employees and their areas of expertise and responsibility
- Previously undocumented office procedures often assigned to co-op students (e.g., how to answer the phone and direct calls).

Work completed

Interviews conducted: content selected

This project is progressing well, for the most part. So far I have hit my deadlines to this point, having selected the content for the manual and drafted the first five pages, which give an overview of the company and its products. I had a little bit of trouble scheduling the interviews at first because two of the three people I needed to talk to were out of town during the week that I had scheduled to interview them. However, I was able to meet with them early the following week, and they were very helpful in suggesting what information they wanted new employees to learn. I drafted an outline of the content and had it approved on September 30.

FIGURE 7.2
Sample status or progress report (first part).

R. McGregor—2

Work remaining

Since I have decided on the manual content and drafted the first third, covering SportSystems' products and specialties, all that remains is to write the personnel and responsibility descriptions and to document the office procedures that I had to learn during the first few weeks of my work term. To illustrate these procedures, I will use a combination of digital photos and screen shots. The owners have given me permission to visit the company this weekend to create the visuals, and I am hoping that I can complete the draft and the graphics by Oct. 17.

Midterms start on Oct. 18, and that may slow down my progress on the usability testing. However, I have built extra time into my project schedule, so I expect to complete the tests on

FIGURE 7.3
Sample status or progress report (conclusion).

time, even if studying for midterm exams delays me actually running the tests. Two employees of SportSystems have agreed to help me test the manual, and my roommate is going to serve as the third test user.

Overall progress

There has been no major delay to this project. I still have two-thirds of the work to do to complete the draft, but the original schedule seems reasonable, if I continue to complete the tasks as listed. Since I have already lined up my test users and tentative dates for testing, I expect that this project will be completed, tested, and revised by the deadline for this project, December 3.

Note how McGregor has divided her discussion into "Work completed" and "Work remaining," a reasonable method given that her project is fairly straightforward. If she were reporting on a huge project, she might have organized it based on the tasks outlined in the proposal or tied her discussion more closely to the budget line. In other words, for an expensive, large-scale project, she might have ended the discussion of each task with reference to how much of the budget had been spent, how closely expenses matched projected figures from the proposal, and how much money remained. This strategy would respond to a supervisor's implicit question about how well the project was staying on budget.

White papers or information reports

White papers (information reports) are reports that provide information about a particular topic. They are distinguished from other types of reports in that they argue a specific position on the issue or pose a solution to a problem by introducing innovations in technology or new products. In technical fields, especially in the high tech industry, white papers are both technical documents and marketing documents. From the company's perspective, their purpose is generally threefold:

- to inform readers,
- to educate them about the advantages of a new product or service, and
- to persuade them that this innovation is the superior solution to a particular problem.

These goals make the white paper both an informative and persuasive genre of technical communication. From the reader's perspective, white papers are useful sources of information about innovative products and services: busy executives review them to find solutions to problems and to justify the solutions they choose. In fact, more

LAB ASSIGNMENT 7.1

WRITING A STATUS REPORT

Using the information in this section, write a status or progress report on one of your major assignments for the technical communication course, for example, the technical manual or the recommendation report. Accurately report the work that you have completed this far, and also explain the work that still remains. Remember to report your progress as positively as possible, but don't minimize problems that you've encountered in your project.

MAJOR PROJECT 7.1

REPORTING PROGRESS ON YOUR TECHNICAL MANUAL

Write a relatively short (one to two pages) status report on your manual project (Major Project 8.2 in Chapter 8). Address the memo to your instructor, and organize your discussion around the points below (taken from this section of the chapter).

Status report content
Summarize your progress in terms of your goals and your original schedule.
■ Use measurable statements.

Work completed
■ Describe what you have already done.
■ Be specific to support your claims in the first paragraph and so your instructor can appreciate your hard work.
■ Acknowledge the people who have helped you.
■ Describe any serious obstacles that you've encountered, and tell how you've dealt with them.

Work to be completed
■ Describe the work that remains.
■ If you are more than three days off your original work schedule, draw up a new schedule, showing how you will be able to meet the original deadline.
■ Discuss "observations" or "preliminary conclusions" if you want feedback before completing your manual.

Overall assessment of progress
■ Express your confidence in having the manual ready by the due date, or request a conference to discuss extending the due date or limiting the project.
■ If you are behind in your original schedule, show why you think you can still finish the project on time.

than three-quarters of information technology professionals review white papers on a topic before they make a purchasing decision.

As both technical and marketing documents, white papers present unique challenges for writers. They often present complex technical information to a broad audience of readers, many of whom lack expertise in the subject matter. Given the non-specialist character of your audience, you should avoid using technical jargon or acronyms (i.e., letter combinations substituted for noun phrases) that can make readers impatient. If a technical term is essential to enable discussion of the product or service, make sure that you define it for readers in non-specialist terms. On the other hand, you can also run the risk of being too promotional in a white paper, selling the product or service too hard, which also turns readers off. Your goal in writing a white paper, then, is to strike a balance between informing and persuading your reader.

WHAT INFORMATION DO YOU PUT IN A WHITE PAPER?

The most effective approach in organizing a white paper is to begin by describing a common problem or scenario, which both grabs readers' attention and illustrates that you understand the kind of problem confronting them that they need to solve. After describing the problem, you explain the solution and introduce the new product or service. Next, you show how the product or service helps to solve the problem. Finally, you conclude by emphasizing why the product or service is the best solution. Figure 7.4 outlines the format for an effective white paper, and Figure 7.5 and 7.6 excerpt sections from a sample white paper following this format and written by Lisa Richards on a new product called "Web-Time."

There are a number of rhetorical challenges to writing a good white paper. Basically, you are writing an argument in which you demonstrate that the new product or service is really the best solution to the problem that you have identified. So identifying the problem correctly is the first step. To do this, you need to analyse and understand your readers and their needs.

HOW DO YOU REACH THE AUDIENCE FOR A WHITE PAPER?

Experts recommend using HTML to post your white paper on the Internet because it will be easy for individuals to find using search engines. You can also post it on the Internet as a "PDF file" for the same reasons: it will be easy to locate and easy to download and read. While your organization might be tempted to have readers register before they can access the white paper, it is better just to have the paper readily available since registering often involves malfunctioning forms that easily discourage readers (and potential customers). If the paper is easily available, then it can accomplish its purpose of educating and convincing readers. Another strategy for making your white paper easily available is to link it to news and information websites that your target audience visits regularly. When the white paper is posted online, it becomes readily available not only to customers but also to competitors as well, so consider carefully the degree of detail you include in your description. You might decide to omit those details that might enlighten the competition.

OUTLINE FOR A TECHNICAL WHITE PAPER

Total length: 5 to 50 pages (optimum length found to be 15 to 20 pages)

Abstract or Executive Summary

LENGTH: One paragraph

CONTENT:

- Summarize the purpose of the paper
- Summarize your findings
- Some controversy over whether to include conclusions in your abstract:
    - Not including the conclusions entices the reader to look beyond the abstract.
    - Including the conclusions results in busy executives not reading further.

Problem statement

LENGTH: Two to three paragraphs

CONTENT:

- Describe the problem
- Give a brief background or context for the problem:
    - Avoid technical jargon
    - Define essential technical terms.

Description of solution

LENGTH: As long as needed, as short as possible

- Describe how product or service works in general (informing goal)
- Enumerate the features of the product or service
- Explain how product or service applies to the problem state above
- Include visuals that illustrate the product or explain the service

How product/service solves the problem

LENGTH: As long as needed, as short as possible

- Show how the product or service applies to the problem (persuasive goal)
- Include evidence
- Show how features of product/service benefit the reader
- Explain why this product/service is superior to other possible solutions
- Acknowledge one or two limitations to demonstrate an unbiased assessment of the solution

Conclusion

LENGTH: One or two paragraphs

- Summarize why your product or service is the best solution to the problem.

FIGURE 7.4
Outline for effective white paper.

Figure 7.5 reproduces the executive summary and first part of the problem statement from a white paper by Lisa Richards on "Web-Time," a new online service that allows temporary employees (temps) to submit their hours through the Internet rather than by filling out paper timesheets. Figure 7.6 excerpts the solution she proposes.

FIGURE 7.5

Abstract and first part of problem statement from a white paper by Lisa Richards on an online service that allows temporary employees to submit their timesheets over the Internet.

Executive Summary

This report evaluates the existing methods for employees to submit the hours that they have worked to their respective temp agency. Currently, many temp agencies use a paper-based method that encourages waste, inefficiency, and can reduce company productivity.

A new service called "Web-Time" gives employees a valuable alternative to filling out paper timesheets by submitting them online instead. Throughout this report, the costs and benefits of using Web-Time as opposed to paper timesheets will be compared and contrasted. Web-Time has proven itself to be the most useful and effective method of submitting time cards, and the reasons for its successes will be evaluated and explained in further detail.

Problem Statement

Technological advancements have created more efficient ways to cope with situations that we face in our daily life. These new methods of doing things are not only more efficient, but can be environmentally sound and financially profitable. Businesses are embracing these technologies by shifting from paper-based systems to electronic processes. Examples include online banking, online course registration at universities, and e-mail. These systems have proven themselves to be invaluable as they save time, frustration, and (occasionally) money for the people who use them.

In the past, employees used to have to punch time cards to mark the beginnings and endings of their shifts as a means of logging their hours. Punched time cards became outdated and society advanced to filling in timesheets that could be mailed (or even better, faxed!) to employers. Once again, old methodology has become obsolete and has been replaced by a new process.

At First Data Merchant Services, most of the employees have been contracted by assorted temp agencies; they all have different schedules and work in various departments of the business. In order to keep track of the number of hours worked, each week, employees must fill in timesheets that detail what specific hours they worked between, how long their breaks were, and what days they worked. (See Figure 1) ...

In Figure 7.6, the solution to the problem is reproduced from Lisa Richards' white paper. Note that she also includes a visual (one of three) that illustrates and supports the solution she describes.

HOW WEB-TIME SOLVES THE AFOREMENTIONED PROBLEM

Web-Time allows employees to log their hours online and then submit the hours to their respective supervisors. Each supervisor is then able to log in at his/her own convenience, verify the hours of the employee, and then submit them directly to the temp agency online. (See Figure 3.) The goal of Web-Time is to reduce the amount of time that is wasted by both employees and supervisors and to make it more convenient to submit/verify hours at one's own leisure.

Figure 3: Completed Timesheet

Web-Time is a cost-effective solution for both the temp agency and the company (in this case, First Data) because it reduces printing costs of timesheets and the individual sheets of paper wasted from the fax machine. This system alleviates the stresses of manually filling in a timesheet, rechecking the hourly figures to ensure accuracy, finding a supervisor for a signature, faxing the timesheet, and then waiting for a confirmation to ensure that it was received by the temp agency. Since employees will be able to complete and submit their hours quickly online, they will be able to concentrate on doing their job efficiently and to the best of their ability, which can lead to increased performance and productivity ...

FIGURE 7.6
An excerpt from the solution section of Lisa Richards' white paper on "Web-Time".

WHAT ARE SOME USEFUL STRATEGIES THAT WILL INCREASE THE EFFECTIVENESS OF YOUR WHITE PAPER?

1. Stand back from your subject matter and summarize the key points that newcomers need to know to appreciate the new product or service.
Sometimes when we are too familiar with a topic, we assume that everyone else is equally knowledgeable, so we start the discussion at too high a level. To ensure that you include contextual and background information, outline the basic requirements. For example, for a computer-based product, you should list the following basics:

- Is it hardware or software?
- What support equipment or conditions are necessary?
- What platform is it designed for?
- What language is it written in or does it assume some knowledge of?
- Who will find this product useful?

If you address these kinds of issues clearly in the white paper, readers can quickly and easily assess whether to keep reading: if the product is compatible with their current system, they will be interested in your argument; if not, they will move on.

2. Assume your reader is a newcomer to the subject.

If you are addressing a newcomer, you assume that they are not aware of the significant issues associated with this topic: your discussion should fill them in on the key points they should know. You should also lay out the associated points as you highlight for them what is at stake in the discussion. Once they are familiar with the basic issues, then they will be equipped to follow and appreciate the argument that you build in support of your solution.

3. Describe the problem in specific and personalized terms.

One expert recommends using a case study or narrative as an interesting and attention-grabbing way to set up the problem that your product or service solves. Case studies employ characters and situations that make the problem come to life: a narrative approach is much more likely to draw in readers, who will want to keep reading to find out how the problem is resolved. This approach also allows you to present a fully developed example of how to solve the problem set up in the case.

4. In describing how your product or service works, distinguish its features from the benefits it confers on the reader.

When you are describing how the product or service works, detail the special features that make it useful and desirable. Describe these features clearly and accurately. Once you have described the special features, *then* go on to show readers how those features provide them with specific benefits. Describing reader benefits helps readers to imagine the ways in which the product or service might be useful to them.

Generally, reader benefits are based on appealing to readers' basic needs or wants. For example, here is a list of humans' basic needs:

- Physical well being
- Feeling safe and secure
- Being loved and feeling that one belongs
- Esteem and recognition
- Self-actualization.

This list is based on Maslow's hierarchy of needs and is in order of importance, with physical well being coming first and moving through to self-actualization. Individuals will not be motivated by the need for self-actualization unless their other needs are already being met fairly well.

In *Business and Administrative Communication*, Kitty Locker translates Maslow's hierarchy of needs into organizational terms. Her list is useful because it helps us see how the basic categories apply as motivations for employees in organizations. Table 7.1 identifies some of these needs.

Basic need	Organizational motivation
Physical	▪ Earning enough to pay for food, shelter, clothing, ▪ and medical care ▪ Having safe working conditions
Safety, Security	▪ Earning enough for a comfortable living ▪ Being treated fairly ▪ Saving time and money ▪ Having pleasant working conditions
Love, Belonging	▪ Having friends, co-workers who like you ▪ Collaborating on projects ▪ Feeling needed
Esteem, Recognition	▪ Having achievements recognized ▪ Being promoted or gaining authority ▪ Having status symbols
Self-actualization	▪ Using your talents and abilities ▪ Solving problems ▪ Developing your talents as fully as possible ▪ Serving the larger community

TABLE 7.1
Hierarchy of needs expressed as organizational motivations (adapted from Locker's BAC).

You can develop reader benefits by thinking about what motivates your readers. This list of basic needs provides ideas that you can build on. Generate your own list of potential motivations for readers based on these basic needs. Then consider how the features of your product or service can meet these needs. You have converted the product features into user benefits when you write several points for the white paper that show readers how the features of the product or service can benefit them and help them reach their goals. See Figure 7.7 for an example of how to analyse a product's features and potential reader motivations.

Katrice Blackwell is writing a white paper to inform potential customers about new cellphone technology that allows them to photograph printed information. The phone will then convert the image to a text file that they can download onto their computer and edit in a word processing file. She has created a list of the following features:
▪ PC and Mac compatible
▪ USB connector for downloads
▪ Cellphone contains software to enable link
▪ CD supplies software for PC/Mac programming
▪ Converts image to Notepad file
▪ High resolution image file (X pixels per inch or X pixels per cm)
▪ Operation manual shows you how to use the new functions

FIGURE 7.7
Blackwell's analysis of products features and readers' motivations.

She then creates the following list of possible motivations for her readers, based on Maslow's hierarchy of needs:

- To do their job well and efficiently
- To have the tools to do their job well
- To have access to cutting-edge technology
- To help employees do their jobs better
- To find a way to minimize lost documents (i.e., potential problem)
- To be promoted (or get a raise) because of improved job performance.

When she compares the list of features with the needs she has identified, Katrice realizes that many of the features will help readers (or their employees) do their job well and more efficiently. She also sees that she has several potential audiences here: the employees who will use the phone and the managers who will authorize the purchase of the phone.

Employees:
- To do their job well and efficiently
- To have the tools to do their job well
- To have access to cutting-edge technology
- To be promoted or get a raise because of performance improvements.

Managers:
- To do their job well
- To have access to cutting-edge technology
- To help subordinates do their jobs better
- To minimize potential problems (i.e., lost documents)
- To gain recognition for improving unit's performance.

Of these two groups, she decides that the managers will be the primary audience for the white paper because they can allocate funds for the purchase. So she decides to adapt employee needs and appeal directly and broadly to managers, who want to improve the performance of their subordinates and set themselves up for promotion based on overall improved productivity.

The third step of the process is to then link up the product features with the readers' motivations to create reader benefits. In Figure 7.8, Katrice Blackwell converts her cellphone's features into benefits that correspond to the motivations that she has identified. Note how she combines several features in point 2 to argue the benefit more convincingly.

In her white paper, Lisa Richards includes several well-developed reader benefits as she explains the "Solution" section of her paper. (See Figure 7.9.) She notes that the program provides these benefits:

1. Security for workers
2. Reduced interruptions for supervisors
3. Increased efficiency in the workplace

4. Cost savings for both the temp agency and the client company.

ONE EXPERT'S HELPFUL HINT

Here is one pointer that expert writers of white papers recommend to increase your chances of success. Wade Nelson recommends that you mention one or two limitations in your product description so that you present a balanced view. He notes that, by acknowledging some limitations, you also add more persuasive weight to your claims for the product's advantages.

Following this advice, Lisa also includes the following limitation at the end of her discussion of the solution to show her balanced view of the situation she describes: "A limitation that Web-Time could potentially face is servers becoming overloaded when multiple employees try to log into the service simultaneously. Also, should the website be down for whatever reason, they will not be able to submit their hours online. These limitations have not occurred yet, but, in a worst-case scenario, the paper timesheet is a fallback option." These points help to strengthen her persuasive case.

READER BENEFITS TO USE IN THE WHITE PAPER

1. Machine compatibility feature means this phone can download the converted files to Mac or PC, so the type of machines your organization runs is not a barrier to using this technology (contributes to efficiency)

2. Phone already has all of the hardware and software needed, so once you purchase the package, after a quick installation, you are ready to use it (relatively limited start-up time contributes to efficiency)

3. Converts image to Notepad file that can be opened easily and edited in any word processing program (wide compatibility = efficiency)

4. Ways the phone can improve job performance:

- Use it to record notes taken at a meeting (you don't have to retype them)
- Photograph business cards so you have the contact info when you need it
- Photograph short documents, brochures, ephemeral stuff that you can use for a creative presentation later (contributes to efficiency, innovation)
- Increase employee satisfaction by equipping them with cutting-edge technology (status symbol)

5. This phone will help you improve the overall productivity of your employees, resulting in improved performance and, then, promotions and possibly other types of recognition. (This last part is a bit self-serving, so any reference to this type of benefit should be subtle.)

IN-CLASS EXERCISE 7.1

Converting Product Features to Reader Benefits

Select a product or device that you know well and like well enough that you could sell its merits to someone else.

- Generate a list of at least 10 features that the product has that make it useful and desirable.
- Brainstorm a list of potential motivations based either on Maslow's hierarchy of needs or Locker's adaptation of these needs to a business organization.
- Create a third list of the features (listed in #1) that can meet some of the motivations (listed in #2).
- Finally, develop as many reader benefits as you can from your analysis.

Write two paragraphs, one that describes three or four of the most important features of the device and one that elaborates some of the reader benefits of owning it.

FIGURE 7.8
Blackwell generates a series of reader benefits by connecting the phone's features with her anticipated reader motivations.

USABILITY TEST YOUR WHITE PAPER

When you feel that your draft is just about finished, you should have several non-technical people read and respond to it. Do this by sitting down with each reader one at a time, with both of you looking at your own printed copy of the white paper. Observe the tester as he or she reads the draft aloud, and, during the reading, make a note of any comments, pauses, stumbles, and so on. When the reader is finished, ask for a description of her or his personal experience of reading the paper. Have the tester point out any passages that seemed difficult to understand or confusing. Ask what kinds of changes might improve the paper. Carefully take note of all of the reader's remarks so that you have a detailed record of the test.

Later, go over your notes and revise everything that you think might have caused a problem for the reader. Assess whether suggestions are useful, and act on the ones that you think will improve your paper. When you believe that you have clarified all of the issues raised by the first test have the same people (and one or two new ones) read the draft again, using the same method, to determine whether you have fixed the problems and to ensure that you have not introduced any new ones while addressing the earlier ones. Your goal is to produce a draft that it is completely clear and convincing to non-specialists. Only when your test readers agree that it is clear, readable, and persuasive, should you put it online.

MAJOR PROJECT 7.2

WRITING A WHITE PAPER

Select a new product or device that you know something about, and write a white paper introducing it to readers who will find this innovation helpful.

LAB ASSIGNMENT 7.2

USER TEST YOUR WHITE PAPER DRAFT

Bring three or four copies of your draft white paper to class with you. In groups of three people, user test your drafts, one draft at a time. Distribute a copy of your draft to the members of your group and have each person read it aloud, one at a time. Take notes, as first one reads the paper and then the other, to record places where readers pause or stumble over the wording. Use the discussion above to help you plan and execute your usability test.

The laboratory report

Each field that uses the laboratory report has its own specific requirements about how to write it well. This section will *not* detail the specifics of biology, chemistry, physics, or engineering lab reports

In addition to all of the practical features that Web-Time boasts, this system provides security for workers, who can rest assured that they will be paid consistently on a weekly basis (depending on the pay period specified by the temp agency) and that their paycheque will be an accurate reflection of the hours that they have submitted. Supervisors also benefit from Web-Time by being able to complete their tasks with less interruption, freeing office equipment (i.e., fax machines) to be used solely for business purposes and minimizing the risk of potential problems such as their employees not being paid as a result of timesheets getting lost amongst other faxes.

Since implementing Web-Time, the supervisors have been able to schedule their noon hour on Mondays to scroll through all of the timesheets of their employees and verify hours. They no longer have to be interrupted for signatures when they may have been focusing on another task at the time.

Web-Time is superior to other forms of hour tracking as it is efficient, allows the company to maintain solid productivity without interruption, and is financially sound for businesses. This saves the temp agency money by reducing its costs since the agency does not have to print sufficient timesheets for employees, distribute them (normally by mail, which then adds the cost of a stamp), and then print one faxed timesheet per employee. The reduction in paper waste is also environmentally friendly.

FIGURE 7.9
The reader benefits that Lisa Richards describes in explaining her solution to the problem.

because doing so is beyond the scope of this book. However, this section *will* introduce you, generally, to the rhetorical strategies and genre requirements that make a good lab report. Your instructors in the specific fields will provide you with details about their specialties' preferences, which you can then use in adapting the more general information here.

There are two parts to writing a good laboratory report. One is, of course, the report itself, but the initial step that directly affects your report quality is how well you record your experiment in the laboratory notebook, while doing the experiment. For this reason, this section reviews the basics of keeping a good laboratory notebook and then describes how to transform the notes into a laboratory report. Generally, the laboratory report is an academic exercise in which students gain experience replicating common experiments while they learn how to use equipment, perform common laboratory-based activities, and report their results in written form. Some instructors argue that the lab report gives students practise in writing the genre in which experimental research is published. However, there are some fundamental ways in which lab reports for school differ from research articles published in journals. For example, in the literature review in an article manuscript, writers focus on demonstrating the existing gap in knowledge in the area that justifies publishing their new insights. In contrast, the introduction in a lab report explains the reason for the experiment (creating new knowledge in the student, not in the disciplinary specialty). However, the lab report does point students towards understanding the genre of the experimental report and the fundamental ways in which it is different from something like an essay or even a recommendation report.

THE LABORATORY NOTEBOOK

Experimental descriptions originate in the laboratory notebook. Laboratory reports rest on a foundation of experimental evidence, first recorded in the notebook, so they are only as good as the records made during the experiment. While you are conducting the experiment, you should be recording clear and detailed notes about the following:

- Your actions
- Your observations
- Your thoughts.

With detailed notes, you will find the laboratory report much easier to write later because it won't depend on your short-term memory. The key elements here are that you record this information as it takes place, in a systematic fashion and in a permanent place—the laboratory notebook.

Your lab notebook and scientific integrity

Your laboratory notebook should have the following qualities:

- It should be a bound volume.
  Experts recommend that you use a bound notebook. Don't use a loose-leaf binder for your notebook because the pages can fall out easily or be moved out of sequence. Don't use a spiral notebook because pages can be removed without it being noticeable.
- All of the pages should be numbered and dated in sequence.
- All entries should be in waterproof, non-erasable ink.
- Don't leave blank pages.

These qualities all have to do with scientific integrity. It is critical that the notes you take during an experiment are as accurate and clear as you can make them. You can change your notes during the experiment as long as you record what you changed and why, but they should not be altered later or even crossed out beyond a single line drawn through the entry so that it remains legible. While this degree of care and accuracy may seem excessive at your level of study, remember that these activities are establishing good habits. If you get used to keeping an accurate and careful record of your actions during an experiment, you will not have to unlearn bad habits later, when the stakes of having inaccurate observations and fudged data might be much higher and more serious. For example, in an industrial lab, the notebook is a legal record of discovery. If the researchers maintain a high level of detail and accuracy in the notebook, it can stand up in a court of law to prove what was done and when it was done. In disputes over who was the first to discover a new idea or who is entitled to the patent on it, the notebook is central to the discussion of the legal issues.

In higher education settings, instructors often prescribe how to write laboratory entries as part of the course lab manual, sometimes setting out strict penalties for not following the requirements. They specify how they want data kept in a notebook, and their requirements usually include rules about content, structure, level of detail, and quality of the descriptions and written text. For example, one chemistry instructor informs students of these rules:

1. Buy the required laboratory notebook at the bookstore. It must be formatted for duplicate pages and recording page numbers. [Duplicate pages are used in pharmaceutical research.] Do not tear out any pages—not a single one. [These points are relevant to training students to work in a patent or research lab.]

2. The lab notebook must have a Table of Contents. Leave the first *two full pages* blank so that you can fill in the name and page number(s) of each experiment as you enter it into the book.

3. Keep your lab notebook up to date. Add to the table of contents with each new experiment. Your TA [teaching assistant] or instructor will check your lab book after every second or third experiment.

4. When you are in the laboratory, write only in this notebook. Do not jot down ideas on scrap paper.

5. Write all relevant information related to the experiments on the right-hand page of the notebook. Record in your notebook all data and other information needed to complete the lab assignment.

6. Write all entries in blue or black *ink*. Do not record entries first in pencil and then trace over them later in pen. Do not erase any entries. Marks will be deducted for pencil, overwritten, or erased entries.

7. Use correct units for all data. Clearly label all of your data, and tabulate it so that readers reviewing your notebook can easily understand it.

FIGURE 7.10
Goldberg's lab notebook from chemistry experiment, "Gravimetric Determination of Calcium as $CaC_2O_4 \cdot H_2O$." The left page presents the pre-lab or introduction while the right page presents the narrative—the observations and measurements made during the experiment in the lab.

Note that these rules all have to do with maintaining the integrity of the data in the notebook. They also try to ensure that the student will conduct the experiment as intended rather than attempting to "back engineer" the data to get the expected results. While these rules may seem prescriptive, they are no more so than the procedure followed in industry to maintain the integrity of data developed there. Industrial laboratories often have rules that notebook pages must be signed and researchers must have important results and data witnessed to verify accuracy and reliability. Why all this concern about the veracity of scientific or experimental data? All records should be accurate and truthful in case they are needed as evidence in legal disputes. For example, in lawsuits over intellectual property and patent issues, the dates, details, and raw data from research become crucial evidence to support claims in law courts.

How should you organize the information in your notebook?

Some instructors will direct you to leave the first two or three pages of the notebook blank, so that later, when you have filled the rest of the pages, you can come back and add a table of contents that will help you (and others) locate the data for specific experiments.

Usually, experiment notes are divided into two parts: the introduction (or pre-lab) and the narrative (or in lab). To reduce the amount of work that you need to complete during the lab itself, you can prepare the introduction in advance of actually conducting the experiment. See Figure 7.10 for a two-page spread from Aaron Goldberg's lab notebook prepared for a second-year chemistry experiment, "Gravimetric Determination of Calcium as $CaC_2O_4 \cdot H_2O$." Note that the left page contains the introduction or pre-lab information, while the right page displays the narrative—the observations and measurements made during the experiment in the lab.

INTRODUCTION (OR PRE-LAB)

In the introduction, include the kinds of details that establish a context for the experiment:

- The title
- The location and date
- The aim for this experiment
- Citations of relevant background literature
- A description of the materials used and information about safety data
- An account of experimental conditions and reactions
- A description of the experimental procedure you plan to follow (not to be confused with a description of the procedure that you *actually* followed, which appears in the narrative section).

NARRATIVE (IN LAB)
Write a detailed account.

The narrative section provides a detailed account of the experiment the way that you actually conducted it. This means that you should pause every few minutes throughout the experiment to record clearly and accurately what you have just finished doing. Describe your actions and your observations. This level of detail will help you reconstruct the activity when you write the laboratory report later. The goal is to have more information in your notebook account of the experiment than you will need when you actually write the report.

Separate speculation from reality.

If you have ideas about how to explain what is happening, make sure that you distinguish the way you record them from your method of recording the actual happenings, so you separate the real from the speculative. When you write the report later, you want to avoid confusing what actually happened with what you thought you were seeing at the time or what you hoped might be happening.

Record every measurement.

The notebook is the appropriate place to record all of your raw data. Even though you will find some of your measurements irrelevant to the experiment when you later interpret the data, you still want to have a permanent record of everything associated with the experiment. You should also include any sources of error that may have affected your results and made them different from what you expected. The notebook is the appropriate place to preserve these numbers. That way, at a later date, if you need to correct a calculation or check some aspect of your results, you may find that the so-called "irrelevant" data were what you should have used in the first place. If you had discarded these data, the experiment would be worthless.

WRITING THE LABORATORY REPORT

Writing the laboratory report is the final stage in the process of research where you interpret and communicate the results of your study. It provides an account of the experiment(s) that you conducted in the lab, and it is a permanent record of your activities and observations. Other individuals should be able to repeat your activities as described in the report and arrive at similar results and observations (that is, your results should be replicable or repeatable).

The laboratory report is used in higher education to assess and evaluate your performance in the lab. It is also an exercise that helps you to learn how to process the raw data that you collect, analyse data into an interpretation, and then present that interpretation in the report as an argument supported with data. It also provides a chance for you to evaluate your knowledge of the topic and argue the significance of your work.

Before you can begin writing the report, you will have to make decisions about what information and data you should include. Spend some time analyzing your data—that is, applying the theories and principles that drove the research to the data and observations that you collected to help you make sense of your findings. After the experiment is complete, you should have more insight into the event than you did while you were in the middle of it. Use this insight to help you distinguish the useful data from the erroneous or irrelevant. You may also need to decide whether or not you should include any of the erroneous or irrelevant data to help clarify the meaningful results.

Do not be tempted to adjust any of your data at this point to improve your results. Tampering with your data is a grievous sin in scientific research at any level. A lab report is assumed to be based on truthful data, and your findings are taken as facts based on truth. Making adjustments to the data undermines the integrity of the knowledge you present in your report and, through it, of the whole scientific enterprise. Even findings that seem impossible should be acknowledged, never altered or discarded.

To begin writing you need to have the following:
- Data (drawn from the narrative in your lab notebook)
- Results calculated from the raw data of the notebook
- Knowledge of the theories or principles underlying the experiment
- References or sources for the theories or principles.

Format of the lab report

The laboratory report has an established format. All of the information presented in it should appear in one of the headings listed:
- Title (and author[s])
- Introduction
- Procedure and materials
- Results
- Discussion
- References.

TITLE (AND AUTHOR[S])

Choose a short but informative title for your report. It should reflect the content of the paper and catch the reader's interest. List the key words from the subject matter of the experiment, and include them in your title.

Don't forget to also include such information as your name (and the names of collaborators, if applicable), the course and section number, the day and time of the lab, and the date that you conducted the experiment. Your instructor may also request additional information on the title page of your report: be sure to include it too.

INTRODUCTION

The introduction of the report should accomplish a number of goals. It should explain the purpose of the experiment and include enough background information on the subject matter to establish the context for the experiment. That is, readers should gain a general but clear sense of what you did, why you did it, and why it matters. The introduction should be as brief as possible while still including all relevant information:

- Clearly state the purpose of the experiment.
- Describe the nature and scope of the problem being investigated.
- Review relevant literature to give readers a context for your experiment.
- Limit the background to only what readers need to know.
- Identify clearly how your data refers to what is known and not known about the topic.
- Include any definitions or principles that your reader needs to understand the experiment.
- State methods of the experiment only if they are part of the purpose (e.g., evaluating two techniques).
- Briefly summarize the principal results of the experiment.

Figure 7.11 is a sample introduction section taken from Kavita Patel's microbiology lab report. Given space limitations in this volume, only part (three-quarters) of the introduction is reproduced here.

In the introduction to this lab report, Patel has briefly identified the purpose for the experiment (to determine the optimal environment for growing micro-organisms) and the reason this knowledge is important (micro-organism growth affects human health and food safety). She then outlines the types of micro-organisms that were studied and provides some background or theory about the experiment (temperature is the most important factor in promoting or preventing micro-organisms' growth).

PROCEDURES AND MATERIALS

In this section, you describe the procedure you followed to obtain the results that you present. A rule for this description is that it should contain enough information to enable someone else to perform the same experiment successfully. That said, this description should be as clear and concise as possible.

Some science courses will provide you with a manual that details the procedure you should follow for some of the experiments. If this

THE EFFECTS OF TEMPERATURE AND PH ON ENCOURAGING AND DETERRING THE GROWTH OF BACTERIA VS. FUNGUS

Introduction

This experiment was done to determine the optimal temperature and pH conditions for different micro-organisms. These two environmental factors have the greatest impact on the growth of a micro-organism, which makes them both important and straightforward to study. It is important to know the optimal temperature and pH for the growth of different bacteria and fungi because they both affect our food and our health. In this experiment, the amount of growth of micro-organisms was determined using a spectrophotometer as well as visually. Using both methods also highlights the strengths and weaknesses of both techniques.

For the determination of optimum temperature, four bacteria and two fungi were used, and for the determination of optimum pH, three bacteria and one fungus were used. The bacteria used grow at different optimal temperatures, but were all capable of growing well on the same nutrient agar plates or nutrient broth solutions. Similarly, the fungi used in the temperature determination were both grown on Sabouraud's agar. Every micro-organism that was used for this experiment can be found in some type of food, either as an aid to processing it or as spoilage.

Temperature is the most influential environmental condition that affects cell growth and survival (Madigan *et al.*, 2003). At the optimum temperature for a specific micro-organism, its biochemical reactions run quickly, allowing the cell to grow at its maximum rate. This is the optimal growth range for temperature for a specific organism. If the temperature is increased too far past this point, the maximum temperature of the organism is reached. This is the temperature at which the micro-organism's enzymes begin to be denatured by the heat, prohibiting the growth of the cell. The minimum temperature is the lowest temperature at which the organism can grow. Below this temperature, the reactions within the cell occur too slowly, and the cell membrane begins to gel, prohibiting growth (Madigan *et al.*, 2003). The optimal growth range of temperatures that micro-organisms grow best at can be anywhere from below 0°C to above 100°C (Madigan *et al.*, 2003). Increasing or decreasing the temperature of an organism's environment to within the micro-organism's optimal temperature range encourages growth. Conversely, if the environmental temperature is moved not only out of the optimal range for the organism but also past the maximum or minimum temperature, the micro-organism can no longer survive. The closer that the environmental temperature gets to the maximum or minimum for a specific organism, the more growth is deterred.

FIGURE 7.11
The introduction section of a microbiology lab report. Only three-quarters of the section is reproduced here because of space limitations.

is the case, then often you won't need to detail your procedures in the lab report. Instead, you can just refer the reader to the procedures outlined in the manual, as Patel has done in Figure 7.12. Give the full citation of the procedure that you are referencing (i.e., title, course number, author, year of publication of manual, and page numbers of the lab you are referring to), so the connection is clear. At the same time, if you deviated from any part of the manual's description, you should note and describe in the "Procedures and materials" section the changes that you followed during the experiment.

As with the introduction, aim for clear and concise coverage in this section of the report.

FIGURE 7.12
The procedures
and materials
section of Patel's
microbiology lab.

METHODS AND MATERIALS

This experiment was performed as outlined in the *Biology 140L Fundamentals of Microbiology Lab Manual Fall Term 2004*, experiments 20 and 21, from pages 77–81. No changes were made to this procedure.

RESULTS

This section of the report presents your findings from the experiment(s). In the first half of this section, describe how you got your results, and, in the second half, explain the significance of the results (i.e., what the results mean).

This organizational division means that the early part of this section should present processed data to the reader in a comprehensible fashion. Organize the information, perhaps by placing it in tables or by laying out the critical calculations upon which your interpretation is based. The finished results (as you present them in this section) should support the interpretation that you have decided to present for your data.

The laboratory report should include all of the data that you collected from the experiment. However, the raw data should be assembled in an "Appendix" at the end of the report. Also include in the appendix any computer printouts or instrument tracings that you used to derive data for the experiment.

Occasionally, you may have to use in your report data collected by someone else. If this is the case, you *must* state the sources of your data, giving credit to the collector. Passing off someone else's raw data as your own is fraudulent and an academic offence.

ORGANIZING AND PRESENTING YOUR DATA

There are three ways to present data that is easily understood and processed by readers. Select the method that best presents the point about your data that you want to make. Compare some of your data to other data you collected; if appropriate, compare your data to the data gathered by others in your class.

TABLES

Use a table when the precise numbers—including decimal places—are important. They allow your reader to quickly scan and compare columns of numbers. Arrange your table so the numbers are read down the columns and not across the cells. In Figure 7.13, Patel has used tables to present observational data from a microbiology experiment. This format helps readers to make quick comparisons between the microbes.

CHARTS

Use charts to display data that shows a trend or relationship.

Provide a caption and title for each figure or chart. Convention dictates that you label the axes with the dependent variable (the one that you measured) on the vertical axis and the independent variable (the one that you manipulated) on the horizontal axis.

RESULTS

TABLE 1. Growth of Micro-organisms Under Different Temperature Conditions

Organism	4–6°C	20–25 °C	37 °C	55 °C	Optimal (°C)
Staphylococcus aureus	−	++ yellow	+++	−	37
Serratia marcescens	+	+++ red	+++	−	20–25
Pseudomonas fluorescens	++	+++	−	−	20–25
Bacillus stearo-thermophilus	−	+	+	+++	55
Saccharomyces cerevisiae	−	+++ yellow	+++	−	30
Aspergillus niger	−	+++ green fuzzy centre	++	+	20–25

A majority of the micro-organisms in this experiment grew the most when they were incubated at either 20–25ᵒC or 37ᵒC. Four of the six were more coloured when grown between 20–25ᵒC than when they were grown at other temperatures, even though some of these other temperatures produced an equal amount of growth.

TABLE 2. Visual Analysis of Micro-organism Growth at Each pH

Organism	pH 3.0	pH 5.1	pH 6.9	pH 8.1
Saccharomyces cerevisiae	+++	+++	+++	++
Escherichia coli	−	+++	+++	+++
Lactobacillus plantarum	−	−	−	−
Staphylococcus aureus	−	++	+++	+++

S. cerevisiae had the most growth at the widest range of pH values. Except for *L. plantarum*, the organisms grew best closer to neutral pH values....

FIGURE 7.13
Part of the results section of the same microbiology lab report by Kavita Patel. The observations are presented in table format for easy comparison and effective organization.

DIAGRAMS AND ILLUSTRATIONS

Use diagrams or illustrations to present data that is not numerical. If appropriate, include the magnification of the image. Make sure that you include a number and caption with the figure.

Verbally describe your results

Even though you have presented your data in tables, worked examples, diagrams, or charts, the results section should also include a textual description of the data. This does not mean that you repeat the specific numbers in words but rather that you provide a verbal overview of the various data you present, pointing out general trends and important features. Think of this verbal overview as a tour guide's commentary on the numbers. If you don't direct your readers' attention to what you believe are the key points, then you miss an opportunity to prepare your readers for the interpretation of the results that you will make in the next section. They may well pay attention to quite different aspects of your data than you had intended, resulting in their resistance to the argument you present in the discussion. Note that, in Figure 7.13, Patel summarizes the data under each table, drawing readers' attention to her major insights about each data grouping. These summaries are helpful in directing the reader toward your broader conclusions about the data, which follow in the next section of your report.

Remember, however, to confine yourself to presenting the data in the results section. Avoid getting into the interpretation that should rightfully appear in the following section, the "Discussion." At the same time, if you find yourself adding details about the procedure or materials, move them to the appropriate and previous section.

Discussion

This section should follow inevitably (from an argumentative perspective) from the information presented to this point. In your discussion, do not restate your results; instead, make clear to your reader what the results mean and why they are important. In other words, explain the significance of your results and findings.

Remember how in the introduction you described the problem or reason for conducting this experiment? In this section of the report, you return to this point and explain how the work that you have done illuminates our understanding of the original problem. If your results contradict the findings of other published reports, say so, and try to explain what you think accounts for your different results. If your results are consistent with earlier studies, then you can point this out and underscore the importance of this agreement in results.

If there are broader implications for your results, then explore those in your discussion as well. If appropriate, bring in established theory or principles that help explain your findings. You can also suggest other experiments that need to be done or could be done, based on your findings from this one.

Conclude with a clear, concise summary of your conclusions and the main evidence upon which they are based. This summary gives

DISCUSSION

The published optimal pH and temperature values for the micro-organisms in this experiment are as follows:

Table 5. Published Optimum Temperature Values for Micro-organisms

Organism	Optimal Growth Temperature (°C)
S. aureus	37
S. marcescens	12–36 (for red pigment)
P. fluorescens	4
B. stearothermophilus	55
S. cerevisiae	28–35
A. niger	25–30

Table 6. Published Optimal pH Values for Micro-organisms

Organism	Optimal pH
S. cerevisiae	4.5–6.5
E. coli	6.0–7.0
L. plantarum	5.5–5.8
S. aureus	4.5–6.5

Staphylococcus aureus has a published optimal growth temperature of 37°C, which is what was found in the experiment (*Staphylococcus aureus*, 2001). The bacteria have a published optimal pH of 4.5 to 6.5 (*Staphylococcus aureus*, 2001). This makes sense because *S. aureus* is bacteria that reside mainly in the human respiratory tract and on human skin, which have a near neutral pH and are maintained around the normal human body temperature of 37°C (*Staphylococcus aureus*, 2001). The bacteria can also be found in cows, chickens, pigs, turkeys and unpasteurized food (*Staphylococcus aureus*, 2001). *S. aureus* does not compete well with other bacteria and is consequently found more often on cooked food than raw food (*Staphylococcus aureus*, 2001). *S. aureus* is normally a yellow colour, so both the colony grown at 20–25°C and the colony grown at 37°C should have been yellow (*Staphylococcus aureus*, 2001).

Serratia marcescens grew best at 20–25°C. The published range for optimum growth and pigment production agrees with this result (Rafii, 1999). The red pigment is a combination of prodigiosin and pyrimine, which are produced by the bacteria in this temperature range when they are grown on peptone-glycerol agar aerobically (Rafii, 1999). *S. marcescens* only produces this pigment when grown under the correct conditions (Rafii, 1999). *S. marcescens* are found in soil, air, water, plants, and animals (Rafii, 1999). In the food industry, the bacteria have been found in milk, ice cream, coffee, fruit juices, eggs, and meats (Rafii, 1999). These bacteria are involved in opportunistic human infections as well as in food spoilage (Rafii, 1999). The experimental results agree with the published information about *S. marcescens*...

FIGURE 7.14
Part of the discussion section from Patel's microbiology lab report.

you the opportunity to recap for your reader the main points that you want them to take away.

In Patel's discussion of her results, she presents her key findings—the optimal temperature and pH values for the micro-organisms that she studied—in a table, so readers can quickly scan and compare the values from one strain of micro-organism to another and assess the accuracy of her measurements. In the textual discussion following the tables, Patel integrates established findings for this type of experiment with her own results to show their validity as well as to explain their significance.

REFERENCES

Use the style sheet for your discipline in preparing your references for the report. You may also find that the conventions for formatting references change from class to class. Be sure to find out (in advance, if possible) what is considered the acceptable format in each class. Usually the references are listed in alphabetical order. They generally include the following information, but the order and method of presentation can vary widely, depending upon the citation style being used:

For a book

Authors' initials and last name, book title, publisher, city, and the year of publication.

For an article

Authors' initials and last name, article title, journal title in which it appeared, volume and issue number, year of publication, and page numbers.

For websites

Include as much information as you can, including authors' initials and last name, date that the file was created or modified, the title of the page and/or the title of the site.

REFERENCES

Batt C. 1999. Lactobacillus. In: Encyclopedia of Food Microbiology. San Diego (CA): Academic Press. p. 890.

Cousin MA. 1999. Pseudomonas. In: Encyclopedia of Food Microbiology. San Diego (CA): Academic Press. p. 1290.

Department of Biology. 2004. Biology 140L: Fundamentals of Microbiology Laboratory Manual. Waterloo (ON): University of Waterloo. p. 77–81.

Escherichia coli [Internet]. May 2001. New Zealand Ministry of Health [updated 2004 Oct 24; cited 2004 Nov 25]. Available from: http://www.nzfsa.govt.nz/science-technology/data-sheets/index.htm

Kozekidou P. 1999. Bacillus. In: Encyclopedia of Food Microbiology. San Diego (CA): Academic Press. p. 110.

Madigan M., Martinko J., Parker J. 2003. Brock biology of micro-organisms. 10th ed. Upper Saddle River (NJ): Prentice Hall. 1088 p.

Radke-Mitchell LC, Sandine WE. 1986. Influence of temperature on associative growth of *Streptococcus thermophilus* and *Lactobacillus bulgaricus*. J Dairy Sci. 69:2558–2568.

FIGURE **7.15**

A partial list of references from Patel's microbiology lab report formatted in Council of Science Editors (CSE) style.

If the reference is associated with an organization, include its name in the reference. Also include the date when you accessed the reference and the complete URL.

Do not use footnotes in a lab report.

Some libraries have purchased citation software that helps you format your references properly. Check with your school's library to find out whether you can gain access to software such as RefWorks to help you put your references section together correctly.

LAB ASSIGNMENT 7.3

REVISING A LAB REPORT TO IMPROVE ITS ARGUMENT

Revise a lab report that you've already written to improve its organization and the quality of its argument. Incorporate the suggestions in this chapter and the ones in Chapter 4 on writing arguments.

When you have finished rewriting the lab report, write a short memo report to your instructor detailing the ways in which you changed the original draft to take into account the advice in this chapter for improving your lab report.

MAJOR PROJECT 7.3

WRITING A LAB REPORT

Using the data from your lab notebook for an experiment that you've recently conducted, write a lab report following the advice in this section of the chapter to write a strong report of the experiment. Include several visuals, as appropriate to the subject matter of the experiment.

Recommendation reports

Another type of report that is common in technical communication is the recommendation report. It is the written outcome that often follows a study or research into a particular problem. In a recommendation report, the technical communicator (or engineer) describes the problem and then presents several possible solutions that he or she has devised based on extensive research. If the writer has been asked only to recommend several solutions, the report ends with a neutral description of the possibilities. If the writer has been asked to solve the problem, then he or she will generally end by recommending one solution over the others, explaining what makes it superior. A variation on the recommendation report is the feasibility report, which discusses the viability of applying one recommended solution to a problem. This section of the chapter examines the genre of the recommendation report, looking at the typical structure that it uses and the rhetorical challenges that it presents for the writer.

VALUSPEC
Home Inspection Service
NORTH AMERICA'S NUMBER ONE HOME INSPECTOR

July 5, 2006

Dear Client:

Re. Home Inspection
947 Woodbury Dr., Winnipeg, MB.

ValuSpec Home Inspection Service has completed a visual inspection of the property and building at the address above. Thank you for choosing ValuSpec, and we appreciate the chance to work with you at this time. The enclosed report provides you with extensive information about the general condition of this property after a visual examination of the accessible areas of the house, based on the enclosed Inspection Agreement. Please note that no aspect of the home was dismantled, so the inspection judgments are based only on the evidence visible without further probing.

We found three major areas of the home and property that you would want to address within a year or two of purchasing this property. There are a number of minor issues, and they are detailed in the report. We recommend that you complete the following at your earliest convenience:

1. Replace the roof.

2. Improve ventilation in interior to reduce overall humidity levels.

3. Improve drainage around base of foundation at southeast and northeast corners of the house.

The inspection began at 9 a.m. and concluded at 11:30 a.m. on June 27, 2006. The current owners of the property were in residence at the time, so our inspection was limited to a visual examination with little moving of personal effects.

I would like to thank Robert Stafford, P. Eng., who allowed me to accompany him during the inspection as part of my responsibilities as a student worker at ValuSpec. He also reviewed a draft of this report, and his comments were helpful in sharpening my analysis and clarifying my explanations, especially of obvious humidity problems on the premises.

Again, thank you for the opportunity to undertake this inspection. It has made a valuable contribution to my education as a civil engineer.

If you have questions or concerns after reading this report, please contact me at mtrottie@engmail.uwinnipeg.mb or telephone me at 321-123-4567.

Sincerely,

Michel Trottier

Michel Trottier

FIGURE 7.16
The letter of transmittal for a home inspection report written by Michel Trottier during a work term at ValuSpec Home Inspections. This report was written as an assignment for a writing class as part of Trottier's degree. Please note that the actual report submitted to the homeowners was significantly longer and more detailed.

REPORT STRUCTURE

- Memo or letter of transmittal
- Title page
- Executive summary or abstract
- Recommendation
- Report body
- Conclusions
- Notes, references, works cited.

Memo or letter of transmittal

Usually, the memo or letter of transmittal is separate from the report, but it accompanies the report to provide a context for the reader, especially the reader who requested the report. It is usually directed toward your boss or the individual who requested the research.

Use general conventions when deciding whether you should use a memo or a letter:

- For an internal report going to your supervisor use a memo;
- For an external report, submitted to an organization from your consulting firm, use a letter.

See Figure 7.16 for a sample letter of transmittal, written by Michel Trottier, after a work term as a building inspector for an engineering company. The report from which this letter is taken was prepared for a writing class that was part of his degree program; the actual report submitted to the clients would be longer and more detailed than the version prepared for the class. The letter or memo of transmittal should communicate the following information:

- Transmit the report—that is, formally release or publish this document. The report can then be circulated for public consumption.
- Summarize the conclusions and recommendations from the report. Usually the conclusions and recommendations are stated in one-sentence summaries that signal the direction of the report but don't provide any details to explain. Readers will need to consult at least the executive summary for a more detailed discussion of these.
- Explain any problems you encountered and how you solved them. If you ran into any minor problems while you were researching and writing the report, describe those in the letter or memo of transmittal and explain how you solved them. Usually this part will require only one or two paragraphs.
- Thank those who helped you with the report. In a sentence or two, acknowledge the help of any co-workers or individuals whose efforts made your work on the report easier or better.
- Point out any additional research, if it is needed. If you found over the course of the project that additional research should

be done but was outside the scope of the project, include this advice as well in the letter or memo of transmittal. For example, you might recommend that the client study some aspect of the problem further before making a decision about that point. Include this information here, even if you also mention it later in the report.

- Thank the reader for the chance to do this work. An appropriate close to this part of the report is an expression of your appreciation for the opportunity to work on this project. Note the ways in which you found the work of benefit. This kind of closing establishes a positive conclusion for the letter and helps the reader to anticipate the rest of the report.
- Offer to answer questions. The final point in the letter or memo of transmittal should be an offer to answer any questions. Include your contact information, so the reader can easily reach you should he or she have questions.

Title page

The title page should be the first bound page in the report, and it should present this information:
- The full title of the report
- The individual(s) who prepared the report
- Whom it was prepared for
- The release date of the report.

Obviously, the title page contains the information needed to help readers orient themselves and begin making immediate sense of the document that they are reviewing.

Executive summary or abstract

The executive summary or abstract is generally no more than two or three pages long. The goal of this section is to provide a brief but clear overview of the whole report. It is designed so that busy executives can read the abstract instead of the whole report and know what the report is about. The interior discussion in the report is available for anyone who is interested, but readers can still understand the conclusions and recommendations without reading all the way through it.

This section summarizes the recommendations of the report and explains the reasons for these recommendations. It outlines the topics discussed and indicates the depth of the discussion. Don't organize the executive summary to reflect the organization that you've used in the report body. Instead, decide on the most effective order of presentation for the executive summary. What will your readers want to know and in what order?

EXECUTIVE SUMMARY

This report documents a visual inspection of the yard and building at 947 Woodbury Dr. in Winnipeg, MB with the goal of identifying any major defects of the property, evaluating their severity, and recommending appropriate solutions.

CONCLUSIONS:

Overall the dwelling and yard are in fair condition. There appear to be no major structural problems that would affect a potential purchaser's decision to buy this property. That said, the house is eighteen years old, and some of its systems do show wear and tear equal to a residential property of this age.

RECOMMENDATIONS:

We recommend that the client consider the following maintenance projects within the next two years:

1. **Replace the roof.** Currently, the roof consists of one layer of asphalt composite shingles. Noted were worn, curling shingles; loose or missing gravel; and evidence of patching. We were unable to determine whether these repairs were effective. Based on these observations and information obtained from the current owner, the shingles are nearly 18 years old. The shingles currently in place average 15-20 years, and they show normal wear and tear for their age. The age of the roofing membrane appears to be reaching its useful life, so we recommend that the client plan to replace it in the near future.

2. **Improve interior ventilation to reduce overall humidity levels**. We noted a potential environmental issue with the presence of mould on interior portions of several windows in the home and basement. A more intrusive examination would be needed to determine the scope and nature of the mould growth. We recommend removing all sources of moisture: install or repair kitchen and bathroom exhaust fans; disconnect furnace humidifier, and use dehumidifier to remove excess moisture; seal the building envelope to prevent water entering from the outside. If mould persists after completing these actions, consult a qualified mould abatement contractor for additional evaluation and treatment options to ensure safe air quality indoors.

3. **Improve grading around building foundation.** We saw evidence of some leakage around the windows in the basement. Ground levels around the foundation also show some compression against the concrete where rainwater and other moisture could pool, presenting a potential leakage problem. We recommend redoing the grading by building up earth in compression areas. The earth against the house should slope away so that water will run away rather than pool around the foundation.

The report provides a detailed discussion of all of the major systems in the house and evaluates their condition, making suggestions where appropriate about solutions that the client should undertake to improve conditions. Minor problems to be aware of include several inoperable systems: electrostatic air cleaner on the furnace, garage door opener,....

FIGURE 7.17
Part of the executive summary that Trottier prepared for his report.

Recommendations

The next section of the report (usually on a separate page from what has gone before) presents the recommendations. In this section, you list the action items that you recommend to solve the problem identified in the report. After each recommendation, describe your rationale for making this suggestion.

Note that this is the only place where your recommendations are discussed fully, so include everything readers will need to know to understand and make decisions about your recommendations.

Body of the report (Note: do not use as a report heading)

The sections discussed previously are all preliminary to the actual report. At this point, you finally get to the report itself. Your goal in the report is to assemble all of the research that you did to explain what you see as the most viable solutions to the problem that prompted this project in the first place. So the report should address the following general topics:

- An outline and overview of the problem
- Your purpose in undertaking the report
- How you collected the information that forms the basis of this report
- The results and analysis of your research
- A discussion of what you see as the findings of your research.

While the content of every report will be different, there are a number of rhetorical moves that you want to make in each part of the body of your report, despite its topic.

INTRODUCTION

In the introduction, you provide a brief overview of the problem that initiated the report. Explain any background information that readers need to understand the topic. If there are technical terms that you must use, define these terms clearly and concisely. If there are several specialized terms or concepts that readers will need defined, consider including a glossary or list of terms at the back of the report, and direct readers to it in the introduction.

Explain the significance of the problem, its cost in terms of money or time, and the importance of finding an appropriate solution. Even if your main reader (i.e., your supervisor) already understands the problem and agrees that it exists, you should still provide a coherent account of the problem because most reports have a much wider circulation than the original individual who requested them. For this reason, you should include in the introduction of the report information that will educate readers who have little knowledge about the immediate problem, so they can understand and evaluate your assessment in the rest of the report.

Depending upon the seriousness of the problem and the complexity of the background, your introduction can be anywhere from two or three paragraphs to several pages. Your goal is to provide all of the information readers will need as clearly and concisely as possible.

Introduction

This report provides information about the condition of the home and property at 947 Woodbury Dr. It was written in response to a request by Charles Fields for an inspection of the home in connection with the possible purchase of the property. He requested that we examine the systems within the house with the goal of identifying any that needed repair or replacement, with an emphasis on evaluating the potential seriousness and costliness of addressing any structural or system-related problems that were noted.

This report details the condition of the home as it was observed during the inspection on June 27, 2006. As is routine in reports of this nature, we have summarized the overall condition of the house before detailing the specific condition of the various systems of the house. The discussion moves from the exterior of the building to the lower level and then to the main level. The major systems demanding immediate attention are summarized in the Recommendations section of the report. More minor problems are noted during the general description of the survey results.

Please note that the following terms are used in the report:

S = serviceable, meaning the materials and workmanship associated with the part being inspected are acceptable, and it is in generally satisfactory condition.

N = not applicable, meaning the part does not exist or apply to the property.

Also note that the point of reference given to locate a particular component is the front exterior of the building, facing the main entrance (e.g., the sump pump is located in the lower level at the rear right side).

Limitations

Please remember that the personal effects of the current owner occasionally limited the scope of the inspection because the inspection team was unable to undertake extensive moving of these effects. However, we have noted in the report those instances when the belongings limited the examination.

Purpose

The purpose of this report is to evaluate the overall condition of the building and property at 947 Woodbury Dr. in Winnipeg, MB, and to assess the extent of any structural or system-related problems that will require repair or replacement.

FIGURE 7.18
The opening of the body of the inspection report by Trottier. Note that he has added the section "Limitations" to draw his readers' attention to one of the limitations of the inspection—the presence of the current owner's belongings, which occasionally prevented thorough inspection of a room or closet. He added this heading because he was concerned that embedding this point inside the introduction might make it easy to miss.

Figure 7.18 presents the beginning of Trottier's home inspection report in which he summarizes the reason for the report as well as its limitations and goals. The introduction to the report is quite brief, mainly because a home inspection report generally deals with a well-recognized problem that doesn't, as a rule, need extensive elaboration. The home inspection and the report that follow generally arise from a real estate transaction; a potential buyer wants to uncover any costly structural or system-related problems that the seller has not disclosed but that the buyer will have to repair or replace upon purchasing the property. Usually, by identifying the report as a home inspection report, the writer communicates the context for the report and for anticipating the types of problems that it solves. For this reason, Trottier doesn't need to explain further after he identifies the location of the property, names the individual who commissioned the inspection, and defines any specialized terms.

Assess the amount of detail that your report will require to bring readers up to speed. You may need to provide several pages of details to explain the nature of the problem if you are writing a different kind of recommendation report than the home inspection report. Given the broad nature of the potential situations that your recommendation report may address, you need to analyse your subject matter, your readers, and your situation to determine how much introduction will be needed to help your readers become oriented to your topic. As stated elsewhere in this book, these guidelines and strategies are general, and we intend that you adapt the relevant ones to your particular project and omit the ones that seem redundant or ill-fitting.

PURPOSE

In this section of the body of the report, you outline the purpose of the project and the goal of the report. It is usually a brief statement that summarizes why the report was written.

METHODS

The third section of the report's body describes how you collected the information that you are presenting in this report. If you interviewed individuals, surveyed large groups, read published studies and books on the subject matter, and so on, you include all of these details. Your aim in this section is to show that you did a competent and thorough job of studying the problem and looking for a range of viable solutions. If you conducted survey research on which to base your results, then describe briefly how the sample population was selected and how you developed the questionnaire that was used. Include a copy of the survey in the report appendix, and refer your readers to it for additional information. If your results are based on statistical analysis, then explain how you calculated your results. The goal here is to provide readers with information about how the study was conducted, so they can judge your work as thorough and of high quality. The methods discussion should be as long as it needs to be to answer the questions readers will have about the validity of your data, but no longer.

RESULTS

While the previous section of the report talks about how the data and results were collected, this section summarizes the data and results themselves. Use tables, graphs, charts, and figures to present statistical or numerical information as legibly and comprehensibly as possible. Of course, you are presenting the processed data not the raw data. Include the raw numbers from the survey results (or other sources) in an appendix. In the results section, you present and highlight the data that support the argument that you want to make in the report. Presumably, your solutions are based on what you found in your research, so the presentation of results should be laying a foundation for your decisions about what they mean (which you will discuss in detail in the following section).

While this section presents your results, note that it does *not* present your interpretation of these results. Instead, you discuss the meaning of the results at length in the next section, the "Discussion." The results and interpretation are discussed separately, so readers can focus on the nature and quality of your research data before they must digest what these data mean. In some ways, you can use the results section to anticipate and begin to support your discussion by laying out and emphasizing those results that are most relevant to the solutions that you intend to propose.

DISCUSSION

As noted previously, this section finally gives you the chance to discuss your results thoroughly and to explain the thinking behind the decisions that you've made about solutions. You can highlight what you see as the most important findings and show why you believe they are the most important. Then you can discuss the implications of these findings—that is, the ways in which they lead inevitably to the solutions that you have proposed in your recommendations. The discussion section of the report, like the earlier sections, should be as long as it needs to be to clarify and explain the significance of the results but also as concise as possible.

CONCLUSIONS

The final section of the body of the report presents your conclusions. In this part, you summarize the main points that you want readers to take away from the report. Never introduce new information in the conclusion. The ideas that you express here should all be drawn from what you have said elsewhere in the report. To emphasize your conclusions, present them in a bulleted or numbered list.

Notes, references, appendices

The final sections of the report are comprised of any notes, the references, and any appendices. If you used published sources, such as articles, books, data sets, or websites, include these in your "References" or "Works Cited" section after notes but before appendices. If you have data or questionnaires or computer printouts of statistical analyses, then include these in an "Appendix" or an "Appendices" section as the final part of the report. Consider how numerous the appended information is when deciding how to arrange it. If this information is fairly limited, think about gathering it together in one appendix. If you have many pages and various types of data, consider putting each grouping in its own appendix. At the relevant point in the body of the report, refer readers to this appended material, indicating which appendix contains which type of information.

MAJOR PROJECT 7.4

WRITING A RECOMMENDATION REPORT

Major Project 6.1 (option 2) in Chapter 6 asked you to write a proposal to create a recommendation report based on a topic of your choice. Create the report that you outlined in your proposal. Follow the development plan and work schedule described in your proposal to complete the report.

Many of the topics that are covered in this book will be important to consider as you write your report, including document design, adding visuals where appropriate to present statistical or technical data, organizing information, and making your writing clear for specific audiences. Follow the format outlined in this chapter on how to structure a recommendation report.

Purpose and Audience

Before you begin, you should have a clear sense of whom your primary and secondary readers are for the report. Include the background information that they will need to understand your discussion, and tailor your arguments to match those that your readers will find convincing and compelling. Also make sure that you understand why you are writing this report and what main points you want to convey to your readers.

Use the outline below to structure your report, and draw on the rhetorical appeals discussed in Chapter 4, "Writing technical prose," to develop and explain the solutions that you found for the problem that you identified and analysed:

■ Letter or memo of transmittal
■ Title page
■ Executive summary or abstract
■ Recommendations
■ Body of report (introduction, scope, methods, results, discussion)
■ Conclusions
■ Works cited or references
■ Appendices.

CHAPTER EIGHT

Writing how-to documents
instructions, procedures, and manuals

Who reads instructional manuals? Some people claim that they never use the instructions provided with a new product, and some companies seize on this anecdotal evidence to justify spending little money on the documentation that accompanies their products.

Is it true though? In fact, researchers have found that more than 80 per cent of users actually *do* use the manual sometimes. Usage also depends on the nature of the product: people tend not to refer to the guides that accompany devices such as cordless telephones and answering machines, but more than 90 per cent of VCR users *have* used the instructions that came with this appliance. More complex devices are not self-explanatory, and high quality instructions can make a big difference as to whether users are satisfied with a new purchase or return it to the store for a refund when they can't figure out how to use it. As one participant in a study said,

> I have a Master's degree, and I work with high-end computers all day, but when it comes to my VCR, I never seem to be able to program it. I read the manual, and I saw the onscreen menus. They were useless. I had to ask for help. I hate that feeling.[1]

Many people share this person's experience, and they dread having to consult the manual because they often have difficulty finding the information that they need when they need it. In fact, many manuals don't actually have instructions in them at all. For example, cellphones generally come with reference manuals that supply detailed information about the features of the phone but few explicit instructions about how to use them. Of course, experienced users don't need an operations manual: they already know how to use the various features and have a repertoire of strategies to draw on to quickly figure out the nuances of the new model.

But what about new users? Another study shows that 60 per cent of users (regardless of age or sex) tend to blame themselves when

1   Quoted in Karen Schriver, *Dynamics in Document Design* (New York: John Wiley & Sons, 1997), 215.

2   Schriver, 220.

they can't figure out how to use a new product, although researchers concluded that, in the majority of cases, the problem was not with the users but with the manual, the equipment, or both.[2]

This would seem to let companies and technical communicators off the hook, wouldn't it? If people are going to blame themselves for poor instructional documents, why do we need to improve them? Karen Schriver argues that, over time, people will resist buying and using new technology because of their previous negative experiences learning to use it. This resistance means that they will continue to use their old electronics because they already know how to use them, and they don't want to invest time in learning a new system. Instead of expanding sales, manufacturers may find their profits failing to meet their shareholders' expectations. On the other hand, when Schriver asked study participants whether they would buy a product if they knew it had a clear manual, 79 per cent of them reported that they would. In fact, they would pay extra to get instructional documents that they *knew* they would be able to use without frustration. This point suggests a business opportunity for companies and the technical communicators that they employ.

What makes instructional documents good?

There are a number of ways to make instructions, procedures, and manuals easier to use:

- Know your audience or user group
- Include an overview of the procedures
- Subdivide processes
- Write usable steps
- Illustrate procedures
- Design an effective page layout
- Do usability testing.

KNOW YOUR TARGET AUDIENCE OR USER GROUP

While many of the instructional manuals for software that you can buy at the bookstore are produced for the broadest possible audience, the most effective technical communication is targeted towards a particular group, for example, basic beginners or advanced beginners or expert users. Think about two activities, one that you know virtually nothing about and another about which you are an expert. Now consider the type of instructional documents you would want in each case. For example, if you decide to change the oil in your car for the first time, how detailed would you need the information to be to ensure that you service your car properly? Would you need a photograph of your car's engine with the relevant parts labelled? Would you need the instructions to tell you what kind of engine oil to buy and how much? On the other hand, if you have spent the last three summers in your cousin's auto shop helping out with various clients' cars, would you need a labelled visual? Even if you had never actually changed the oil in a car by yourself, you would likely have assisted enough times to be quite familiar with the procedure. In this case, you would need some refresher-type instructions, reminding you of one or two key points—for example, don't over tighten the oil filter—but you would skip impatiently over instructions that told you where to find the plug in the oil pan.

Knowing how much your target user knows about the subject matter is critical to writing good instructions. How do you find out what your target user group knows? Review the discussion in Chapter 1 for ideas about analysing your audience. The list that follows is reprinted from Chapter 1 and summarizes the kinds of information you need about your target user group:

- Level of experience with the subject matter of your instructional material
- Educational background, both generally and specifically in subjects related to your subject matter
- Experience with and attitude toward learning new things
- Experience with and attitude toward technology generally and toward technology related to your topic specifically
- Relevant demographic characteristics such as age, sex, race, socio-economic background or class, culture, and first language.

As noted in earlier discussions, you may already have this information if you are familiar with your target user group, but, if you are not, then you will need to do some research to find out general answers. Interviewing members of your target audience is a good way to start. Review the proposal by Jason Nguyen in Chapter 6: in it, he plans to interview first-year engineering students from his programme, as well as undergraduates from other majors who are assigned oral presentations as part of their discipline-specific training. Nguyen is, in effect, gathering insight from his target user group to decide the best way to organize and present his information. Even if you can't mount a full-scale study of the group, informal conversations with three or four people who would fall into your target user group can give you invaluable feedback in understanding the needs of your audience.

A second way to collect information is to observe your target users as they work with other similar types of documents. You would do this to determine the level of background knowledge they bring to the subject matter as well as their attitudes and habits of use with this type of educational material. If you have limited ability to contact or work with your user group, then another strategy is to draw on the expertise of your co-workers who do have some knowledge of the target user group so that you can test and verify your assumptions about their needs and preferences. Usability testing at the earliest stage can also help you head off serious misunderstandings, which can happen if you started with only second-hand knowledge of your target user. This testing gives you the chance to meet and learn more about the preferences of actual members of your primary audience.

INCLUDE AN OVERVIEW OF THE PROCEDURE

Another feature of good instructions is that they include, at the beginning, some type of introduction to or overview of the content covered. The introductory material should accomplish four goals:

- Allow users to gauge whether this document is the right one to help them answer their questions
- Help users decide whether the instructional level is appropriate, too elementary, or too advanced for their current skills
- Provide a list of requirements or equipment needed to complete the procedure
- Provide a conceptual overview of the content of the document to assist users in processing the new information.

Introductory material can help users to quickly gauge whether the document covers the topics they need. This information makes their search for help more efficient by revealing, up front, whether this manual covers the function about which they need to know more. Instead of paging through the volume, they can tell from skimming through your introduction whether to look further inside.

Users also appreciate being able to find a clear statement early on as to the level of background knowledge assumed in the instruction. They can assess whether it matches their own level closely enough and decide whether they want to try to accommodate the level to their actual skills. For example, if the manual is more basic than they need, they may choose to overlook the statements that don't apply to their level of knowledge. Or if the manual is geared to a more expert audience, they may choose to use it while seeking additional help, from a reference book or more knowledgeable friend, for instance. But knowing the anticipated skill-level of the audience up front can reduce the frustration users experience with the instruction, because they go into the volume knowing what to expect.

Third, the overview should include a list of equipment or requirements that are needed to complete the procedure. Users can scan the list and identify any items or conditions that they don't have or may be unable to fulfil. For example, to create electronic instructional design materials using Dreamweaver's e-learning toolkit, users must have a copy of Dreamweaver MX (also Windows XP). When these versions first came out, individuals had to buy both the new operating system and the new version of Dreamweaver if they wanted to create lessons that incorporated the quiz function and the learning sites. Some people got a rude shock after they purchased the e-learning toolkit when they learned that they would need to upgrade their whole operating system. Had they known this at the point of purchasing the toolkit, they would have understood the extent of the investment they were making.

Finally, the overview helps to orient the reader to the organization of the instructions or manual. They can begin to build a conceptual basis from which to work as they process the content. Also, they can easily find the material of direct and immediate relevance to them.

If you are writing a set of instructions, then your overview will be brief, maybe no more than three or four sentences. In a longer educational document, you may need a paragraph or two to set up the larger context for the content discussed in the manual. But the key element of your overview is that it should be accessible and help your readers to understand and make decisions about whether this is the right set of instructions for them.

WRITE USABLE STEPS

The actual instructions or procedures themselves often seem straightforward to write. However, there are several conventions that you should know and apply to ensure that your documentation is as satisfying to use as possible. First-time writers of instructions often format their work as a series of paragraphs, as if they were unaware that documenting procedures is an entirely different genre from writing an essay or a report. For example, many cookbooks provide the directions for making a dish in one long paragraph under the list of ingredients. While experienced cooks will have little difficulty figuring out how to work through the steps, newcomers may find it difficult to keep track of where they are in the process or discover that too much information has been left out for them to prepare the dish successfully.

Examine Figure 8.1 in which Daniel Brisebois has written a first draft of the procedures for an experiment to measure amino acid titration. As you read the draft, think about what—beyond the scientific subject matter—makes this procedure difficult to follow. Note that the various steps of the procedure are embedded in paragraphs, with "then" used as a transition between the steps but there is no way to keep track of which step is next except the chronological order of the sentences. It would be easy for someone trying to use this procedure to miss one of the steps and make an error. A second characteristic that makes this procedure hard to read is the use of the impersonal "one" as an indirect means of instructing the user. This form of address is ultra formal (in everyday conversation, most people don't use "one" in speaking to each other), and this formality distances the writer from the reader. Many people are put off by someone who speaks to them in the third person. The form of address is also not consistent: mostly Brisebois uses "one" to instruct the reader, but he also occasionally uses "you" or imperative verbs. This use of "you" is more informal, changing the tone. A more effective strategy would be to maintain a consistent tone throughout—likely one that reduces the distance between the technical communicator and the user.

AMINO ACID TITRATION

Procedure
The first step is to calibrate the pH meter. To calibrate the pH meter, one should turn the meter to standby, and then plug it in, and allow it to warm up for about 10 minutes. Then one should adjust the temperature dial to the temperature of the solution. The third step is to rinse the electrode with DI (de-ionized) water and remove the excess water with a Kimwipe. One should submerge the electrode 1/2 inch into the buffer with a pH of 7. Then you should switch dials on the pH meter to read. Next, one should turn the calibration dial so the meter reads 7.0. Next, one should turn the dial back to standby, and remove the electrode from the buffer. Then one should rinse the electrode with DI water, and dry it, and place it in a buffer solution with a pH of 4.0. Next one should re-calibrate the pH meter as with the pH 7.0 buffer. If one finds the calibration is off, one must re-do the 7.0 buffer reading and compromise between the readings for the two buffers. The next step is to accurately weigh a .3 g. sample of unknown amino acid into a 150 mL beaker. One should then dissolve the sample in about 50 mL of DI water (one should just use enough to cover the electrode tip when it is high enough that the stirring bar doesn't hit it). If one finds the amino acid won't dissolve, one needs to heat the solution a bit, but then let it cool before titrating. Then titrate with standardized .1 M NaOH, using 1 mL increments for the additions. If one notices a large pH change occurring during titration (>.3 pH), one must decrease the additions of base to .5 mL or less.

Now one should continue the 1 mL incremental additions after the large pH change has passed. Next continue the addition of base until the pH reaches a value of 12.5. Once you have done this, then draw a graph of the pH vs. mL NaOH added. You should also calculate the molar weight, pKa, and whether the acid is monoprotic, diprotic, or triprotic. If your molar weight does not match any on the list, then one must re-do the titration using smaller increments of NaOH around the suspected endpoints.

The last step is to report the molar weight, pKa, and name of amino acid.

FIGURE **8.1**
First draft of procedures
for chemistry lab.

AMINO ACID TITRATION

Procedure

1. Calibrate the pH meter:
    i) Turn the meter to standby.
    ii) Plug it in.
    iii) Wait about 10 minutes until it warms up.
    iv) Adjust the temperature dial to the temperature of the solution.
    v) Rinse the electrode with de-ionized (DI) water.
    vi) Remove the excess water with a Kimwipe.
    vii) Submerge the electrode ½ inch into a buffer with a pH of 7.
    viii) Switch dials on the pH meter to read.
    ix) Turn the calibration dial so the meter reads 7.0.
    x) Turn the dial back to standby, and remove the electrode from the buffer.
    xi) Rinse the electrode with DI water.
    xii) Dry it.
    xiii) Place it in a buffer solution with a pH of 4.0.
    xiv) Re-calibrate the pH meter as with the pH 7.0 buffer.

    If your calibration is off, re-do the 7.0 buffer reading, and compromise between the readings for the two buffers.

2. Accurately weigh a .3 g sample of the unknown amino acid into a 150 mL beaker.

3. Dissolve the sample in about 50 mL of DI water.

    Use enough to cover the electrode tip when it is high enough that the stirring bar doesn't hit it.

4. If your amino acid won't dissolve, heat the solution a bit, but then let it cool before titrating.

5. Titrate with standardized .1 M NaOH, using 1 mL increments for the additions.

    If a large pH change occurs during titration (>.3 pH), decrease the additions of base to .5 mL or less.

6. Continue the 1 mL incremental additions after the large pH change has passed.

7. Continue the addition of base until the pH reaches a value of 12.5.

8. Draw a graph of the pH vs. mL NaOH added.

9. Calculate the following:
    ■ molar weight,
    ■ pKa, and
    ■ whether the acid is monoprotic, diprotic, or triprotic.

    If your molar weight does not match any on the list, then re-do the titration using smaller increments of NaOH around the suspected endpoints.

10. Report the following:
    ■ molar weight,
    ■ pKa, and
    ■ name of amino acid.

FIGURE 8.2
Revised
procedure
for chemistry
lab report.

IN-CLASS EXERCISE 8.1

Strategies for Writing Good Instructions

Compare the procedural steps in two drafts written by Brisebois: his first draft (Figure 8.1) and his revision (Figure 8.2). Record all of the different aspects that are changed, and assess whether they make the procedure easier to follow. Evaluate what specific elements related to the writing make instructions clearer and easier to read.

In the revised version, Brisebois numbers his steps because the order is important.

In reference to tone, he abandons the distancing use of "one" for a direct address. He substitutes commands or the imperative (e.g., "re-do the titration"). This choice closes the gap between himself and his users, creating a more user-friendly tone. It also makes the procedure much more concise.

Next, assess the individual steps in the procedure. Each numbered step contains one single action. Research has shown that most users read to the end of the first action and then jump to the next numbered step. If you have packed several actions into each number, many of your users will skip the second and third action and move on when they assume they are finished after the first one.

Note that step 4 includes a condition that may apply to the users' situation. Brisebois has placed the condition first to be sure that users read it. If it applies to their situation, they will follow the rest of step 4; if not, they can skip directly to step 5. When you find yourself in this writing situation, similar phrasing will enable you to bring conditional situations to users' attention and provide solutions to potential problems early on in the process.

Fifth, Brisebois has both numbered steps and indented italicized sentences. How is the information contained in these two formats different? The numbered steps are actions that users must perform. In contrast, the indented sentences are often reactions—that is, they summarize what has happened in response to the previous action taken by users. They may also contain explanatory or advisory information. For example, Brisebois provides alternate information in the italicized sentences that begin with "if"—"if this happens, then do this, etc." The key point is to format explanatory information in ways that distinguish it from the numbered steps so that users can easily differentiate the two.

What is your response to Brisebois' use of italics for these sentences? The italics format the information so that it stands out, but it also makes it more difficult to read. If the information is critical, then you want to format it to be as noticeable *and* readable as possible. What are some other choices Brisebois might have made to emphasize the explanatory information but maintain maximum readability?

- Put these sentences in a text box.
- Bold the sentences.
- Use a contrasting or coloured font for these sentences.
- Add a symbol or other decorative element on either end to draw user attention.

The list below summarizes the strategies that Brisebois has used to improve the quality of the writing in his instructions. Using these as guides for your own composing will greatly increase your chances of creating instructional information that users will follow easily and successfully.

Five strategies for writing readable instructions

1. If the steps must be done in chronological order, then *number* them; if the order does not matter, use bullet points.
2. Phrase steps in the imperative, i.e., as commands (verb + object).
3. Put one action in each step.
4. If conditions apply to the action, include them in a phrase or dependent clause *before* the imperative.
5. Format actions differently from explanatory information.

Brisebois' revisions to his original draft greatly improve the quality and readability of his instructions. At the same time, he has 14 steps in a sub-procedure and 10 steps altogether, resulting in a visually daunting page describing the procedure.

The psychology of writing good instructions responds to the belief that users can be intimidated by long and complex new processes or procedures that they must learn. One way to reduce the complexity of a procedure is to take the 135 individual actions that might be involved in a process and subdivide these into a number of stages with between 7 and 10 steps in each stage. As users move from stage to stage, they are able to mark their progress through the manual or procedure. The staged approach also allows them to more easily keep track of their stopping point when other commitments interrupt. The general topic that they last completed can be much easier to remember than step number 74 on page 27.

SUBDIVIDE THE PROCESS

Any type of process or procedure can be conceptualized as a series of stages that the user moves through on his or her way to successful completion. For example, if you are creating a set of instructions for how to change a flat tire on a car, you could number each step separately as Tyneka Porter has done in Figure 8.3.

One major change that Porter has made to her original draft is to subdivide the process into stages: Before you begin; Set up the jack and loosen the lug nuts; Jack up car and remove flat tire; Install spare tire; Finishing up. This process of subdivision is called "chunking," in other words, re-grouping the procedure into chunks of information, usually with between seven and ten steps in each chunk. Once you find yourself moving on to steps beyond ten in a single chunk, you can take this as a sign that you need to think further about subdividing the process again.

IN-CLASS EXERCISE 8.2

Organizing Information for the User

Consider the set of instructions in Figure 8.3 from the perspective of the first-time user, that is, someone who has never changed a flat tire. Answer the following questions to help you analyse and evaluate the effectiveness of this set of instructions.

- How do you think the first-time user would respond to these sixteen steps?
- What parts of the instructions do you think they would like? Dislike?
- Are there any steps that you don't understand?
- What do you think makes them hard to understand?
- If you are familiar with the process of changing a flat tire, assess these instructions to determine whether Porter has omitted any important steps.
- Are there steps that you would leave out because you think they are unimportant?
- How might Porter reorganize this set of instructions to make it easier to follow?
- What document design changes could be made to make these instructions easier to understand and follow?

CHANGING A FLAT TIRE

1. Pull over to side of the road. Make sure that you are far enough off the shoulder that you and your vehicle will be safe throughout this process.

2. Place blocks behind the tires to prevent vehicle from rolling when you start to work on it.

3. Locate spare tire and jack.

4. Place jack under back or front axle, depending upon which tire needs changing.

5. Loosen lug nuts in a crosswise pattern about 1 turn.

6. Jack up car until flat tire is off the ground by about eight inches.

7. Continue loosening lug nuts and remove them.

8. Remove the flat tire.

9. Place spare tire onto axle.

10. Replace lug nuts and tighten in crosswise pattern.

11. Lower jack until full weight of car rests on spare tire.

12. Tighten lug nuts as tight as possible.

13. Remove jack and replace in trunk.

14. Load flat tire into trunk.

15. Remove blocks from behind tires carefully, in case car weight shifts slightly or car rolls.

16. Return blocks to trunk (or wherever you store them).

FIGURE 8.3
This draft is a long, unorganized list of steps that will intimidate many users, especially if this is the first time they've changed a flat tire.

CHANGING A FLAT TIRE

This set of instructions is intended to help the first-timer change a flat tire easily and safely. Before you begin, review the list of equipment, locate it in your car, and assemble it in a safe location near the flat tire.

Equipment
- Jack
- Lug nut wrench
- Four heavy triangular blocks
- Spare tire
- Car manual, turned to information about changing your car tire

Before you begin
1. Make sure your car is pulled well off the road so that both you and your vehicle will remain safe throughout this procedure.

FIGURE 8.4 & 8.5
Page one of Porter's revision. Note how she has subdivided the process into stages and re-started her numbering at 1 under each heading. What could be added to this set of instructions to make it even better?

2. Choose a flat, level area, if at all possible.

3. Place one heavy, triangular block behind each of your rear wheels and in front of your front wheels.
   These blocks will prevent the car from rolling once you have the flat tire jacked into the air.

Set up the jack and loosen the lug nuts

1. Assemble the jack.
   Usually you need to insert the handle into a slot on the jack.

2. Set the jack under the axle and behind the flat tire.

3. Locate the slot on the axle where the jack will engage to lift the flat tire off the ground.

4. Line up the tabs on the top of the jack with the slots on your axle.

5. Wind the jack up until the tabs engage with the axle.
   At this point, do not lift the car off the ground.

6. Using the lug wrench, loosen the four wheel nuts one turn, working in a crosswise pattern around the tire.

Jack up car and remove flat tire

1. Continue raising the jack until the car begins to lift up and the flat tire is well clear of the ground (usually about 8 inches).
   You need to have space under the axle to fit the inflated spare between the car and the ground.

2. Loosen the wheel nuts the rest of the way.

3. Remove them from the wheel bolts.

4. Place them together on a sheet of plastic or newspaper so that you can easily find them in a few minutes.

5. Remove the flat tire.

Install spare tire

1. Place the spare tire on the axle, lining up the holes with the wheel bolts.

2. Replace the wheel nuts, tightening them finger tight.

3. In crosswise fashion, tighten wheel nuts using wrench.

4. Lower car using jack.

5. Tighten lug nuts as tight as you can, using wrench.

Finishing Up

1. Remove jack.

2. Replace jack, lug nut wrench, flat tire, etc. into your trunk.

3. Carefully remove triangular blocks and replace in trunk.

YOU DID IT!

IN-CLASS EXERCISE 8.3

"Chunking" Techniques and Your Target Audience

Compare the set of instructions in Figure 8.3 with the revised version in Figure 8.4 and 8.5. Answer the questions below to help you identify the specific revisions that improve the usability (or ease of use) of these instructions for a first-timer needing to change a tire.

In her revision, what specific changes has Porter made to the following areas?
■ Overview
■ Equipment
■ Subdividing process
■ Numbering
■ Labelling
■ Separating action from explanation

Why do these changes improve the quality of her instructions?

Do you see any aspects that could be improved even more?

HOW DOES "CHUNKING" IMPROVE THE QUALITY OF THE INSTRUCTIONS?

Chunking is a useful strategy because it encourages you to organize and subordinate the information that you want to present to your readers. You need to make decisions about which stages of the procedure you will give prominence to by selecting these as your topic headings. As you make decisions about these stages, you also review the suitability of each one for your target user group. Will users need the detail that you include in a particular section? For example, Porter adds information when she has clearly identified her audience and subdivided her information. In the original draft, she includes no mention of how to operate the jack, implying that such knowledge is obvious. Once she has described her target user, however, she also realizes that first-timers will not already know how to do this. She also includes a tip about keeping track of the wheel nuts once they are removed. Chunking helps technical communicators think through the procedures they are documenting. It is also useful to users.

The headings—which should be informative and descriptive—serve as guideposts to your users as they move through an unfamiliar process. They can use the movement from one "chunk" to the next as confirmation that they are making headway in learning the new information. The headings and chunks also serve as conceptual guides to the process, highlighting its major steps. Even if you don't consider yourself a teacher, when you document systems or procedures, you are, in fact, teaching someone else how to use or do something. One of the best ways for someone to "learn" is to grasp the conceptual overview into which they can organize the new information. Headings serve this purpose in a manual or set of procedures.

Another major change that Porter makes to her draft is to include an overview and list of equipment that serve as the users' introduction to the process. The overview underscores the target user group, which also cues readers as to the level of the instructions: basic.

Finally, what revision could be made to Porter's draft to improve it further? Illustrations. Will first-time users know what a lug wrench looks like? Do they know which way is up on the jack? Would an illustration be helpful in indicating where on the axle, approximately, users will find the notch under which they should place the jack? Will they know what she means when she says to tighten the wheel nuts in a crosswise pattern? Visuals would quickly and easily clear up possible confusion on these points.

USE ILLUSTRATIONS

There are few procedures that wouldn't be greatly improved by the strategic use of relevant and appropriate illustrations. You may not need to include a visual for every step of a process; in fact, many users find too many visuals to be as distracting and confusing as no visuals at all. However, an appropriately placed and well-chosen drawing or photograph can make a complex step both simple and crystal clear.

In the past, illustrating procedures could be difficult and time-consuming, but, with the advent of digital cameras and screen shots, technical communicators have access to a variety of ways to illustrate procedures, ways that are fairly easy and somewhat reasonably priced. You may still need to hire an artist to create line drawings of a piece of machinery, but, for the most part, the options for creating visuals are much easier than they were a decade or two ago.

Visuals in software documentation: Use screen shots

The easiest way to illustrate most computer or software manuals is to use screen shots. A screen shot refers to the use of the "print screen" [Prnt Scrn] key on the top right row of your PC keyboard to take a picture of what appears on your computer screen. (Mac users can use "Command-Shift-3" to take pictures of the whole screen and "Command-Shift-4" to take pictures of a part of the screen. The shots are usually stored automatically on your desktop from whence they can be inserted into other programs.) You can then paste the image into a word processing file and manipulate it to fit your needs. Here is a short tutorial for PC users to introduce the basics.

LOCATE THE PRINT SCREEN KEY

1. Locate the [Prnt Scrn] key on the top right row of your computer keyboard.

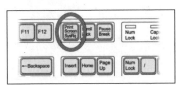

FIGURE 8.6
Locate print screen key.

COPY THE SCREEN IMAGE

1. Select the screen image that you want to copy.
2. Depress the [Prnt Scrn] key.
3. Open a word processing document.
4. Hit "enter" five or six times to put blank spaces before and after your image.
5. Place cursor two or three lines down from top of page.
6. Left click on "paste" icon (or CTRL+V).

A picture of your screen should appear in the open file, as in Figure 8.7.

MANIPULATE THE IMAGE

1. Left click on the image to select it.
2. Right click on the image to bring up the picture toolbar. (See Figure 8.8.)

FIGURE 8.7
Screen shot of open Microsoft Word™ file.

- Use the crop tool to cut away parts of the image you don't need.
- Use format picture to wrap words around the image or to resize it.
- Use Autoshapes (in Microsoft Word®) to add arrows or callouts.

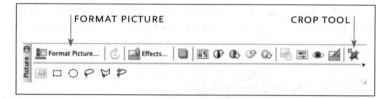

FIGURE 8.8
Picture toolbar

LAB ASSIGNMENT 8.1

CREATING AND LABELLING A SCREEN SHOT

Use the previous set of instructions to create screen shots (or use the "help" documents supplied with your computer's operating system or with particular programs on your computer). With the screen shots as illustrations, write a short set of instructions for using one of the easier functions of your favourite word processing or design (or other) program. Make sure the series of screen shots you create to illustrate these instructions are complete with labels and callouts, as appropriate. Decide on the level of knowledge and the background of your user before creating your instructions, and adapt your level of detail to the needs of your users.

How can you make effective use of visuals?

Whenever you pair text and visuals together, you are setting up a relationship between the two items. Sometimes, the text and the visual present the same information; sometimes, each provides its own particular meaning. When you decide to include an illustration or visual, you want each to contribute its unique features to the rhetorical situation to aid your users' understanding.

Karen Schriver describes several ways that visuals contribute to the meaning of text. When they are used effectively, they clarify the text, support it, or supplement it, depending upon your purpose in pairing them together:

- Stage setting
- Redundant
- Complementary
- Supplementary

FIGURE 8.9
The stage-setting use of a visual to explain the meaning of the common toolbar for Dreamweaver®

STAGE SETTING

Visuals that serve a stage-setting function are particularly useful for technical communicators. Stage-setting visuals convey different information from the text, but they also forecast the content of the text ahead. For example, in a manual for novice users on the latest version of Dreamweaver, you might begin by reproducing images of the various toolbars that show up on the screen and then identifying the function indicated by each of the icons. Placing the visual of the toolbar before the explanation basically sets the stage for your list of definitions. It forecasts the explanation that follows.

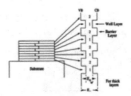

SEMICONDUCTOR BAND STRUCTURE FOR A SUPERLATTICE WITH THICK LAYERS

In a multiple layered film, the electronic structure changes to incorporate the different structures of the different layer materials. This figure depicts the semiconductor band structure for a superlattice structure. The well and the barrier layers are represented by the numbers 1 and 2 in the illustration of the film layers on the left side of the figure, and the band structure on the right side of the figure, reflecting the layered configuration. The presence of these different energy band gap structures in the layers offers the possibility of channels or wells where the electron-hole pairs, the carriers, can collect in the narrower band gap material, in this case, the a-SiN.$_{58}$:H.

FIGURE 8.10
Redundant use of visual and text to repeat complex information, making it more accessible through the paired representation.

Source: H. Graves, Rhetoric in(to) Science (Cresskill, NJ: Hampton Press, 2005), 88.

REDUNDANT

A redundant relationship between prose and image results in both the picture and the text presenting exactly the same information. This type of relationship is useful to repeat the key ideas, especially for processes or concepts that are complex and challenging. Users who are encountering a complex concept for the first time will find the redundant use of text and image helpful in grasping it. However, after they understand the concept, users find the redundant integration of text and image irritating, so it is important to understand fully the needs of your users. An example of the redundant use of text and image appears in Figure 8.10, which explains the semiconductor band structure for a superlattice (multi-layered film) with thick layers. In solid state physics, researchers explore possible useful applications for amorphous silicon as well as conduct basic research to describe its properties. Figure 8.10 illustrates the structure of the superlattice and some of its properties.

COMPLEMENTARY

The complementary use of text and visuals means that each mode presents slightly different information and both are required to

USING WORDART

1. Click on the WordArt icon on the drawing toolbar (See Figure 1).
The window, as pictured in Figure 2, should appear.

2. Select the effect that you want applied to your text.

3. Click "OK."

4. When a window appears, type your text into the box.

5. Choose the typeface that you want to apply to your word art.

6. When you are happy with your choices, click "OK."

Figure 1: the wordart icon is located on your drawing toolbar.

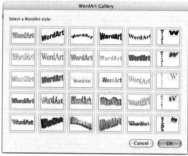

Figure 2: the wordart gallery gives you a range of choices for formatting your text.

FIGURE 8.11
Complementary use of text and image to supply different information.

ensure full understanding. The two modes together communicate the complete idea better than either one would alone. This type of relationship is useful when prose would be cumbersome to explain a detail but a visual would help make the action crystal clear. For example, step 2 in Figure 8.11 needs only a brief instruction to the user because the image fills in all of the details.

Illustrating the menu of choices for WordArt in "Figure 2" of Figure 8.11 supplies the details that no user would want to have to read but will still find useful to see. The image fills two functions simultaneously in this situation: it confirms the outcome of step 1 (action>reaction), and it illustrates the range of choices available for selection.

THE ALLEN KEY

An Allen key differs from an ordinary wrench in that it is shaped with a 90° turn at one end. (See Figure 1.)

To Use

1. Insert one end or the other into the head of the Allen nut.

2. Turn until nut is tight.

In tight areas, you may need to turn as far as you can and then re-insert the wrench and turn several times to completely tighten the nut.

Figure 1. Ring of Allen keys.

FIGURE 8.12
Supplementary use of the visual supports the textual description.

SUPPLEMENTARY

A supplementary relationship between text and image means that one of the modes is dominant, conveying the main information, while the other mode mostly confirms or elaborates the point. This method is the most common way to integrate text and graphics, often with the text being the dominant message and the visual serving as an example. (We are using this technique in this section, by the way.)

DESIGN AN EFFECTIVE PAGE LAYOUT

What makes for an effective page layout of instructions, procedures, and manuals? There are a number of points that you should consider to ensure that your information is easy to access and follow.

Shorten line lengths

Make the length of lines of text shorter than if you were writing an essay or report. You don't want instructions that are 6 inches long and stretch from a one-inch margin on the left to a one-inch margin on the right. Long line lengths are harder to read, and users can lose their place from one line to the next. Aim for a maximum line length of about 70 characters or 4 inches.

Choose a page orientation

Many people choose a vertical orientation for their pages (portrait) automatically without really thinking about the final product and how (or where) it will be used. They just format the page as an 8½ x 11" sheet and staple the pages together. While this is an easy (and inexpensive) way to format and bind your manual, it is definitely not always the best choice, from a user's perspective. Standard-sized sheets of paper take up a lot of space in the working area, and pages tear away from a staple binding surprisingly easily. Without a substantial cover, the pages quickly become dog-eared or lost.

Instead of selecting the "default" choice, think about and make decisions on the overall format for your manual. Would a booklet (generated by folding an 8½ x 11" sheet of paper in half) be easier to use and suit your subject matter better than the full-sized sheet? If so, perhaps you should format your file using a landscape orientation with two columns or a two-cell, one-row table to hold your content in place. Maybe a single page can hold all of your information and visuals about mixing martinis, but the busy environment of a restaurant bar would mean that spills would soon obscure your work. Perhaps laminating the page would make the information sufficiently sturdy and waterproof to last as a reference for employees for years. Think creatively and innovatively about how to present your instructional information so that you can create a finished product that is convenient, easy to use, and lasting.

Design a grid to organize your information

When you have decided on the best basic format for presenting your content, review the discussion in Chapter 6 on how to design a page grid so that you can figure out how to present it in a clear and organized way. Once you have designed the basic grid, you will find it easy to lay out your instructions because you already know where to place certain types of information on the page. For example, if you have decided to fold an 8½ x 11" sheet of paper in half for a booklet, you could then design a two-column, three-row grid for each page. Your visuals will appear in the right column, and the text will appear in the left column. Each page will hold up to three separate visuals and the text that accompanies them.

While the grid aids you as a writer in designing and putting together your pages, it is even more helpful to users because they can quickly assess your organizational strategy and anticipate where to find specific information. For example, they will look to the right side of the page for a visual to confirm or clarify a textual instruction that might, initially, seem confusing.

Include and visually emphasize tips, warnings, and cautions

If you have important information that your users need to know as they proceed through the document, format it using design principles that will help it to stand out and be noticed. The design principle of "contrast" is helpful here. Choose a particular way to format tips, warnings, and cautions so that users cannot easily overlook them in the pressure to finish the process. Reverse textboxes (black background with white lettering) can be effective, as can just placing the information in a text box. The line around the material usually sets it off from the rest of the page, if you have not already used boxes for some other function. Contrasting colour is also another effective way to grab users' attention. But be aware that two- or three-colour printing is considerably more expensive than printing that uses only shades of black on white. You can also use meaningful symbols or icons to mark information in a particular way. The challenge with this method is to select symbols or icons that will be meaningful to users. For example, a government website on responding to disasters relies extensively on icons and pictures to communicate with readers. However, some of the images are no longer self-explanatory. One set of instructions that advises readers to call the police features an icon of a rotary telephone, an antiquated relic to anyone under 30. Icons and symbols are only useful if your users recognize the point they are intended to convey.

Icons and symbols are only useful if your users recognize the point they are intended to convey.

Do usability testing

Once you have completed a draft of your instructions, procedure, or manual, you should arrange to test it with a selection of people drawn from your target user group. The idea is to have several people work through your draft (or, in the case of a manual, through one or two chapters) following the instructions as written while you observe them to determine how clear and easy to use the instructions are. You can verify that your organization and presentation of material makes sense to your users, that they can easily find the section that they need to complete the task assigned to them, and that your assumptions about their background knowledge and level of experience are accurate. Between your observations and their report of their experiences at the conclusion of the test, you gain valuable feedback about which aspects of the draft work well and which aspects could use revision or redesign.

It is important that you observe users while they work with the draft because your observations may vary from the experience they report. For example, several users might skip over the first three pages of the chapter but not report this behaviour to you because they believe it is unimportant. However, from your perspective, not using a portion of the manual is a significant behaviour that you would like to be able to explain. By questioning them about this action, you might discover that your target user group doesn't need the information contained in that section: it is too basic for their needs. If you had not been present at the test to follow up on this seemingly trivial action, your final draft would undoubtedly include unnecessary information, needlessly increasing the cost of the document and reducing company profits (as well as potentially frustrating knowledgeable users without the confidence to skip ahead).

Alternatively, your test might reveal that there are two or three critical steps that are not documented, an omission that prevents users from completing the procedure. In this case, the usability test has saved your company from having to issue a reprint of the manual almost immediately to correct a fundamental oversight. See Chapter 9 for a detailed discussion of how to design and conduct usability testing.

LAB ASSIGNMENT 8.2

EVALUATING GOOD INSTRUCTIONS—ORIGAMI

Requirements: One package of origami paper, with instructions

1. Form groups of three or four people.
2. Select a group member with little or no prior experience doing origami.
3. Choose an origami figure from the instructions.
4. Have the inexperienced member follow the instructions to create the figure.

5. As the inexperienced group member follows the instructions, the other group members should observe, watching for problem areas in the instructions—in other words, where the novice slows down, hesitates, rereads instructions, etc.
6. Observe the novice member and make notes with the goal of rewriting these instructions.

Questions for observers

- Where in the instructions does the experimenter encounter problems, either with the equipment, the instructions, or the activities required?
- What potential solution does the experimenter propose for each problem?
- What does he or she finally decide to do to solve the problem as he or she encounters each difficulty?
- How successful are the solutions that he or she devises?

Revise the original instructions

After the novice member successfully completes the origami figure (or gives up after a reasonable effort), revise the instructions as a group, adding text and visuals where necessary.

Questions for the entire group

- What is your group's assessment of the instructions for the origami set?
- What prior knowledge does the writer assume in the reader?
- What kinds of changes did you make to the instructions to improve their clarity and communication?
- In what ways did you find that the group's level of experience and prior knowledge of the subject matter (creating origami figures) affected the outcome or success of the figure that the (novice) experimenter was trying to create?

LAB ASSIGNMENT 8.3

REVISING A POORLY DESIGNED SET OF INSTRUCTIONS

The set of instructions in Figure 8.13 is poorly written and poorly designed. Revise these instructions on how to use Microsoft Word's WordArt, rewriting text where necessary, adding screen shots for illustration, and incorporating as much of the information in this chapter on writing effective instructions as you can.

DESIGNING AND WRITING INSTRUCTIONS ON HOW TO CREATE SCREEN SHOTS

Create a two-page reference card that explains how to create screen captures using a PC or a Mac. (Choose just one platform for this assignment). This card will be laminated and distributed to first-year technical communication students who have never made screen captures before.

Your Audience:
Undergraduate students in technical communication who need to know how to use a PC (or a Mac) to create screen captures to illustrate their first assignment, a short set of instructions on how to use a common function of Word.

Your Method:
Planning Your Grid Layout
1. Use the discussion in Chapter 5 on designing a grid layout to design your two-page layout.
2. Use the drawing toolbar in Word to create a model of the modular grid that you develop for your two-page layout.

Using Your Grid Layout
1. Use the grid to decide how many and which of the topics listed below you can and should include in your two-page reference card.

   Since you may not be able to fit all nine topics and their accompanying illustrations on the two pages, decide which are the most useful or important functions that the card should document.

2. Use the grid to design the actual layout for your screen capture reference card.

Adding Graphics to Your Prose
1. To illustrate the steps on your reference card, use as many of the four ways to integrate prose and graphics as is reasonably practical. (See the earlier section in this chapter.)
2. Adjust the content of your reference card as necessary to maintain its legibility and usability.

Topics to Select from to Create your Reference Card for Creating PC/Mac Screen Captures:
1. Kinds of screen captures
■ Print screen key (PC) or Command-Shift-3 (Mac) to capture entire screen
■ Alt + print screen key (PC) or Command-Shift-4 (Mac) to capture part of screen

2. How to capture an image of the whole screen

3. How to capture an image of the open window

4. How to crop your screen image picture

5. How to re-size your screen capture

6. How to place text beside your screen image

7. How to add captions to the picture

8. How to add callout boxes to the picture

9. How to add drawing arrows to the picture

HOW TO ADD WORD ART TO YOUR TEXT

When using Microsoft Word, it is helpful to use some special effects to enhance the appearance of the text. You can add special effects in various ways, for example, to create a shadowed, rotated, or colourful text. The following instructions will help you in making some basic changes to your text to make it more interesting for the reader.

Equipment Needed
Computer, Windows 98 or newer, Microsoft Word program

Ready? Let's begin then.
Open Microsoft Word.

Turn on your computer, and click on the start button, which is located in the lower left corner of the screen.

Drag your mouse to "programs," click on it, and then drag the mouse pointing to Microsoft Word and click again.

Tip: Depending on if you need to type the body of the text, you might do that or just begin with the WordArt to make a title page.

How to get to the WordArt.
Click on the "insert" button on the toolbar.

Once the insert menu drops, go down, click on "picture," and go to the right to select "WordArt." Click on it to select it.

Welcome to the WordArt Gallery.
Select your preference by clicking on the picture you want and clicking on "OK."

Now you have a chance to pick your font style and its size.

After making your selections click on "OK."

Great. Hopefully you got the art you desired.

Tip: It is often helpful to play around with various fonts and sizes to get the desired effect from WordArt.

FIGURE 8.13
Poor instructions on using WordArt

MAJOR PROJECT 8.1

WRITE A SET OF INSTRUCTIONS OR A PROCEDURE

Identify a procedure that you know in detail and that you have performed but that has not been adequately documented for a particular group. Write a two-page set of instructions for the target audience that you select, showing group members how to complete that procedure.

On a separate piece of paper, identify your audience and its members' level of knowledge about the subject, and turn this in with your assignment (not part of the two-page guideline).

- Break the instructions into groups of steps (maximum 7 to 10 steps to a group), and write headings that identify each group.

■ Orient the readers to the instructions before beginning with the first step.
■ Include cautionary statements to warn readers about dangerous outcomes (e.g., stirring the sugar mixture at this point will cause the sugar to crystallize, making your fudge sugary rather than smooth; save your new file every five minutes to minimize loss of data).
■ Include ways for readers to get started again in case they have trouble along the way.
■ Design a modular grid layout for your instructions that will make it easy for readers to find the instructions and follow them quickly.

MAJOR PROJECT 8.2

WRITE A TECHNICAL MANUAL

Major Project 6.1 in Chapter 6 asked you to write a proposal to create a technical manual based on a topic of your choice. Create the manual that you outlined in your proposal. Follow the development plan and work schedule described in your proposal to complete the manual.

Many of the topics that are covered in this book will be important to consider as you write your manual, including document design, visuals, organizing information, and making your writing clear for specific audiences. Make sure that you take time to design a modular grid for the page layout of your manual, including where to place images and text, what kind of headings to use, and what kind of navigational aids to provide (table of contents, list of figures, page numbers, indexes, etc.).

Purpose and Audience

Before you start writing your manual, you should have a good sense of which kind of document you are trying to write. Are you trying to teach someone something (tutorial)? Are you trying to help someone find a specific piece of information (reference manual)?

When you've got that figured out, focus on your readers:
■ What is the best way to get the information to them?
■ Should the manual be printed, on a website, or both?
■ Should it be in the form of help cards encased in plastic?
■ Should it fit in a pocket for easy portability and convenience?
■ Should it be spiral bound so that it stays open on any page?

After you have some ideas about what the end product will look like, start thinking about how to organize the information. What should come first? Should there be an index? Tabs?

Your next task is to draft at least part of the manual and then test it out, formally or informally, on someone who will use your manual when you are finished. Watch your tester try to use your draft and ask for suggestions on how to improve it. If you think you are going in the right direction, draft the rest of the manual and then test it again. Manuals are far more complicated than they appear to be, but you can ensure that you write a useful one if you know your audience and keep checking your draft over with that audience or someone who resembles that audience.

Constraints and requirements

As you write your manual (or section of a manual), keep two general constraints in view:

1. Your audience is a lay reader rather than a specialist.

2. Your manual must describe how to perform the kinds of tasks discussed in this book.

The function that you choose to document must be substantial (resulting in about 15 pages of text).

If it is appropriate, include a note to readers to locate them in your text. (For example, what section is this of the manual? Or how does it connect to related subject matter such as the other functions of a program, the larger process of which this manual is a part?)

You should also include screen captures or other appropriate visuals to complement your written text. Indexes, tabs, and a table of contents are some of the other features you may wish to include to improve the usability of your document.

Here is a list of topics that students have successfully completed in the past:
- Describe your part-time (or full-time) job functions as a receptionist, help desk attendant, etc.
- Contact a local service organization and volunteer to write a procedures manual for their volunteers.
- Document how to create and use a free email account for first-time computer users.
- Show how to create a website using HTML.
- Write procedures for choosing, installing, and automatically updating free software for virus, firewall, and spyware protection.
- Describe setting up a wireless network and protecting it against unauthorized users.

CHAPTER NINE

Testing and reporting document usability

What is usability?

Usability refers to the actual conditions under which a document is used by real people to accomplish a task. Usability tests of documents are designed to answer questions such as these: How easily could users retrieve the relevant information? Have all the essential steps been included? Does every step that needs a visual have a visual? Ready-to-assemble furniture, for example, usually comes with a short set of instructions detailing how to put the item together. Usability testing would determine the quality of the instructions as measured by how they helped or hindered the people trying to assemble the furniture.

While it may seem like common sense to have users test the draft of an instructional document before publication to ensure that it is written as clearly and accurately as possible, many organizations do not do so, resulting in documentation that is frustrating and alienating to use. Alexandra Peers makes this point in a review of one of Martha Stewart's books of homemaking projects: "The recipes and projects in the book are often so complicated and require so many obscure items—you just try finding Japanese Moriki paper—that even someone comfortable in the kitchen seems doomed to defeat. Of course, you wind up blaming yourself, not Ms. Stewart, if something fails because it lacked all the 'right' ingredients."[1] Peers's comment suggests that, as a technical manual, the book needs additional revision before the average user would be able to create the projects successfully.

Although he's talking about web usability (i.e., the ease of navigating websites) in *Don't Make Me Think*, Steve Krug makes an important point about usability testing by many organizations. He notes, "This is how most usability testing gets done: too little, too late, and for all the wrong reasons."[2] He urges companies to begin

1   Alexandra Peers, "But Martha Made it Look so Easy," *Wall Street Journal*, December 12, 1997, B10.

2   Steve Krug, *Don't Make Me Think: A Common Sense Approach to Web Usability* (Berkeley, CA: New Riders Press, 2000), 140.

user testing at the beginning of project development and to keep it simple, so they do enough of it to get the project right.

Why test for usability?

If members of a target audience purchase a product and find themselves able to use the accompanying instructions to quickly and easily assemble and use it, they are much more likely to purchase other products from the same company. In contrast, if they are unable to assemble or use the product, even after wrestling extensively with the instructions, and have to return it for a refund, how likely will they be to purchase other products from the same company? They are more likely to buy from a competitor, hoping the documentation will be better, or they may decide not to purchase the new product at all but make do with what they already have at home and know how to use.

Between returned products and lost sales, bad documentation can cost a company big money. Usability testing is one way that technical communicators and their employers can ensure that their documentation will do the job it is supposed to do, creating satisfied customers and guaranteeing further sales. Gathering user feedback can help writers to gauge the quality of their documentation and to determine what kinds of revisions are needed.

Here are some of the ways you can make your documents more usable:

- Organize information into manageable chunks.
- Position information for emphasis.
- Provide structuring devices (such as tabs or indexes).
- Identify the background knowledge of users.
- Include labels and headings.
- Use graphics and typefaces as locating devices.

What is a usability test?

A usability test is a test that researchers or technical communicators run to determine how easy a document is to use. It generally involves giving a draft of the document to potential users and asking them to perform the activities covered in it.

However, there are several ways that you can collect user feedback to assess the quality of a set of instructions or a manual. You can observe individuals attempting to use the draft. The observation can be done in person, or you can videotape their experience to view and analyse later. In the case of computer manuals, special programs exist that can record keystrokes, enabling you to re-construct the steps that people take as they try to do something explained by the manual. You can analyse the keystrokes to assess where a user might have had difficulties. A usability test can also involve interviewing test subjects after they finish the task set for them. Based on their responses, you can make recommendations about the kinds of revisions that would improve the draft.

This chapter focuses mainly on the type of usability test that observes users working through a draft and then interviews them about their experience and perceptions at the end of the test. This type of test can be done to assess both print and web usability. It is one of the more accessible methods of testing and is available to many students of technical communication because it is cheap (when conducted using volunteers) and low tech (requiring no expensive equipment). However, it is time consuming. It does take several hours to organize and run the test with each different user. Usability testing run by professionals in an organization is considerably more expensive because of the time involved as well as the expense of having to pay researchers and testers for their time. However, it also provides critical feedback that is difficult to obtain in any other way.

The test itself is only the first stage of a complete usability test. After you've run the test, you assemble and analyse the data that you collected through your observations and interviews. After analysis, you compile your findings into a usability report that documents the test, the users' experiences, the outcome, and the revisions suggested by the test. The usability report generally provides a summary of the outcomes of the testing and a record that the testing was done. It can serve as a reference and a model document for technical communicators or researchers at a later date.

What is the purpose of a usability test?

The point of a usability test is to observe users to identify
- omissions or ambiguous passages in the document or
- better ways to organize and present information.

Beyond these general points, you can of course establish more specific goals for your test.

Planning the test
SELECTING TEST SUBJECTS

The individuals that you want to participate in your test should fit your target user group. In other words, their backgrounds and their knowledge of and experience in the subject area should be similar to those of the people who will purchase the product and use your documentation for it. Only by testing with individuals who fit your user profile will you gain accurate feedback about the draft's possible shortcomings.

HOW MANY TEST SUBJECTS?

One rule is that the more subjects you can test, the more accurate and representative will be the feedback you receive. That said, time and money often restrict what is possible. However, you do want to test with more than one or two people, if possible, in case a particular individual's response is idiosyncratic. Comparing an individual response to the responses of others will help you determine whether the problem is unique to one respondent or general among a majority of your test users.

Researchers recommend that, for large-scale projects, you should test as many as twenty to fifty people. However, with small projects (and small budgets with tight timelines) you might find that between five and fifteen people are sufficient to give you accurate and useful feedback. Research by web usability experts Jakob Nielsen and Tom Landauer has shown that five users will usually uncover up to 85 per cent of the problems with a website.[3] However, in *Don't Make Me Think*, Krug makes a critical point: "Testing one user is 100% better than testing none." And he notes, "Even the worst test with the wrong user will show you things you can do that will improve your [draft]."[4] His experience has shown that any testing can be helpful in pointing out problems with your draft. He also argues that "testing is an iterative process"—that is, after you test, you fix the draft and test again to see if the solution actually works.[5] He recommends three or four users for each stage of usability testing.

For the purposes of school projects, we usually recommend that our students test their drafts with three people. This number highlights common problems while avoiding the issue of idiosyncratic responses. However, as Krug says, testing with even one person is more helpful than not testing your draft at all. Even one person can help you make your draft better by pointing out problems that you, as the writer and designer, can't see.

WHAT SHOULD I TEST FOR?

Of course, you can collect feedback about a range of aspects. You will be the best judge of the list, based on your sense of the strengths and weaknesses of your draft. Here is a list to get you started thinking about aspects you might want to evaluate:

- Organization of information (including grid design)
- Accessibility (table of contents, page numbers, headers, tabs, graphics)
- Clarity and readability of prose
- Completeness of prose
- Appropriateness of visual aids.

---

3   Cited in Krug, 146.

4   Krug, 142.

5   Krug, 143.

WHAT SHOULD I HAVE USERS DO DURING THE TEST?

The first step in planning your usability test is to decide what it is you want your users to be able to do after working through your draft: Do you want them to follow instructions? In this case, you might assign them a task of performing a function using the set of instructions that you've written. Do you want them to make judgments about something? In this instance, you may want them to read through a discussion, digest and understand the information, and then apply it to arrive at specific conclusions. Do you want them to make decisions? In this case, you might have them work through a list of criteria that they apply to achieve the final goal of recommending a course of action. Each of these scenarios relates to a different type of document and suggests a particular activity for your test subjects, and both the document type and the activity will shape the kind of test that you design.

In deciding what task you will have users perform, you will also want to consider other aspects of the users' experience or of the test situation:

- the characteristics of the work environment that may affect them during the test;
- the attitudes or level of expertise and/or experience that they bring to the task; or
- the possible ways that they might misunderstand the task you have set them.

For example, if end users will operate a piece of machinery in a noisy factory environment, consider whether you can recreate this type of environment during the test. To what extent will your results still be valid if you test the draft in a relatively calm and quiet atmosphere? Would providing loud rock music be an adequate substitute for the noise on the plant floor?

If your documentation is an update for users who are already familiar with the procedure or equipment, then you will see more relaxed attitudes from users than when a brand new procedure or operational manual is being tested. Are there things that you can do during the test that will help your users relax and feel less anxious about learning a completely new procedure?

If possible you might try to interview present users of the current version of the device or program that you are documenting to find out what they think is essential to the final document. This way you can assess some of their pet peeves regarding the current version, and these may give you insight into how to improve the documentation of the next version. Generally, people who are familiar with earlier versions of manuals or instructions have some excellent suggestions as to what could be improved in a revision. While these recommendations may not necessarily represent the final word, they can at least give you ideas about how users interact with and view earlier versions, so you can sharpen your own thoughts about both your draft and the test that you are developing.

Designing the test

Once you have made decisions about what aspects of the document you would like to receive feedback about and how best to organize the usability testing, then it's time to sketch out the design of the test. Develop objectives for the test that describe how users should be able to use the document that you plan to test. Write out a list of three or four key objectives that you intend the test to meet. You will later review these objectives to determine the success of your test. If it accomplished all of the objectives, then you can feel confident that your test was a success.

Next, identify and contact participants who are willing to participate in the test. Ideally, you want them to be people who might actually use your document in a non-test environment, so they are conceivably part of your target user group. They should have a similar basic knowledge of and background in the subject matter as your target users so that any problems they have with the draft will be more likely because of your error rather than their lack of experience or understanding. You don't want to add basic details to the revision that your target users may see as extraneous and distracting. At the same time, if your test participants have more knowledge and experience than your target audience, they may recommend that you remove steps or information that your actual users need (and would miss). However, if you can only find volunteers for the test whose experiences and backgrounds don't match those of your users, you are better to have them help you with the test than to forego any testing at all. You could ask that they consider, as they do the test, the needs of someone with perhaps less experience than they have. They may be able to alert you to areas that could be improved even though they don't exactly match your user profile.

The next step in designing your test is to figure out where you will run it. If possible, you should set usability testing in the actual work environment, where users will make use of the finished document. You want to try to replicate a real user's possible experience, so your test users can bring to light problem areas of the draft that might not be revealed in an artificial work environment. For example, if actual users will be exposed to noisy, active, and distracting work conditions, your test users might be able to help you brainstorm ways to maximize readability. Based on their experience in an environment resembling the actual one, they might suggest that you organize your process so that each stage is clearly marked, making it easier for users to find where they left off before the latest interruption. Using a calm environment for your user test would prevent users (as well as you) from perceiving this external complication.

When you have completed the organizational details of setting test objectives, locating willing participants, and creating a realistic work environment for the test, the next step is to create a handout that you will distribute to test users, one that will explain to them what the test will involve. (See Figure 9.1 for a sample handout created for a usability test.) The reason for creating a handout is that you want users to have something to refer to during the test in case they forget an oral explanation. You also want to ensure that each participant has the same amount of information about the test so that you are creating a similar experience of the draft document for each one. Address these points in the handout:

- Summarize the purpose of the test.
- Outline what you want them to do.
- Thank them for participating.
- Inform them that they can quit if they become too frustrated.

Thank you for agreeing to help out with evaluating the ease of use of the attached instructions on how to set up a buddy list and send photos using AOL instant messenger.

Test Objectives
I have three goals in setting up this test:
- to uncover errors or confusing passages in the draft
- to identify whether each step that needs one has a visual
- to reveal whether these instructions are too basic for users who know MSN but haven't used AIM before.

Tasks to Perform
The attached instructions should help you move smoothly through the process of getting and using an AIM account. Please use these instructions to
1. sign up for an AIM account
2. create a buddy list, and
3. send an image file to the people you select on your buddy list.

As you work your way through these instructions, please remember that the focus of this test is to find errors and problems with the instructions. Any difficulties you might have are entirely due to the draft and in no way reflect on you.

If at any point in this test you feel uncomfortable or too frustrated to continue, please remember that you are helping me out here, and you can quit at any time. Thanks so much for taking the time to help me create great instructions!

FIGURE 9.1
Sample handout for a usability test. It lists the objectives and the tasks to be performed, and it thanks users for participating.

SUMMARIZE THE PURPOSE OF THE TEST

You need one or two sentences that explain the point of your test. From a user's perspective, the purpose of the test is generally to find out where the draft is unclear, ambiguous, or lacking key information. It might also focus on organizational issues, for example, the ease with which users can locate particular pieces of information or instructional steps.

From your perspective, you might not want to explain every detail of your purpose. For example, if a goal of the test is to determine how quickly users can find a specific section of the manual, then you might not want to tell them that time is important because you don't want them to speed up their search just to help your test be a success. For this reason, then, a general statement of your broad goals is sufficient.

You also want to emphasize that you are testing the document and not them. Stress that, if they run into problems, these are likely the fault of the instructions—*they are not to blame, and they are not being tested.*

OUTLINE WHAT YOU WANT THEM TO DO

This section of the handout is usually fairly general as well. Ask them to perform tasks that you expect an actual user of your document would want to do. You want the test to be as authentic as possible. Write the tasks out as short, simple numbered steps. Leave white space around the tasks so that they are easy to see and also find later when users want to check that they have completed all of the tasks.

At the same time, you don't want to provide too much detailed information to your users when assigning tasks in case you give them clues regarding how to overcome obstacles in the document that you are testing. The task descriptions should be enough to inform test users but not enough to compromise the integrity of your test.

THANK THEM FOR PARTICIPATING

The main point you want users to understand as they finish reading your handout is that the goal of the test is to improve your draft, not to evaluate their performance in any way. Given that users often blame themselves when they have difficulties with a poorly written step, you want to minimize any negative psychological effects they might experience because of participating in the test. You can make this point clear by expressing your appreciation for them volunteering their time, energy, and perhaps patience, in helping you improve your document.

INFORM THEM THAT THEY CAN QUIT

You also want your test participants to understand that, by volunteering to do this test, they are helping you. Consequently, if they experience excessive frustration or feel uncomfortable at any point during the test, they are free to quit. Since your testers are volunteers, you want their experience to be as positive as possible. Making them feel as if they cannot escape, no matter now gruelling the test, will certainly not encourage them to volunteer for a similar experience another time. Recording this option on your handout can serve as a reminder to users later in the test, when they may run into a problem that they can't solve.

Conducting the test

When you have prepared your handout and are generally satisfied that your usability test is well planned and ready to be executed, move on to the next stage of the process, which is conducting the test. Schedule dates and times with each of your volunteers when you can observe them working with your draft. You do want to be present through the whole test, so you can watch and take notes while they work and then debrief them at the end to get any thoughts or comments they have about the experience or the draft.

Plan to be present during each test so that you can do the following:

- Record any comments users make during the test.
- Note problems they have or requests for help.
- Identify passages in the draft that confuse them.
- Note problems they have finding information.
- Note information that was not used (skipped over).
- Note any strategies they use to overcome obstacles they encounter.

Obviously you should take notes during the test. In addition, you can also consider audio taping the session or videotaping it (or both) to analyse later. Of course, you need to have access to technology if you want to tape the tests. If you decide to tape the tests, you should still take notes during the session in case your equipment malfunctions at some point. At the same time, the notes that you record will help you to pay closer attention to what's happening during the test. Sometimes people become complacent when they videotape because they believe everything will be available to them on the tape, and, although this might be true when everything goes according to plan, if your equipment breaks down, you may find your tapes are much less helpful than you would have liked. The second point to remember is that audio and video tape have to be viewed in real-time, and

IN-CLASS EXERCISE 9.1

Modelling Usability Testing

The purpose of this exercise is to model the procedures for designing and conducting a usability test. To complete this exercise you will need

- a craft kit, such as beading or paper airplane instructions, and
- several volunteer test users.

The point of this exercise is to evaluate the usability of the documentation that accompanies the supplies provided in the craft kit. To determine the usability of the accompanying instructions, you must have someone from the target user group try to use them.

There are four steps to this exercise:

1. Design the test.

2. Create a handout describing the tasks that you want your participants to perform during the test.

3. Observe three or four people using the instructions.

4. Write a report describing your evaluation of the instructions.

Design the test

Set several objectives for the test that identify the kind of information that you want to gain from your users about the instructions:

- What are you trying to determine about the instructions?
- Which part of the instructions do you want to test?

continued...

Describe the tasks you want performed

Prepare a brief handout (one half to one page long) describing the tasks that you want your participants to perform during the test.

Observe users performing the tasks

Make notes as you observe several people attempting to follow the instructions from the craft kit. Note any problems they have or strategies they use to complete the assignment (including when they don't use the instructions at all).

Write a report

In the form of a memo addressed to your instructor, write a report describing the objectives of the test, the test itself, and the results of the test. Also include a section explaining how you would revise the instructions you decided to test, based on the experiences of your test users.

Address each of the topics below in your report:

- The test objectives
- The audience for the craft instructions
- The test subjects
- The tasks assigned to the subjects
- What happened during the test
- Comments from subjects
- Plans for revision of craft instructions

reviewing recorded material can be enormously time consuming. Not only will you have spent the time running the tests, but you will also need to "re-live" them when you watch the tapes again, adding several more hours to the total time taken up by this project.

DEMONSTRATE THE EQUIPMENT

If your test users need a particular piece of equipment to complete the test, be sure that they are familiar with how to use it (unless, of course, the point of the test is for them to figure out how to use it based on your draft document). You don't want their inexperience to slow down the test. Before they begin the actual test, make sure that you have explained the purpose of each piece of equipment that they might need and how it will be used in the test. Demonstrate any equipment that they might have to use to complete the test.

EXPLAIN HOW TO "THINK ALOUD"

Not only do you want to observe your users while they work through the tasks that you've set them, you also want them to talk aloud as they do so. Ask your users to speak aloud what they are thinking as they perform the activities that you've assigned to them. While you cannot, of course, get at everything that is going on in their minds as they work, having them "think aloud" does give you some insight into what they are experiencing at each moment. Explain why you want them to think aloud, and demonstrate how to do it. Some people feel self-conscious speaking aloud, but if you show them what you want and how to do it, they will feel less strange about it. From your perspective, this thinking aloud helps you figure out what is going on inside as test users move from one step to the next. If they pause for a few seconds, if they voice their confusion, you are alerted to a potential problem with the draft. It is always useful to hear users' unedited responses to layout, phrasing, and visuals, directly at the users' point of contact with them. You can make notes about details and features of the draft that you want to pursue further (at the end of the test) as you watch and listen.

DESCRIBE THE TASKS

Explain what it is you want your user to do first. This is when you give test users the handout that you created earlier and allow them a few minutes to read through and ask any questions they have about any part of it. Describe generally what the task is, but do not demonstrate the parts that you are trying to evaluate. If you give them too detailed an overview, they won't need to follow your document to complete the task.

ONCE THE TEST BEGINS, DO NOT TALK TO YOUR TESTER

Once testers have read through the handout and you have answered any questions they have, you should retire from the main stage and keep a low profile while they work. Do not talk to them about what they are doing; do not answer questions that arise during the test. The only point at which you might intervene is if a tester reaches an impasse in the process and is unable to proceed. If the tester is ready to end the test because of some small omission or ambiguity in the draft, then you may interrupt to supply as little information as possible to help the person continue.

The points where your users run into difficulty are incredibly valuable to you as an opportunity to observe and understand the type of strategies your users will attempt in overcoming an obstacle as they interact with the text. You may decide to include trouble-shooting information in your final version based on the types of obstacles users encounter and the efforts they take to remove them. You may also consider adding strategies to help users get started again after they run into a roadblock. The usability test can often reveal to you areas where this type of information could be critical to users' successful experience with the document.

CONCLUDING THE TEST

When the test ends, either with the task being completed or the user becoming too frustrated to continue, explain to the user what you were trying to find out specifically during the test. If testers have questions at this point, be sure to answer them. If you noticed any interesting behaviours during the test, this is your chance to have people explain what they were doing. Finish the interaction with an interview of your test users. Ask them to give you their overall impressions about the document and how easy it was to use. Ask them what they liked about your draft, as well as what they think could be improved. Take notes during the interview part of the test as well so that you have a written record of all of the crucial points that came up during the test.

When you have run the test with each of your users, you should be developing a clear idea about the strengths and shortcomings of your draft. Users' responses, along with your notes and observations during the test, provide the data that you need for the next step of the usability testing process, which is, of course, reporting the results.

Reporting your results

The next step is to assemble and analyse the data from each of your usability tests. If you have taped the tests, then you should go through the tape at this point and make notes about key events that signal problems with your draft. In your written notes, look for points that corroborate or illuminate the taped incidents. If you don't have tape, then review your notes to identify points in the test where users found an opportunity to improve your documentation. Examine the specific suggestions made by your test subjects, and assess whether you think their points are valid and whether revisions addressing these points will improve your draft. Determine whether each problem area was reported by all users or by only one or two; were users' experiences representative or idiosyncratic, do you think? If a problem seems broadly experienced, then it is likely you will need to find a solution.

When you have finished analysing the test results, you are ready to assemble the data and your analysis into a report. Generally, a usability report is two or three pages long, depending upon the number of test subjects to report on and the nature of the problems that arose during the test. You want to include enough detail in the report to show that the test was done properly and the results are reliable, but the report should also be as clear and concise as possible. So you are aiming for brevity and completeness. Here is a list of the information to include and discuss in the report:

- The objectives of the test
- The target users' level of knowledge within the subject matter of the document (optional)
- The test subjects
- The task assigned to test subjects
- What happened during the test
- Comments of the users (optional)
- Plans for revising the document.

Use this list of topics as the headings for your report, and discuss the details in each section.

THE OBJECTIVES

You can base this section on the objectives you listed in your handout to test users. Do remember that your audience for the report is slightly different, so you may want to reword the objectives to better fit your main readers for the report. Also consider whether you should revise these objectives in light of what happened during the test. Perhaps you feel that one of the objectives was not achieved or you now realize that it wasn't appropriate for the test that you ran.

You may change it at this point to better reflect the actual (rather than the projected) experience.

You may also need to revise the tense of these objectives: since the tests are completed, use the past tense in discussing the objectives. If you leave your objectives in the future tense, you can confuse your readers by making them think that maybe you haven't completed the usability testing after all. Avoid creating this kind of confusion because it can undermine your ethos as a competent writer, researcher, and employee.

In Figure 9.2, Lisa Chang opens her usability report with an explanation of how she set up her test and why. She explains that it wasn't feasible to test the draft with people who were actually travelling from Hong Kong to Saskatoon, given that she was then attending school in London, Ontario. However, she did try to compensate for the altered circumstances by testing her subjects orally rather than having them write down responses. She also lists the objectives for her test as bullet points for quick reference.

MEMO

To: Dr. Roger Graves
From: Lisa Chang
Date: February 21, 2007
Re: Manual for first-time flyers travelling from Hong Kong to Saskatoon by Air Canada

Test Objectives:
The best approach to demonstrating the usability of my manual for first-time flyers travelling from Hong Kong to Saskatoon by Air Canada is to ask people from my potential audience to use the manual. However, it is almost impossible to achieve this goal because it is extremely difficult to look for such users in such a limited amount of time. Instead, I devised a set of oral questions for conducting the usability test of my manual. I decided to conduct an oral survey rather than a written survey because I wanted to increase the degree of difficulty. This allows me to simulate the many unpredictable situations, such as time pressure, that will happen to the manual users in real-world situations. I geared the questions towards the novice users who had never travelled from Hong Kong to Saskatoon by Air Canada. This allows me to determine how well they understand the manual and which part of the manual I need to improve upon. I constructed the survey to answer the following questions:

- How easy is it for the users to understand the content of my manual?
- Do the users find the Tips and Cautions helpful?
- Would the users be well prepared for the trip?
- Can the users follow the maps?
- Can the users find the direction to specific locations?
- In actual situations, would the users be able to apply what they have learned?
- Would the users be able to travel successfully on their trips?

FIGURE 9.2
In the objectives section, Lisa Chang explains how she organized the test, given that the typical approach was not feasible for her project.

TARGET USERS' LEVEL OF KNOWLEDGE

This is not a mandatory discussion in a usability report, but, if you do decide to include it, it serves to remind readers of your target audience for the document. It notes your expectations for the background of your target users and for their level of experience with the subject matter of the document. This section is useful depending upon how closely your test subjects fit your user profile. If they were not a perfect match, then this section will help readers understand and evaluate the discrepancy between your test subjects and your actual user group.

This section of the report is usually written in the present tense, since your assessment of the target user group is an ongoing process, taking place neither in the future or past.

The Audience for the Manual:
I decided to aim the test towards English as a second language (ESL) students at U of S who had never travelled from Hong Kong to Saskatoon by Air Canada. This would assess whether my potential audience could comprehend the content of my manual.

The Test Subjects:
Lina Chu, Age 22, travelled by plane twice
Abi Chang, Age 22, travelled by plane twice
Liu Ma, Age 30, travelled by plane three times
John Guan, Age 21, travelled by plane once
Victor Chen, Age 24, travelled by plane twice

The Tasks Assigned to the Subjects:
I provided the subjects with my manual, along with nine specific questions that reflected the three different parts of the trip. The first three questions were designed to reflect the first part regarding how well the users prepared for this trip. The next three questions were designed to reflect the second part concerning whether the users could successfully reach the plane on time. The last three questions were designed to reflect the last part relating to whether the users could successfully exit the Saskatoon airport after landing. The subjects were asked to answer the following questions:

1. How much cash can you legally bring into Canada?
2. How soon should you arrive at the airport before your flight departure?
3. What is the phone number used to confirm the flight reservation?
4. Can you locate the Air Canada check-in counter?
5. Can you tell me the direction from the Hong Kong Immigration to Boarding Gate #28?
6. When must you arrive at the boarding gate if the departure time is 2:30 pm?
7. How would you go to the CBSA if you leave from Gate #5 at the Saskatoon airport?
8. How would you go to retrieve your checked luggage from the CBSA if the Baggage Claim for Air Canada is located at Baggage Claim #5?
9. Where is the Lost & Found?

FIGURE 9.3
In these sections, Chang describes the test subjects and the task assigned to them.

THE TEST SUBJECTS

This section gives relevant details about each of your test users. It explains how closely their demographic profiles fit the profile of your target audience, as well as giving some insight into the variations among test subjects and between test subjects and end users, so your report readers can assess the validity of your usability test. Variations in demographic information might help to account for major differences in the results from each test. Usually, you include first names, ages, background in and level of experience with the subject matter, and any other details that help to provide a context for understanding a later section of the report: what happened during the test.

This and the following sections of the report should be written in the past tense because you have completed all of the stages associated with the usability testing. However, in describing test subjects, you may use the historical present (for example, "Karen is a 45-year-old Canadian woman with extensive travel experience who has lived in Hong Kong for three years but has never flown Air Canada to Saskatoon"). But be sure to switch back to the past tense when describing what happened during the test. Avoid the future or present tense for discussing the tests themselves because either tense raises questions in your readers' minds about whether you have completed the testing: you should not be writing the report if you haven't finished the testing.

In Figure 9.3, Lisa Chang reminds her reader as to the target user group for her manual, and then she lists the test subjects, plus relevant demographic details (age, familiarity with air travel), so report readers can see how closely the testers fit her target audience. In this case, she was able to use test subjects who fit her user profile closely.

TASK ASSIGNED TO USERS

This section summarizes for your reader the task(s) that you assigned to your users. You might copy the series of steps from your test handout into this section, but also provide some brief explanation to supply a context for the steps. The goal in this part of the report is to ensure that readers understand what you had your users do to test the draft document. If the basic test varied slightly from test to test, then you want to make the variations clear in this description. For example, Kat found she couldn't afford the ingredients needed to perform two tests of an old family recipe that she was finally writing down, so she bought the ingredients needed for one test and had her testers create a half batch each. This way she could have two different people work through the recipe without spending all of her grocery money for the month on her usability test. In describing the task assigned to her users in her report, she explained the decisions she had made to solve her financial problem while maintaining, as much as possible, the integrity of her test.

WHAT HAPPENED DURING THE TEST

This section is an important part of your report, so don't skimp on the details. Describe the central experiences of each user separately, even if they seem quite similar. Your goal in this section is to recreate concisely for your reader your experience as an observer during the test. You want to include individual experiences that were informative while also giving a flavour of how the tests went. Your reader is evaluating the validity and reliability of your results based on this section of your account especially. If your discussion is too brief and you lump all of your users together, you create the impression that you were a casual and uninterested observer during the tests because you didn't notice the inevitable, subtle differences between each user's experience with the text. This is also the section of the report that sets the foundation for your recommendations for revision, for the final section of the report. Be sure that the information that you include describing the tests lays out the appropriate evidence that will support those recommendations. For example, if you have decided that you need to reorganize the layout of your instructions, then you should recount in this section of your report the incidents during the usability tests that suggested such a reorganization was necessary. If you plan to add several more visuals to your draft, then, in this section of the report, you want to include some description of your users' difficulties during the test because an important detail was not represented in your existing visuals.

COMMENTS OF THE USERS

This section of the report can be useful because it provides an opportunity for you to make the usability tests come alive for your reader. By including comments made by users during the test, you can bring the different personalities of your test users into the report, a tactic that helps your readers to better imagine the test itself while also strengthening your credibility as a competent researcher. This kind of detail shows that you did conduct the tests, that they were well planned and well run, and that you gathered some excellent feedback with which to improve the next version of the document. This section can also help strengthen your argument in support of the various changes that you are recommending as a consequence of the usability testing. Real people provide important feedback that transforms the quality and clarity of a draft.

PLANS FOR REVISION

Your plans for revision, based on the discussion that has gone before, are the most important part of the report because they distil for your reader the outcome of the tests. In three or four bullet points, you can highlight the main areas that the tests have shown require revision.

This part of the report may be written in future or past tense, depending upon whether you've made the revisions to the draft. There is a strategic advantage to you as the writer to be able to write this section of the report in the past tense; i.e., you've already made all or some of the changes to your draft. If you've already made most of the changes, it helps you to demonstrate your proactive approach to your work. If the usability tests uncovered the need for major, time-consuming changes, you probably can't make those in a few hours. However, you can emphasize the value of the tests for revealing areas that will significantly improve the product documentation

We have found that, sometimes, a student will have difficulties with usability testing because all of his or her test users are so effusive in their praise of the draft that they don't give useful feedback. This uncritical response is sometimes due to a lack of experience with writing or designing instructional material. Sometimes, it is because many of us have become accustomed to using poorly written instructions—as long as we can *eventually* figure them out, we consider them "good enough." While it might be tempting to believe your users when they say your draft is perfect, you should rather assume that there must be something you can do to make it better.

Note that, in Figure 9.4, Lisa Chang uses her test subjects' actions to figure out areas that she might be able to improve in her draft, even though testers didn't have significant suggestions. For example, in the places where the information was complex and required extra time to decipher, she improved the layout and design to make the content more accessible.

Very few technical communicators—even experienced ones—produce a perfectly clear and usable draft the first time. If you review the advice in Chapter 7 on design and in Chapter 8 on writing good instructions, you can probably identify several changes that could improve your draft. Sometimes co-workers, peers, or fellow technical communicators can also make suggestions when your usability testing goes off *too* smoothly.

Here is a list of some of the aspects that can improve the usability of a document:

- Organize information into manageable chunks (See Chapter 8 on chunking information.)
- Position information for emphasis (See Chapter 6 on using emphasis in document design.)
- Provide structuring devices (e.g., tables, index, etc.).

- Identify background knowledge of users (See Chapter 1 on audience.)
- Add labels, headings, and arrows (See Chapter 6 on document design.)
- Use graphics and typefaces as locating devices (See Chapter 6 on using contrast.)

The Results of the Test:
Every tester went through my manual once before answering the questions. The average amount of time it took to go through the manual was six minutes. After users went through the manual, I asked them the questions one by one, and they figured out the answers using the manual. Overall, they seemed to understand the manual very well according to their average response time for the questions. Actually, the average response time was faster than my expectation. Having said that, some of the questions, such as questions 5–8, are strict and comprehensive. These questions resulted in the longest response times. In fact, two people spent much longer than the average response time in answering those questions. Afterwards, I went back to examine those four questions, and I found that they are indeed a lot more complex compared to the remaining questions. However, all those questions that seemed difficult for the testers simply reflect real-world scenarios that might well determine the success of the trip. I believe they provided a good way to test my users. According to the test results, I found my manual offers high usability.

Comments from Participants:
All five participants said the manual was easy to read and understand because of the clear maps and simple language. They found that it would be useful for the trip. One tester even asked me if he could send the manual to his cousin who would be flying to Saskatoon in August!

Revision:
In order to improve the usability, I decided to revise the second part and the last part of my manual. I expanded several sections to improve readability. I also added signs to the maps to identify the user's current location.

FIGURE 9.4
Chang's results from test subjects, and plans for revision.

Rhetorical challenges of writing a usability report
ANALYSING YOUR DATA

Writing a usability report is not particularly difficult, if you run your usability tests well and make good notes about what happens during each test. To make the report as easy on yourself as possible, do the planning up front to ensure that your tests are carefully thought out and well organized. Schedule enough time to both conduct the tests carefully and interview your test subjects adequately at the end.

If you have detailed data from the tests, spend some time analysing your data to sketch out the results of your testing. Sometimes, the major outcomes are obvious because your users point out two or three significant changes that you can make to radically improve your document. Other times, your user feedback isn't as clear or useful. In this case, you will need to study your notes and compare among each of your tests to find common threads and patterns that arise from them. Or you may find that one or two of your users had difficulties, while the other one or two just breezed through with no slow downs or questions at all. This situation also will require some effort on your part to decide whether the difficulties are signs that the draft needs revision. Consider whether your problem-free users share experience or knowledge that you can add to your draft to smooth the way for users with slightly less knowledge or experience.

WRITING THE REPORT

One mistake inexperienced technical communicators may make when writing a usability report is not including enough details about the tests. You may have found your tests uneventful or routine, with each one rather similar to the others, but remember that your readers have no knowledge at all of your test process. So you want to include some specific information about the test subjects and their experiences to recreate what the test was like and how it proceeded.

Your goal in writing the report is basically threefold:

1. to include evidence from the tests that support your later claims regarding essential revisions
2. to demonstrate your skill and competence as an employee (or student) in planning and executing the tests, and
3. to show that the usability testing process yielded valuable insight that will significantly improve the quality and usefulness of your draft documentation.

Evidence for your revision plans

The first three-quarters of the report generally set up an argument outlining the problems that the usability testing revealed with the draft version of the document. The description of the test (its objectives, activities, test subjects, etc.) serves to provide context for your readers about the planning, design, and execution of the tests. Provide enough detail to demonstrate your competence but not so much that the description becomes tedious and overblown.

When you get to your plans for revision, they should evolve logically and naturally out of the preceding description, which noted the different incidents during the tests that identified the major problems. Your revisions should solve each of the problems that came up during the test. If you plan a revision that is unaccounted for in your test narrative, then you will need to explain in the "plans for revision" section why you see this change as necessary: what motivates this change? If too many of your revisions seem spontaneous and unconnected with the testing, then you undercut your implicit argument for the value of usability testing: why should your employer pay you to test documents if the activity doesn't result in a superior product?

Demonstrate your skill and competence

Any document that you write becomes an example of your abilities as a writer. From this perspective, then, you want your usability report to be a clear, concise, and correct piece of writing. Check your spelling and grammar, and also proofread the final version carefully to ensure that the report represents your best work.

The content of the report is equally important. Consider your descriptions in each part of the report as contributing evidence of your competence as a researcher (i.e., usability tests research the ease of use of your drafts) and as an employee. Include enough information to create a context whereby readers can judge your usability tests as well organized and well executed. Also, include a few telling details that add personality to your report—that recreate the tests for your reader. If readers experience a (positive) emotional reaction to your account, they will feel more receptive to your plans for revisions, as well as to any plans you have to continue to test draft documents.

USABILITY TESTING IS VALUABLE

You may wonder why this point is included in this discussion. Usability testing is an expensive activity, and, as Steve Krug points out, many organizations do "too little, too late, and for all the wrong reasons."[6] If executives and bosses understand the value of usability testing early in the production process, you will have the support and time to conduct this testing properly. If they don't understand, you will be part of the process that turns out to be too little and too late, resulting in documentation that causes frustration, alienation, and the refunding of returned products.

Use your usability report as an opportunity to demonstrate the value of the process—how it alerts technical communicators early on to potential problems with particular designs and organizational patterns. When issues are resolved before the eleventh hour, technical communicators can significantly improve the usefulness and quality of documents, boosting product quality and usefulness. Include enough detail to demonstrate the value of the process without belabouring the point.

DESIGN CONSIDERATIONS

Usually a usability report is an internal document, so you can format it as a memo, especially if the testing process was relatively limited in scope and time, testing only half a dozen people. You should address the memo to your supervisor on the job or your instructor if it is a class assignment.

Make sure your memo includes headings as guides to help readers follow the discussion. Standard headings, such as those listed earlier

6   Krug, 140.

in the chapter and in each of the exercises, will help your readers recognize the genre and immediately begin to comprehend your report.

Document design considerations for a report include leaving enough white space to separate and mark section changes and choosing a contrasting typeface for heading titles. Otherwise, make design choices in your usability report that are generally traditional and conservative. The central focus of this type of report is communication, so avoid any design choices that may distract or confuse readers about the message being delivered.

At the same time, include visuals if they support your argument or present test data in an accessible form. For example, technical communicators sometimes graph results from user tests because the visual presents the main point clearly and concisely in the report. Readers can quickly compare different users' experiences through the graphs rather than having to read the same information embedded in two or three paragraphs of text. Of course, the text should refer to the graph and provide the basic context for explaining its contents.

LAB ASSIGNMENT 9.1

REPORT ON USABILITY TESTING YOUR INSTRUCTIONS OR PROCEDURE

Design and conduct a usability test for the assignment you completed for Major Project 8.1.

In designing the test, you want to set several objectives identifying the kind of information you want to gain from your participants. What are you trying to determine about the instructions?

Next, sketch out a brief description of the task or tasks that you want your participants to perform during the test. Prepare a handout (one half to one page long) to give to your test subjects at the beginning of the test. The handout should outline the tasks you'd like them to complete during the test.

Observe three or four people attempting to use your set of instructions or procedure. Make notes about any problems they have or strategies they use to complete the assignment (including when they don't use the document).

After at least three people use your document, write a report describing the objectives of the test, the test itself, and the results of the test. Also include a section detailing how you plan to revise your instructions or procedure based on the results of your test.

Address each of the topics below in your report:
- The test objectives
- The audience for the instructions or procedure
- The test subjects
- The task or tasks assigned to the subjects
- What happened during the test
- Comments from test subjects
- Plans for revision.

For more information about using visuals effectively, see Chapter 2 on using visuals to be clear.

Acting on your plans for revision

Of course, all of your usability designing and testing is wasted if you don't follow through on the plans for revision. Incorporate the suggestions from the report into your draft. When you feel that you have revised the draft to the best of your ability, you should test out this new version again with another set of test subjects to verify that the changes have solved the problems identified in the earlier round of tests. You also want to determine that the changes solve the earlier problems without introducing any new problems. Also, sometimes fixing a glaringly obvious problem helps to reveal some other less obvious but still significant problems. A further round of testing can assure you that your revisions have generally improved the documentation. As Steve Krug notes, "Testing is an iterative process. Testing isn't something you do once. You make something, test it, fix it, and test it again."[7]

7   Krug, 143.

EVALUATING THE USABILITY OF YOUR MANUAL

Design and conduct a usability test to evaluate how easy it is to use the manual that you wrote for Major Project 8.2.

In designing the test, set several objectives identifying the kind of information you want to gain from your participants. What are you trying to determine about the manual?

Next, sketch out a brief description of the tasks that you want your participants to perform during the test. Prepare a handout (one half to one page long) to give to test subjects, a handout that outlines the tasks that you'd like them to complete during the test.

Observe three or four people attempting to use the part of your manual that you have selected for this test. Make notes about any problems they have or strategies they use to complete the assignment (including when they don't use your manual).

After at least three people use your document, write a report addressed to your instructor describing the objectives of the test, the test itself, and the results of the test. Also include a section detailing how you expect to revise your manual based on the results.

Address each of the topics below in your report:

- The test objectives
- The audience for the manual
- The test subjects
- The tasks assigned to the subjects
- What happened during the test
- Comments from subjects
- Plans for revision.

CHAPTER TEN

Taking technical communication online
Sharing documents electronically and writing online documents

What is structured documentation?

An ongoing problem that faces organizations is how to continue to make company documents easily available as they update their hardware and software. For example, when BrilliantTechSolutions Ltd. decided to replace its now dated machines running Windows 98, it had to upgrade all of its company software, the operating system, and associated software programs. After doing so, BrilliantTechSolutions had hundreds of important files created with the old system that it still needed to be able to use. While most new versions of a software program allow you to continue to open files created with older versions, a straight transfer can sometimes lose the formatting in a complex document because of fundamental changes to the structure of the program.

To minimize this kind of disruption and the wasted effort needed to reformat complex documents, most organizations have moved to structured documentation as a way to maintain continuity as they upgrade their systems. Structured documentation refers to the use of software style sheets to accomplish two goals:

- Emphasize the organizational structure of the document
- Facilitate transferring the document from one program to another.

Writers use the style sheets to assign a specific format to each aspect of the document, such as major and subordinate headings, ordered and unordered lists, or typeface changes. When you use style sheets to format your document, it forces you to first articulate the document's organization to yourself and then reveal this organization as you write the document, so your use and formatting of headings, tables, bold and italic fonts, numbered sections, etc., then makes clear to your reader the organizational structure of the document. For example, when you have to decide what level of heading applies to a particular section, your choice signals to the reader important

FIGURE 10.1
The "Styles and Formatting" menu bar in Word.

information about the relationship between this section and the document as a whole.

Style sheets work by coding particular types of text in particular ways. If you apply a heading style to the titles of your major sections then each one will be formatted using the same size, weight, structure, form, and colour. A different level of heading then uses a different size, weight, structure, form, or colour, and the change in formatting signals a changed level and importance, as well as the relationship between this section and the rest of the document. For example, a major heading suggests that the information in this section is both important and general; sub-headings signal that this information is more specific and detailed. Understanding how the different heading levels communicate importance helps you to decide which level to assign and how to format more specific, detailed, and perhaps less important information. Figure 10.1 illustrates the styles and formatting menu bar in Word, and it depicts the style choices for the chapter of a book. Other word processing programs also have available style sheets that you can adapt to your document.

You can either generate your own style sheets for a document or use the default formatting established in your word processing program. Some organizations have a style sheet that they prefer their employees to use on all documents. In this case, the main challenge for writers is to figure out how to use the style sheet to format the document that they are preparing.

However, if you can create a style sheet to suit your document, your process of design can be quite creative as you select the font forms, weights, and structures that best represent your subject matter. Think of the style sheet as an aid to improving the usability of your document by making its organization visible.

Style sheets are also valuable because they enable you to format long, complex documents and then automatically generate tables of contents, indexes, lists of figures, etc., for the final version, whether this version is printed and bound or posted on the web. If you have formatted the file using a style sheet, then even radical revisions to your draft will not mean increased time regenerating the table of contents; each chapter title, heading, and subheading is easily discerned because of the style you have assigned to it.

When all of the organizational features of a document are coded with a particular formatting, the document can be transferred into a different program or program version, and the style sheet application will ensure that all formatting and design are preserved. Consider the time it would take to re-enter and reformat a long, complex document, and you will understand what makes the use of style sheets so important. This valuable feature enables organizations to upgrade their technology without losing the hundreds or thousands of documents essential to their success.

What this means for you as a potential employee is that you should make yourself proficient in the use of style sheets, whether for word processing or web design. You can begin by figuring out how to use the style sheets associated with your software programs as you prepare the assignments in this volume.

Converting documents to portable document file (PDF) format

One of the issues associated with transferring document files around an organization is the potential for changing or editing the draft. When multiple writers collaborate on a document, then having each contribute her or his share is a good thing. However, when you need to distribute a document that you don't want changed or edited, a useful solution is to convert the file to a PDF, or portable document file. In the past, the only way to create PDFs was through purchasing Adobe Acrobat and adding it to your word processing program, but the recent version of Word offers the capability of turning a document file into a PDF without the expense of a second program.

Many organizations have found PDFs to be extremely useful for distributing technical and company documents. For example, a software engineer at a robotics company notes that he creates products and then documents them in PDF files that clients can download from the company website. This publishing of instructional technical documents online is a growing trend because customers can quickly and easily locate the most up-to-date documentation; then they can read it on screen or print off the pages that they need to use.

One point to note when converting a document file to a PDF is that the conversion should be your last step before distributing the file, because, after you have converted your document to an uneditable PDF, *you* can't make changes to it either. Any changes have to be made in the original source file, and then the document has to be converted again to a new PDF file.

Sharing documents electronically

There are a variety of different ways to share documents electronically. You are likely familiar with email attachments, which allow you to send word processing files or images with an email message. Documents sent as email attachments represent the fastest and easiest way to disseminate information or projects around a company. One problem with sending email documents, however, is the potential incompatibility of the senders' and recipients' operating platforms or word processing software. For example, documents composed on a Mac and written using some word processing programs will sometimes not open with a PC.

HOW TO USE RICH TEXT FORMAT (RTF) FILES TO SOLVE SYSTEM OR PROGRAM INCOMPATIBILITY

While some organizations regulate the word processing programs that their employees may use to create company documents, others let theirs select whichever program they prefer. As files are sent back and forth between individuals with different word processing programs and sometimes operating systems (e.g., Mac vs. PC), the incompatibility of file formats can cause headaches for recipients who cannot open attachments that are incompatible with their machines or software.

An excellent solution to software or machine incompatibility is the rich text format file (RTF). For example, if you save a Word or WordPerfect document as an RTF file, you preserve most of the formatting of the original file, while also creating a version of the file that will open for different operating systems and software programs. Figure 10.2 shows you how to convert a Word document to an RTF file.

Note that when recipients wish to retrieve an RTF file, they need to enable all types of files after the "Open" command. This step requires making sure that Word has not, by default, allowed access only to "Word Documents." Scroll through the file type menu until you come to a more general category (e.g., "All Files" or "All Documents") and select it.

Shared folders and documents posted online

A growing trend in many organizations is to make documents available on line and in shared folders on the company intranet. When documents are posted in shared folders on a server, people at differ-

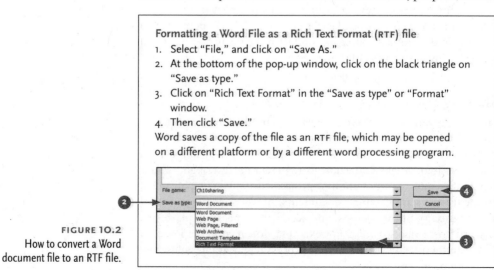

Formatting a Word File as a Rich Text Format (RTF) file

1. Select "File," and click on "Save As."
2. At the bottom of the pop-up window, click on the black triangle on "Save as type."
3. Click on "Rich Text Format" in the "Save as type" or "Format" window.
4. Then click "Save."

Word saves a copy of the file as an RTF file, which may be opened on a different platform or by a different word processing program.

FIGURE 10.2
How to convert a Word document file to an RTF file.

ent locations can help draft documents by accessing the files from the folders, adding information based on their areas of expertise, and then reposting the updated file for others to work on. This technology streamlines the collaborative process and contributes to overall productivity in significant ways. An advantage to using files in shared folders is that access to the files can be controlled. Supervisors set permissions on the shared folders to control who can access the files and who can make changes. Usually, shared folders are only available to the individuals authorized to work on the particular files stored there, and employees must enter their identification information into the system to access these files.

If you do not need to control access to a word processing file, then you can post it as a downloadable document on a web page. For example, many instructors make course syllabi and assignments available on course websites where students can view and download the assignments as needed. Once the file is opened in a word processing program, individuals can make changes to the text of the file or cut and paste text from it into a new file. This function is particularly useful for posting forms that may be downloaded, filled out, and then emailed to the appropriate department or individual.

POSTING A DOCUMENT FILE ON A WEB PAGE

Posting a word processing file onto a web page is relatively simple. It requires three steps:

1. Update the web page by adding a hypertext link to the document
2. Upload the document file and the revised web page
3. Set page permissions (if necessary).

Update the web page by adding a link to the document

There are two ways to add a link to your webpage. One is to create the link by adding it directly into the page source code using HTML. This is the fastest way to update the page if you know how to code.

If not, the second way is to download the page, add the link, and then upload it to the website again:

1. Using a file transfer protocol (FTP) program (such as ssh or telnet) or website development software (e.g., Dreamweaver, FrontPage, or Composer), download the web page file to your local computer.
2. Add a brief but descriptive phrase to the web page to identify the link as the source for the document. For example, "Download the syllabus for English 204." You can use a web design program for this step.
3. Make the phrase into a hypertext link. See Figure 10.3 for an example of an HTML link that enables you to put a docu-

ment file on a web page for users to download.

> NOTE: Figure 10.3 uses a Word file as an example, but you could also save the document as an RTF file and post it on the website to ensure that the file is available to a broader range of users—beyond just those with Word.

4. Save the web page file with the new link.

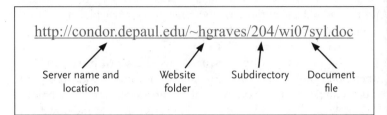

FIGURE 10.3
An HTML link that enables
users to download an
editable document file.

Upload the document file and the revised web page

1. Being sure to place it in the same subdirectory where you found it, FTP the updated web page back to your website.
2. FTP the document file into the same subdirectory as the web page with the link to it.

Set page permissions (if necessary)

1. Set the page permissions to allow visitors to the website to view and download the document file.

You can also use this method to upload other types of files to make them available for downloading: PowerPoint, Lotus Notes, etc., depending upon the nature of the files that you wish to make available to others.

CREATING AN ELECTRONIC PORTFOLIO

One way to use this electronic file sharing technology as a student or practicing professional is to create a portfolio of your technical communication projects that may be accessed on line. You may decide to save all of your completed work as a series of PDF files so that you and potential clients have easy access to past projects, or you might choose to design a special portfolio that presents sections of various exemplary projects. Of course, you can have print and online versions of your portfolio. If you print out your documents and put them into a binder, you have a portable record of your work that you can take to display and discuss at job interviews.

Depending upon the type of work you would like to do and the type of skills you have developed, you should post examples of your work that demonstrate the breadth and depth of your abilities. Some of the examples should be print, and others should be online documents, since technical communicators can be required to work in a variety of media. If you currently lack technical communication skills in a particular area or medium, now is the time to begin enhancing your skills by learning more about the area that is unfamiliar. Good books exist that can help you get started learning the basics of such topics as web design or page layout. Other books teach you how to use specific programs, e.g., Dreamweaver or FrontPage for website development or InDesign or Publisher for the production of print materials.

Of course, learning new software programs requires access to them; many software companies offer academic versions of their programs which you, as a student at your institution, can purchase and download on line for significantly less that the commercial version. While you can continue to use the academic version after you graduate, the software licensing agreements stipulate that you will not use the academic versions for creating documents that you plan to sell commercially. The academic versions of these software programs do not contain all of the functions of the commercial versions, but they are definitely complete enough so that you can become a proficient user of the program. At some educational institutions, you can buy the academic versions of many software programs through the campus bookstore.

If you decide to put together an electronic portfolio, you can probably post it on the personal website allotted to you by your educational institution or by your Internet provider. Do take a hard, critical look at the homepage to which you link your job application materials (including your electronic portfolio), and assess the site for its professionalism. When you send potential employers to your site, you want to make sure that they get a favourable first impression based on your website. If you have personalized your website to the point that it presents too much humorous, casual, or private, non-professional information about yourself, you might consider creating a second website for your professional development materials, so you *can* safely distribute that site's URL to potential employers. The goals of a personal website are usually very different and not necessarily compatible with the goals of a job search website.

What if I don't have a homepage to display my portfolio?

Most Internet providers allot each of their users space on their servers to host a website. This server space can be anywhere between 2 and 10 MB of memory. If you need additional space, it is usually available for an extra charge.

To access your server space, you usually need a program such as telnet or ssh or FTP, which are DOS-based programs that allow you to navigate to the series of subdirectories where you can post your website pages. You also need to know the name of the server where you can upload your files as well as the name of the home folder for your pages. In the example in Figure 10.4, the name of the server is "condor.depaul.edu" and the name of the website or home folder is "~hgraves." If you were to use ssh to look at the files posted in the "hgraves" folder, you would see a series of folders, one of which is named "public_html." All of the website files will be stored in the "public_html" folder: when someone wishes to visit your site, and they type in the URL that you have given them, the web browser automatically looks in the "public_html" folder for a file named "index.htm." The browser displays your "index.htm" page as the homepage for your site.

The index or home page should display links that allow visitors to move beyond the main page to other pages that you have created, including your electronic portfolio.

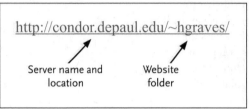

http://condor.depaul.edu/~hgraves/

Server name and location Website folder

FIGURE 10.4
An HTML link that enables users to download an editable document file.

Writing online documents

Internet and wireless technology have paved the way for technical documentation that is inexpensive to distribute and easily and cheaply updated. Electronic versions of documents, whether manuals, assembly instructions, or résumés, can be accessed from anywhere in the world if you have the appropriate technology. Given these facts, more and more organizations prepare technical documents that may be viewed exclusively online or downloaded and printed off. Others develop multimedia support documents intended to be viewed onscreen from a CD, DVD, or website.

This chapter focuses on how to develop web-based documents intended to be viewed and used onscreen. If you want to make the documents available for users to download and print, then a different, print friendly version should be linked to the web page because documents that originate on screen are usually formatted to take best advantage of the screen format and of online capabilities. In this chapter, you will find information about the basics of structuring and developing web-based technical documentation. Good visual design and legible display largely determine how and what your online document communicates.

Online documents are better understood as units of organized information, and the computer becomes a medium of communication or interface between users and the information. In this context, then, you can easily understand that your role as a communicator involves not only finding the right words but also packaging those words in chunks that correspond to the information needs of users.

Documents intended to be used solely online do have some drawbacks, from a user's perspective. They are hard to read, despite the increasing quality of resolution of computer screens. They are also not always available; without access to a computer, or when the website or network malfunctions, people will not be able to get to the information. Comfort levels with electronic technology also vary widely among users: some people dislike and distrust computers, so they find this source of information alien and intimidating. Another drawback relates to lack of portability; for instructions that people will be using in the kitchen or the workshop or someplace their computer is not, print has its advantages.

On the other hand, online versions of texts offer distinct advantages to bound, print versions. If users do have access to Internet technology, they have almost instant access to the information they need. If users have special needs, those can be much more easily accommodated in computer-based information (as opposed to in a traditional book format) through alternate tags that provide verbal descriptions of images, programs that read text aloud, screen settings that magnify text, and other ever-improving innovations.

From a technical communicators' perspective, online documents also represent a number of advantages. You can improve your product quickly and cheaply, correcting errors and ambiguities as they come to light. You can update rapidly by posting new versions online that users can immediately access. It is also much less costly to upload a new version of an operation manual to a website or burn it onto a CD than to print, bind, and distribute a new edition of the same manual. Mind you, distributing CDs requires packaging and postage to get the new version to customers and clients, so such a format doesn't entirely eliminate these costs, the way web-based versions do. Computer files take up less shelf space than do bound volumes, so electronic storage reduces the need for actual storage space. Finally, documents that are available online mean promoting a healthier environment, at least in terms of reduced paper production and recycling: hundreds or thousands of copies of print manuals that fairly rapidly go out of date do not need to be distributed and/or discarded every year. Even if users are printing out copies of online manuals, they rarely print the whole volume; instead they print off the sections that they need.

HOW DO YOU PREPARE DOCUMENTS FOR ON SCREEN USE?

Word processing documents should not be converted directly to web pages, because the onscreen medium entirely changes users' experiences. Creating web-based documents is really all about web usability—that is, can users accomplish their goals using the page design and text presentation of your website? There are two parts to effective web usability: page design and text legibility. But before we get into specific strategies for design and legibility, here are a few general points underlining the ways in which web documents differ from print documents:

- Page orientation is different
- Resolution on screen is poorer
- Blank pages confuse users
- Page navigation requires special attention.

Page orientation is different

FIGURE 10.5
Horizontal orientation
of computer screen.

A computer screen has a horizontal or landscape orientation, while a paper page has a vertical or portrait one. Figures 10.5 and 10.6 compare the two orientations. The change means that lines of text can be much longer on a computer screen than on a printed page. Nevertheless, line lengths of online documents should be short enough so that users don't skip lines as their eyes travel from the end of one line back to the beginning of the next line. A good rule is to format lines of *between 40 and 60 characters long*. This way, your pages will fit on smaller sized screens without users having to scroll side to side.

Resolution on screen is poorer

FIGURE 10.6
Vertical orientation
of printed page.

The resolution on a screen is much poorer than on a printed page, so reading on screen represents a more tiring experience for users, since their eyes must work harder to decipher the text. Online displays can also reverse light and dark, which enables you to create dynamic visual effects. At the same time, poorly designed dark backgrounds with light lettering can greatly increase the eye strain of readers attempting to locate and use information. Make sure your background and text colour choices are high contrast: white background with dark lettering (i.e., black, navy blue, charcoal grey); or dark background (i.e., black, navy blue, etc.) with white or light lettering. Figure 10.7 shows two potential screen design choices: the one on the left is a high contrast choice of text and background, with black lettering against a white background. The design on the right uses a low contrast with dark grey background and a lighter grey text. Obviously, your eyes would quickly get tired of looking at the design on the right, and, if it were onscreen, you might quickly decide not to read this page at all.

Don't use blank pages

Readers of traditional books all recognize the convention of blank pages: a blank page signals the end of one chapter and the beginning of the next. Documents that are meant to be read on screen should not use blank pages, however, because they confuse users: blank pages on screen mean no information—the user took a wrong turn in navigating the website or the page is incomplete. Avoid setting up any visual cue that will confuse and alienate your users.

> This screen design uses a high contrast (i.e., black text on white background). Do you find it easy to read?

> This screen design uses low contrast (i.e., medium grey text on a dark grey background). Which would you rather read?

FIGURE 10.7
Two screen designs, one using high and the other using low contrast in their text-background design choices.

Plan your document navigation

A print book may be accessed by flipping through its pages: using this method, people can often stumble upon the information they need without consulting locating devices such as the index or table of contents. If they do use the table of contents or index, the page numbers help them quickly locate the specific section or page that they need. In contrast, users cannot "flip through" web pages, nor can they consult page numbers on screen to be sure they have found the correct location of the information they need. Since users must use search functions or hypertext links to locate specific pieces of information, you have to plan your onscreen document thoroughly to ensure a clear and logical organization with plenty of visual and organizational cues to help direct users to the pages they need. Such cues include a clear, prominently placed navigation bar or menu on each page; a site map, which illustrates the overall organization of the document, and perhaps a site map link (on each page); and (if you have programming skills or technical support) a search function that allows users to search the site for the particular information they need. (Note: you can also add a search function to a website if you agree to the terms of various search engines, e.g., Google or Yahoo. See http://www.google.ca/services/websearch.html for an example.)

HOW DO YOU ENSURE A GOOD VISUAL DESIGN?

This section outlines some strategies that you can use to create a usable and effective web page design. Here is a quick summary:

- Divide the screen into functional areas
- Group related items
- Guide users' eye movements
- Put action areas near where users will look for them
- Use consistent design throughout the site.

Divide the screen into functional areas

Figure out how much space on the screen will be devoted to your content. (It varies, depending upon the basic screen size, the browser real estate area, the navigational bar or menu, and other factors.) Then decide where, generally, you will place types of content. For example, your navigational bar should appear in the same place on every page. Designate a particular location that is visible and convenient for the navigational system. If your document content is instructional, then you should also designate a general area on the screen page for visuals and text. Similarly, links to previous and next pages should be consistently placed from page to page. Figure 10.8 uses a storyboard to sketch out a potential page layout. Storyboarding is a term borrowed from graphic design that describes the activity of sketching out potential layouts so that you can try various imaginative designs to decide which one will most clearly and effectively convey your information.

Group related items

Put related items in close proximity to one another on the page. Navigational tools should be located close to informational links, so users will look in that general area for other pages that they can jump to. If text and image are related, then a visual and the text that accompanies it should be side by side. Labels should appear beside visuals. Don't make users hunt for related information in case they fail to make the connection that you had intended.

Guide users' eye movements

Even as early as the storyboarding stage, you should think about how to guide users' eyes across the page and how you might most successfully control this movement. You can gain control (and through it users' success at understanding the page content) through your placement of items on the page and the prominence that you assign to specific items based on their location, size, and colour. For example, the key pieces of information on each page should appear above the scroll line when the page loads. Headings should stand out from explanatory text (through the use of white or black space, font size, and colour). The navigational tools should be easily distinguishable from page content, illustrations, or less important information.

Put action areas near where users will look for them when needed

Once you have thought carefully about the path that users' eyes will take across the page, use this information to decide where to place items. For example, in a web-based tutorial, the navigational button that takes users to the next step should appear right after the last step in this stage of the process. Users' eyes will naturally move to the next line, expecting a clue about what to do next. Similarly, when users reach the bottom of the page, they will expect a button that takes them either back to the top of the page or to the next page. As you make decisions about the appropriate location for different items, begin usability testing your web page to verify the accuracy and validity of your understanding of how users will examine the page.

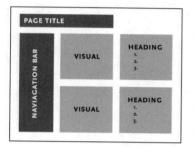

FIGURE 10.8
Storyboard of a web page for online instructions.

Use consistent design throughout

Develop your design for the website or online document, and maintain the design throughout. Use consistency of design as a signal to readers about where to look for particular information, as well as a means for them to understand what they are looking at and make sense of it when first viewing a page. If you locate navigational systems in the same place on the page, with the same design for buttons and labels, then users will quickly learn to look there and recognize the links they need to move around your website. If you use the same size and font choice for headings of equal importance, you can convey at a glance the relationship between major sections and subsections.

Here are some basic rules for designing screens:

- Simplify the display
- Replace text with graphics
- Use black (white) space actively.

SIMPLIFY THE DISPLAY

Prune away all inessential information on the screen. Make sure what is there is useful and related to the main point of the page.

REPLACE TEXT WITH GRAPHICS

Online reading is unpleasant because of the eye strain produced from the relatively poor resolution of the screen. For this reason, reduce the basic text as much as possible: distil it to its essentials. Wherever possible, replace text with graphics. Use the brilliant colours available on screen to depict information in a way that has a high impact. Rather than describing in words what a product or concept is like, reproduce an image of it. The visual attracts the eye, conveys concise information about the item, and reduces the reading load for users. Add some text if it is necessary as an aid to understanding page content, but keep it brief and legible.

USE BLACK (WHITE) SPACE ACTIVELY

The background of a web page constitutes black or white space. Think of this space as a useful resource for emphasizing the items that you place on it. If you want users to notice a particular detail, then leave space around it, so it emerges from the background in a dramatic way. Especially avoid cramming too much information on a screen. Because those who design websites often work on a big computer screen, they may be tempted to create two columns of information or to load up the part of the web page above the scroll bar. But too much can subvert excellence in design by contributing to a busy, confusing presentation, not to mention that those people with smaller screens will be angrily scrolling side to side to view the page.

Think in terms of space around items as a way to help users orient themselves to the important information that you present.

HOW DO YOU ENSURE THAT YOUR SCREEN DISPLAY IS LEGIBLE?

This section deals with techniques for writing effectively for the web. It takes into account how users read or process text during their web surfing activities, and it will help you maximize the likelihood that your onscreen text will be read and your users will find the information that prompted them to go online. Jakob Nielsen, an important figure in web usability, has suggested three simple rules for writing effectively:

- Be succinct
- Write for scanability
- Use hypertext links to split up long information into multiple pages.

Be succinct

Nielsen bases his command to be succinct (i.e., brief and concise) on the fact that reading from computer screens is 25 per cent slower than reading from paper. Consequently, you should write 50 per cent less than you would if you were preparing the same information for a paper-based document.

Check the spelling in your document before you post the site. If you have generated it in a web design program (which doesn't have spellchecking capabilities), you can copy and paste the text into a word processing program and run the spelling check then. Even when you have corrected all the errors that show up, don't consider yourself finished until you also copyedit the text as well. This is a final opportunity for you to catch sloppy language and to remove any extraneous words—to make the online text as succinct as possible.

ADDRESS READERS DIRECTLY

Don't address your readers in the third person (i.e., he/she); instead use the second person (i.e., you). This type of address reduces the distance between you and your reader, resulting in a more comfortable learning situation for your reader. It is also the most concise form of address. You want to use the fewest words to convey the most information.

USE THE ACTIVE VOICE

Active voice is a grammatical term that refers to putting the noun that is "doing" the action described by the verb in the subject position of a sentence. For example, "the dog chased the squirrel" uses the active voice because the "dog," the subject of the sentence, is doing the chasing of the "squirrel," which is the object of the action (the one being done to). The alternative voice is the passive voice (e.g., "The squirrel was chased by the dog"). In the passive voice, the receiver or object of the action appears in the subject position (i.e., the squirrel), and readers must delay understanding the whole sentence until they get to the end. (What is the squirrel doing? Oh, the squirrel is not the main actor in the sentence. It's the dog.) This delay results in a less efficient means of communicating your meaning. It also adds extra words to the sentence, making it longer than it needs to be. A more significant problem, sometimes, is that the passive voice allows people to write a sentence without any real actor, causing ambiguity and imprecision, i.e., "The squirrel was chased." Consider this instruction in the passive voice: "It should be noted that one of the labels listed by Word may be adapted if the desired label is not listed in the Product Number box, or custom labels may be created." Now here is a revision in the active voice: "If you cannot find the label you want listed in the Product Number box, create your own custom label or adapt one of those listed." Use the active voice because it is the most concise, direct, and unambiguous.

WRITE SIMPLE, ACTIVE SENTENCES OR IMPERATIVE SENTENCES

Simple sentences (e.g., subject + verb + object) written in the active voice are direct, short, and easy to understand. They don't contain clauses that add to the complexity of the ideas and the time required to process these ideas. When you are writing prose that will be read or used online, keep your sentences short and simple to compensate for the added difficulty of reading and processing online information. (See Chapter 4 for more information about sentence types.)

Imperative sentences are phrased as commands: "Choose the design that you want to apply to your oral presentation." They address the reader directly, they contain directive statements intended to instruct the reader, and they are concise. When you need to address the user directly, especially in a tutorial or other type of teaching situation, use the imperative to communicate the users' next step clearly and concisely.

UNDER-PUNCTUATE

While you still want to include capital letters at the start of sentences and periods at the end, usability researchers suggest that you can omit many of the commas that you might use in a print document. When read on screen, commas add additional visual interference that users must process, but often they do not help to clarify the meaning of a sentence. For this reason, you can leave out commas from a sentence that is otherwise clear. For example, a comma that separates an introductory element from the main part of the sentence can be left out unless the sentence is unclear without it. Commas separating a "which" clause from the rest of the sentence can usually be omitted as well. Similarly, you can leave off the commas at the end of each item in a bulleted list since, on screen, they interfere with understanding rather than clarify.

AVOID WORD VARIETY

When you are writing text that will be read online, re-use the same words rather than scouring your thesaurus for replacements. Since your goal is to produce clear and concise text, repeat key words to ensure clear connections between sentences rather than using synonyms. The clearer and more concise your text is the quicker your users will be able to scan and understand it. In fact, readers on screen skim rather than read text: the repetition of vocabulary assists them by helping them to fill in the information around the repeated words. When you introduce a new word, they have to pause to determine whether it is a new concept or merely a synonym. If it turns out to be a synonym, they slowed their work for nothing, resulting in some momentary confusion and then irritation.

Write for scanability

Usability research shows that users do not read online text fully: they scan it, picking up key words and phrases. Anything that seems extraneous, they skip. Knowing this, you want to structure your information using two or even three levels of headings to help users assess the relevance of the section to their needs. Also, use headings that are informative and descriptive. Based on the heading that precedes it, users should be able to identify easily what the content of the section will be. Actually, they will make judgments about the content based on your headings whether these are well written and descriptive or not. If the heading doesn't suggest relevance, they will skip over a particular section.

Avoid formatting long, uniform blocks of text. Use bulleted lists to highlight or emphasize specific points. If the order of the points is significant, use a numbered list. After you have formatted a bul-

LAB ASSIGNMENT 10.1

CONVERTING PRINT TO ONLINE TEXT

Find a sample text that was intended to be read in print (it can be one you wrote for this or another class) and rewrite it using the guidelines described in the previous section to make it comprehensible for reading online. Before you begin, decide on the level of knowledge and the background of your target readers and adapt your vocabulary and level of detail to meet their needs. Ideally, this assignment should be done on screen using a web design program such as Dreamweaver, Frontpage, GoLive, or Netscape Composer.

leted list with your key points, add short paragraphs elaborating each point. The idea is to provide users with multiple levels of detail. If they find a bullet point that is relevant or interesting, they will look further for more information on that point.

Use highlighting to emphasize key words, but do not underline text as a strategy to add emphasis. Remember that underlining on web pages means clickable links; underlining text for emphasis will be guaranteed to confuse and annoy users. Instead, use coloured text or a contrasting font for emphasis. At the same time, assess whether your choice of strategy to add emphasis might be confused by some users as signalling a hypertext link. If you think some confusion might arise, look further for a more effective means of highlighting key words.

Use hypertext links to divide long information into multiple pages

Here is one process for deciding how to split your information into multiple pages:

1. Divide your subject matter into coherent chunks that progress logically from one to the next. Each chunk should focus on only one topic.
2. Connect each chunk with a hypertext link.
3. Begin each page with an informative heading that identifies the main topic of the section.
4. Under the heading, subdivide the topic into a bulleted list of key points associated with this topic. (See Figure 10.9.)
5. Under the bulleted list, repeat a short version of each key point as a heading and elaborate the main ideas associated with each point by using another series of bullet points or a two- or three-sentence paragraph. If you use short paragraphs, make sure each one begins with an informative topic sentence.
6. Move on to the next point in the order that you listed them at the top of the page.

Generally, detailed information prepared for online display is written using journalistic conventions with the conclusion and significant information placed at the opening of the discussion. From there, you follow the conventions of the inverted pyramid, moving from the most important details to less important details. The assumption is that readers will quit reading when they reach the level of detail that coincides with their interest in the subject matter. Usability researchers also recommend using informative topic sentences at the beginning of paragraphs and using primarily simple sentence structure. Because of the difficulty of online reading, you do not have to worry about readers becoming bored with simple sentence structure. Since they are not actually reading but skimming the information, a simple sentence structure helps them to skim more efficiently.

How do you decide when to start a new page? A rule proposed by usability researchers is that all of the important information should be visible on the top half of the screen to minimize scrolling. Some users refuse to scroll down on a page, so important points that appear below the scroll line may be overlooked by impatient users. Figure 10.9 provides one example of how to use these guidelines to introduce a topic intended to be read online.

Name titles and headings effectively

When you are writing headings for topic sections (or even titles for your web pages), there are a few points to keep in mind to increase the usability of your pages.

- Eliminate articles (i.e., "A," "An," and "The") from the beginnings of titles because they interfere with users' scanning of the page. Demonstrative pronouns such as "this," "that," or "these," as well as indefinite pronouns such as "some," "many," or "few" can also clutter up the beginning of your titles. If the first word that readers encounter is not meaningful, their attempts to skim are slowed rather than helped.

- Move the information-carrying terms towards the beginning of headings and titles so that the key information reaches the reader as quickly as possible. For example, revise a title that says "A lecture on web usability" to read "Web usability: Strategies and guidelines."

- Give each page a different title that indicates content. Don't confuse the title of a page with the filename assigned to it. When you are setting up the page design, also assign a title to appear in the title bar on the users' Internet browser. If you don't name each page descriptively and individually, you will thwart users' attempts to search for information. Search engines use page titles to locate information about topics: if you haven't assigned a descriptive title to your page, it will be overlooked during the search process. For example, revise a web page title that reads "English 204: Technical Writing" to read "Technical Writing lectures and assignments, Fall 2007."

USE STANDARD WEB DESIGN CONVENTIONS

Web design conventions are your friend. Use them because visitors to your site will be expecting to use your site the way they use other sites. Conventional site design allows users to quickly and easily understand navigational issues: if you subvert the conventions, for example by **not** underlining hypertext links, then users will be momentarily confused about which elements on the page are links and which are not.

In *Don't Make Me Think!*, an excellent book on web usability, Steve Krug explains why you want to design a website or online document that is clear and obvious: "every question mark adds to our cognitive workload [as users], distracting our attention from the task at hand. The distractions may be slight but they add up, and sometimes it doesn't take much to throw us. As a rule, people don't *like* to puzzle over how to do things. The fact that people who built the site didn't care enough to make things obvious—and easy—can erode our confidence in the site and its publishers."[1] To maintain your users' confidence in your ability as a technical communicator, use Internet conventions in your site or document design so that they can focus on the information that you are presenting and not on how to use the site.

WEB USABILITY: WRITING FOR THE WEB

Three rules for writing
1. Keep texts short
2. Write for scanability
3. Use hypertext to split information into multiple pages

KEEP TEXTS SHORT
People won't read a lot of text on a computer screen.
Reading from computer screens is 25% slower than reading from paper.
Write 50% less (not 25% less) than you would in print.

SCANABILITY
Users scan text and pick out key words
To write for scanability
- Use two, even three levels of subheads
- Use meaningful (not "cute") headings
- Use bulleted lists and uniform design
- Use highlight and emphasis

USE HYPERTEXT LINKS
Chunk information into short pages connected by links.
Split the information into coherent chunks that each focus on one topic.
Start with the conclusion; add detail.
Use inverted pyramid
- Put key points at beginning
- List supporting detail in descending order of importance
Use informative topic sentences.
Use simple sentence structure.

What are the conventions?

- Underlined text is a hypertext link.
- Blue underlined text is an active link.
- Purple or red underlined text is a previously visited link.
- Use high contrast colours for text and backgrounds.
- Use plain or very subtle background patterns.
- Never use all caps anywhere on the page.
- Left-align almost all text.
- Use sans-serif fonts for body text.
- Make it obvious what is a clickable link.
- If you use animations or music clips, have them cycle twice and then stop or enable users to stop both by "rolling" a mouse over an accessible part of the web page.
- Make buttons and explanatory text both "hot" (i.e., links).
- Use vertical, left-aligned lists of links rather than centred or right-aligned.
- Use moderate line lengths (i.e., 40 to 60 characters maximum for text blocks).

FIGURE 10.9
Numbered list introduces the main topics. Under each heading are key points. Individual pages, linked to this one, would elaborate on each point in two or three sentences. Underlined text indicates links to related pages.

---

1   Steve Krug, *Don't Make Me Think: A Common Sense Approach to Web Usability* (Berkeley, CA: New Riders Press, 2000), 15. (Italics are in the original.)

UNDERLINING

On a web page, underlining means a hypertext link. Don't use underlining to emphasize titles, unless these are also links. Use bolding or contrasting colours or fonts to emphasize headings or important points.

BLUE TEXT

On a web page, blue text usually means an active link that the user hasn't visited before. For this reason, use the colour blue to indicate hypertext links. Of course, as more and more people become proficient with the Internet, they will be able to navigate past non-traditional design elements such as links in different colours than blue or active links that don't use underlined text. However, to accommodate your site to the broadest number of users, follow as many of the conventions as you can.

PURPLE LINKS

Generally, hypertext links that have been visited change colour to help users see where they have been, so they don't waste time clicking to a page that they've already visited. Traditionally, previously visited links change from blue to purple, and users appreciate being able to see quickly and easily where they have been on the website.

HIGH CONTRAST

Since the computer screen is lit from behind, extended viewing of the screen causes eye strain. Particular colour combinations can make this eye strain worse. To minimize the strain on users' eyes, choose colour combinations that have maximum contrast between the background and the text. For example, combinations such as black and white or a very light colour and a very dark colour offer the most contrast.

SOLID OR SUBTLE BACKGROUNDS

When you place text on a background, remember the importance of high contrast in making your work accessible. Choose solid colour backgrounds for maximum legibility and contrast. If you decide you must have a textured or patterned background, make sure it is subtle enough that users can still read the text easily over top of the background.

AVOID ALL CAPS

A phrase using all capital letters is difficult enough to read on paper, but on screen it becomes nearly illegible. Instead of putting your headings in all caps, choose a contrasting colour, font, or larger font size to give them emphasis.

ALIGNMENT

Left-align text on a computer screen. Justified, centred, or right-aligned text is difficult to read on a computer screen because of the large area of most screens. For users with screens smaller than yours, right-aligned text may vanish from the screen to the right. Justified text spreads the text across the whole screen, and sometimes gaps appear between words as the computer distributes the text evenly from edge to edge. Centred text may not actually be centred on some screens. Because these alignments are non-standard and display text in ways that may hamper legibility, use left alignment as your default to ensure your information is easy to find and read.

SANS-SERIF FONT

Place text that you want users to read in a sans-serif font such as Arial, Geneva, or Verdana. Because computer screens have poorer resolution than the printed page, the serif fonts are more difficult to decipher on screen, and they increase eye strain. Users may not persist in reading your text if doing so is too painful an experience. You can minimize eye strain by choosing a font that is as readable as possible on screen.

OBVIOUS LINKS

Make your links obvious to users by underlining them and putting them in a contrasting (blue) coloured font. If your links appear similar to the non-linked text, no one will know how to move to subsequent pages on your site. While some users may be willing to move their cursors across the page looking for your links, others won't bother, and they will leave your site.

ANIMATIONS AND OTHER MULTIMEDIA ENHANCEMENTS

Animations, video and audio clips, and slide shows are fun and can attract people to your site. However, animations that continue to move after a few seconds or music clips that repeat indefinitely become a distraction rather than an attraction. Adjust your audio-visual presentations (using an animation program, for example) so that they cycle twice through and then stop. (Or allow users to stop them easily at their discretion.) Users will greatly appreciate being able to apply their full attention to your information once they have reached your page.

IMAGE AND TEXT LINKS

If you use both images and text to indicate hypertext links on a page, then make both the button and the text "hot" or clickable so users can click on either one to reach their destination. Well-designed web pages help users move as quickly as possible to the information they need. Having multiple ways of reaching the information makes your site efficient to use.

LEFT-ALIGN LINKS

If you are presenting your links in a column or list, left-align the list rather than centring or right-aligning it, especially if your audience is largely English-speaking. English (and other European) language readers automatically look left to find the beginning of meaningful visual and written communication. Capitalize on this impulse by placing your links where users will look: they will quickly find what they are searching for and therefore be more likely to use and appreciate your site.

MODERATE LINE LENGTHS

Avoid designing a page that requires users to read from one edge of the browser window to another. These lines of text can be excessively long, and readers can easily skip a line as their eyes travel back and forth across the screen. Instead, place your text in a cell or text box that it is never longer than 40 to 60 characters. With moderate line lengths and a larger (14 pt.) sans-serif font, your onscreen text will be as readable as possible.

As more and more users become familiar with the way that the Internet works, these conventions may change, but, in the meantime, by following these conventions, you can assure yourself that your website is as clear and usable as you can make it to the widest possible audience.

MAJOR PROJECT 10.1

PREPARING INSTRUCTIONAL MATERIAL FOR ONLINE DELIVERY

Write a set of instructions that users will access online. Use the discussion in the second half of this chapter to help you design an effective layout. Add illustrations to support the written text of your instructions. When you have completed a draft of your online instructions, user test the site with at least three people from your target user group to help you decide how best to revise and improve your design and instructions. Using the results of your usability test, revise the website before you hand in the final version, either burned on a CD or posted online. If your assignment is posted on the Internet, either email your instructor with the URL for the site or hand in a sheet of paper listing the URL as well as your name and student ID.

CHAPTER ELEVEN

Presenting technical information orally

Many people who are attracted to technical communication or scientific disciplines tend to be uncomfortable in front of audiences.
Drama majors and marketing students tend to be more oriented to
people and to interacting in person with others. For them, the pros-
pect of giving an oral presentation may even seem inviting, a chance
to get in the spotlight and get noticed. For people who tend to feel
more comfortable writing, though, the opposite may be true. When
we write, we feel more in control of the communication situation
because we control the context of communication: we release our
writing when we think it is finished, we control who reads it, and
we can intentionally fashion its tone and style. Presentations invoke
quite different contexts for communication, and some part of the
anxiety many of us feel when giving them is a tacit acknowledgement
of our concerns about communicating effectively in this different
environment.

As veteran technical communicators, we suggest that speaking
opportunities will be presented to you, the novice, often in your
future careers, and your success in life will, to some degree, depend
on whether you take these opportunities to speak publicly. We've
been asked to give wedding toasts in front of over a hundred guests,
eulogies at funerals for similar numbers of people, dozens of formal
academic presentations at conferences with as few as a handful of
listeners to as many as 80, several informal introductions of ourselves to over 100 fellow faculty members, and informal presentations to groups of four to eight co-workers. The list goes on and on.
When we were undergraduate students, the thought of giving this
number and this variety of oral speeches and presentations would
have been enough to drive us into accounting, not that accounting
would have spared us the need to speak formally and informally
in front of others. Our point here is that whatever discipline you
choose, you will make more of your career and your social life if you
become comfortable speaking in front of a group. In this chapter, we

will offer you some guidelines for getting started on what will likely be a lifetime of speaking publicly. Our goal is not to turn you into a politician; we hope only that, when an opportunity to speak about your work publicly comes up, you will have some confidence that you can do so competently.

Common speaking occasions

What kinds of speaking situations are you likely to find yourself confronting as a technical communicator? Speaking opportunities come in a wide variety, ranging from

- Casual, impromptu, short talks to small group meetings (3 to 7 people who know each other well)
- More formal speaking to small group meetings (3 to 7 people who hold various positions within the employment hierarchy or who are from outside the organization or your immediate work unit)
- Informal, prepared presentations (to groups of 10 to15 people within an organization)
- Formal presentations (to groups of 10 to 15 people that include people outside the organization)
- Group presentations (one part of a presentation to a large group).

There are, of course, other presentations that you may find yourself doing: presenting recognition awards, receiving recognition awards, introducing yourself at meetings of your workgroup, or performing skits as part of a planning "retreat" or meeting away from the workplace.

CASUAL, IMPROMPTU, AND SHORT TALKS

These are the kinds of opportunities to speak that come up just in the course of your everyday work. From time to time, you will need to meet with your supervisor, the other people in your workgroup, or as part of a cross-functional work team. Sometimes, these are just short meetings to find out how a project is proceeding; sometimes, groups of workers need to meet to go over policy changes in the workplace, e.g., to consider new health and safety procedures. You may be asked to give a short (30–60 second) update on the progress you've made documenting a section of a manual, for example.

How do you prepare for an impromptu talk, something that by its very definition is not scheduled? The real answer is that no one expects a polished, rehearsed performance in this kind of situation. Instead, they expect you to have some sense of how things are going on the projects you've been working on. Before you go to these kinds of meetings, take a few moments to review the status of each of the projects you are working on. Are they on time? Where are you in the overall development schedule for each one? Is work proceeding smoothly, or are there some challenges you face? How can you phrase these challenges diplomatically?

When you meet with cross-functional teams, the other members may have only a sketchy idea of what you do. Prepare a 30-second sound bite that summarizes what you do or some key aspect of your work. We are often asked to explain how students learn to write, for example, and we have "stock" answers ready to meet this need. If you are working on usability testing of documents or graphical user interfaces (GUI), prepare a brief overview of what this involves and have it ready when you meet with groups who are unfamiliar with your work.

In some cases, the leader of the group may inform the group about a pending change in how things are done at your workplace; they may then ask how that change affects you. While there is no way to prepare for this specifically, your answer will probably make more sense if you have up-to-date knowledge of where you are in your work.

SMALL GROUP MEETINGS

These meetings tend to be called for a reason or to get some work done. To that end, you may be asked to prepare a document or other materials to present to the group. When you actually meet with the group, you may distribute copies of the document or materials before you speak, while you are speaking, or after you speak.

The key difference between these kinds of speaking opportunities and short, impromptu speeches is preparation. If you are giving a status report for a project you are working on, consider preparing a draft of the report in memo form to distribute at the meeting. (For more information on status reports, see Chapter 7.) You could use this as the basis for your comments and summarize the main points for readers as they skim the document. However, resist the urge to read the document to them out loud. Instead, focus their attention on key aspects of it—the challenges section, for example, or a particular breakthrough in the project.

Alternatively, prepare a short handout (one or two pages) that is an example or draft of one section of the manual or document you are working on. This will enable the other members of the group to visualize what you are working on and what it will look like when it is finished. From the small sample section that you give them, they can extrapolate what the rest of the project will look like.

IN-CLASS EXERCISE 11.1

Creating Short Sound Bites

Rehearse short (three-sentence) overviews of what you do and how it contributes to your workplace. If you are a student, prepare answers to interview questions about technical communication:

- What is the most important aspect of technical communication?
- What is the hardest part of preparing a document?
- What is usability testing?
- How do you prepare a PDF?

IN-CLASS EXERCISE 11.2

Introducing Yourself

A common speaking occasion that comes up is the opportunity to introduce yourself to a group of co-workers. In small groups (four to six people), take one or two minutes to prepare a 60-second summary of who you are and where you are in your program of study.

INFORMAL, PREPARED PRESENTATIONS

These are similar to small group presentations but differ in degree: you are the focus for a few minutes, and the point of your remarks is to generate discussion. The meeting itself may still be an informal gathering of team members or committee members who all know each other, but your contribution to the gathering functions to focus or jump-start discussion. The gathering itself may be informal, but your part still needs to be prepared.

In a small group presentation, you could distribute a handout, such as a photocopy of a sample document, and it would be readily accepted. When you have been asked specifically to speak to some issue at some length (over two or three minutes), you may be expected to prepare a more thorough presentation. In this case, determine what you have been asked to do:

- Prepare an overview (for example, of a specific technology)
- Give background or history of a project
- Present two alternative plans of action
- Summarize a policy or procedure currently in place or that is being proposed.

Check with your supervisor to find out how much time will be allotted to discussing this issue and how much of that time should be spent with you talking.

Once you have a sense of the scope of the topic and of the time that will be given to it, prepare a point-form outline of what you want to say. (See Figure 11.1.) You could use presentation software to prepare this and then distribute just the photocopies of the slides without formally showing the presentation itself. The slide handouts would provide some structure for your remarks and would show that you took some time to think about the topic.

Alternatively, you could use the "outline" feature in a word processing program to show only the main headings of your document. You could print the outline view to hand out to the audience and speak from the full text version that included point form notes under each heading. (See Figure 11.2.) Either way, use this part of the preparation process to think of the overall direction and message that you want to convey to the people in the meeting. Any handout should give them an outline that they can annotate as they listen to you.

Once you have a general sense of the main points you want to convey, decide if you need to provide your audience with more detailed information. Do people need the full text of your remarks written out? Do they need a copy of the notes? Will you be referring to documents they have never seen or will need to review later, after the session? These other ancillary materials should not take over your presentation; instead, you should consider making copies of them available at the meeting or upon request. (For example, you could email them or send a copy later to whomever is interested.) The focus of your work here is to consider just how much information your audience needs to know at this point, at this meeting, and to provide it. By making supplementary information available through other means, you are reaching out to the various people within your audience, whose members have different levels of knowledge about or interest in your topic.

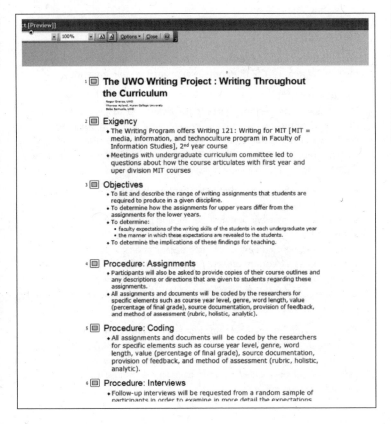

FIGURE 11.1
Outlineview in PowerPoint

FORMAL PRESENTATIONS

Moving from the small group to speaking in front of a larger group (15 people plus) represents a difference in kind not simply in number. These larger groups behave differently: you can't quickly make eye contact with everyone in the group, for example. Several members of the group are likely to be distracted at any one time; if you happen to focus on those few people, you may be discouraged and thrown off by them even though the bulk of the audience is listening attentively. At some point in the presentation, someone may need to get up and leave; if this happens in a small group, that person usually offers an explanation. In a large group, however, the unspoken etiquette is to say nothing but to leave as unobtrusively as possible. As a speaker, though, you may begin to wonder why some people are leaving, whether anyone else will also be leaving, whether you are being boring, and any number of other thoughts. The result is that you may be distracted from what you are trying to communicate. So speaking in front of larger groups presents problems that are distinctly different from speaking to fewer people in less formal situations.

PROPOSAL

That Inkshed's board investigate the possibility of aligning itself with the CATTW and the CSHR to pursue areas of common interest.

Discussion

I have been asked to bring this proposal before the business meeting of Inkshed. Some people who are members of more than one of the three organizations think that the goals of these organizations overlap. Furthermore, having an "umbrella" organization could serve all of these organizations in the following ways:

- Provide a web presence that links them, making it easier to find any one of these groups
- Provide a more authoritative lobbying and public relations presence
- Attract funding for conferences and research by creating a higher profile for the members of all three organizations
- Function as a clearinghouse (directory of members of each organization, support online publications such as Inkshed newsletter, CSHR journal, CATTW newsletter).

Rationale

The overlap among memberships justifies one larger organization that would help facilitate sharing, collaboration, and interchange among members. This grouping might help fund the development and maintenance of websites; on a long-term basis, it may not be feasible to depend on volunteer labour to do this.

FIGURE 11.2
Sample handout

Most invitations to speak formally come well ahead of when you will actually give the presentation. Many organizations have quarterly group meetings or yearly sales meetings at which a number of people will be asked to speak to the entire group. Unless you have been asked to fill in for someone else, you will probably have at least a week and maybe several weeks or even months to prepare for this event. In a technical communication course, you may have been notified by the course syllabus that you will be giving a presentation to the class during the last week of term, a presentation based on your final project, for example. One of the keys to your success will be your ability to use your time well to prepare for the presentation.

The first step in preparing for any presentation involves identifying specific details of the engagement:

- How many people are expected to attend?
- Who, specifically, will be there? Your supervisor? Clients?
- Is this a mixed group with varying levels of knowledge or a group whose members share a common background?
- What is the venue? How large is the room? What does it look like?
- How will the room be set up? Rows of chairs? Tables?
- Can the lighting of the room be controlled to allow for presentation slides?
- Will you be able to set up whatever technology you need ahead of time? Can you use your own technology (e.g., laptop)?
- Is this primarily an information session or a presentation to a decision-making body?

FIGURE 11.3
Formal speaking engagements

You will want to get answers to as many of these questions as possible while you prepare the presentation. Some of these questions dictate the materials you will be able to use in your presentation. For example, if you have been asked to give a presentation on your writing as part of a job interview, you would want to know whether you will have access to the web in order to show examples of your work, say from your electronic portfolio. If not, then you may want to make screen shots and print them out to hand out to the group. (See Chapter 8 on how to create screen shots.) If you will have Internet access, then you will want to create a hyperlink within your presentation to any sites you plan to use. (And, the night before the actual presentation, check that these sites are still active!) If you will not be able to use your own laptop, for example, consider storing your presentation on a USB key drive and running it from the equipment in the room. Sometimes the venue and its setup affect a speaker's preparation in other ways too. For example, you may need to stand still behind a microphone or console, or you may need to move around, in certain circumstances, to be seen by all.

While these material conditions are very important, equally important is getting to know who will be sitting in the seats listening to you. If these people are a homogenous group—at academic conventions we can assume a group of relatively knowledgeable writing teachers will be listening—then you can make assumptions about what they know and what you don't need to explain as you begin your talk. However, if your group is drawn from a cross-section of employees, then you may not be able to assume quite as much about them, and you may have to skew your talk more towards explaining terms and concepts that will be new to many of your listeners. So one thing to discover is how much background knowledge the audience shares.

Another consideration has to do with decision-making: are you giving a presentation to a decision-making group or are you giving an information-rich presentation to a group that wants to learn about something you are working on? The difference is critical because decision-making audiences will be less tolerant of poor preparation, less willing to listen to information if they have not been told why they need to know that information, and more likely to be thinking about the implications of what you are saying. They prefer a direct summary of your main points, and you should consider preparing photocopied handouts that present fuller discussions of what you have to say. These they can read later or during the presentation itself. (For a sample handout, see Figure 11.4.) Of course, it takes time to prepare reports and handouts that elaborate or support some point you want to make, but that time will be well spent. You will be seen as not wasting the time of the committee or group sitting in front of you, and they will think well of you for that. You will enhance your professional credibility through your thorough preparation and foresight.

FIGURE 11.4
Handout distributed to audience

Information-based presentations tend to be less intense than decision-making presentations. Often they are part of an overall sales, marketing, or service programme. While a sales or marketing programme is going to be ultimately decision making, it often also includes an information-based presentation, on the effective use of a product, for example. The focus in an information-based presentation is conveying information about the subject itself rather than attempting to finalize policy changes. The audiences for information-based presentations may be expecting you to inform them about the project you are working on, for example, or some aspect of technology that they need to learn about. As you plan your presentation, think about what kinds of information should be presented in handouts, what kinds could be summarized in a presentation slide, and what kinds of information might best be demonstrated (perhaps by visiting a web site; perhaps by distributing samples). You want your presentation to provide the overall organization of the talk, giving it coherence; in support of the points you want to make, you could show the audience examples (Figure 11.5), lead demonstrations of a particular technology, or engage the audience interactively in a discussion of the topic. These are all ways of informing them in an interesting way.

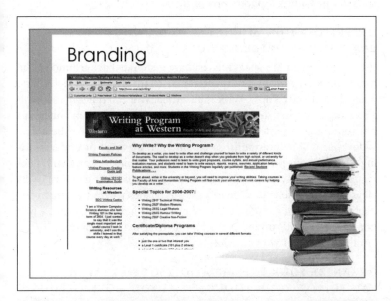

FIGURE 11.5
Presentation slide that shows an example

MAJOR PROJECT 11.1

CREATING AN ORAL PRESENTATION OF THE FINAL COURSE PROJECT

Create a three- to five-minute presentation for your classmates and instructor about some aspect of your final project in this course. Select a topic from or a perspective on your project that you think will interest the class, and create a presentation that includes a visual or a demonstration of a technique covered in the final project.

Guidelines for preparing presentations

Whether you are giving an impromptu introduction of yourself or a 30-minute presentation to the management committee where you work, there are some basic guidelines that will help you make a better impression.

DECIDE WHAT INFORMATION TO INCLUDE IN YOUR PRESENTATION SLIDES OR OUTLINE AND WHAT TO INCLUDE IN A HANDOUT

Presentation slides are good for short phrases and fewer than 20–30 words per slide. If you have more than this number of words, consider moving that information to a handout that you can photocopy and distribute to your audience to read. Similarly, if you have a chart or table of information that you want your audience to review, decide whether they can digest the information in the table quickly. If it will take them more than a minute or so to review the table, consider providing a photocopy of it.

DETERMINE HOW MUCH BACKGROUND TO PRESENT EARLY IN THE PRESENTATION

If the people you are speaking to share a similar background in the topic you are speaking on, it should be relatively easy to determine what they already know. With that settled, you can quickly establish a starting point for your remarks. However, if audience members do not share a common knowledge level on your topic, provide a few slides that will help establish a common framework of understanding. In addition, provide a handout that summarizes any technical language you may be using or perhaps a graphic that gives an overview (for example, a flow chart that establishes where you are in the overall process of creating the new product line). This way, you will not have to spend too much time going over material that is already familiar to half of your listeners.

ORGANIZE YOUR PRESENTATION SO THAT LISTENERS CAN FOLLOW YOUR THOUGHTS AS YOU MOVE THROUGH THE MATERIAL

Provide clear cues (sometimes called *signposts*) to your audience, so they know where you are in the presentation: "The *second* main area we worked on ... " If you provide an outline of your talk or copies of the slides you show, that will also help listeners understand where you are going with the presentation and how the different parts of the presentation relate to each other. One way to organize a presentation on your major project for the term might look like this:

- Interesting opening
- Description of topic

- Definition of any special terms
- Brief description of how information was gathered
- Presentation of main ideas
- Conclusions
- Questions.

Remember that your audience is listening, not reading, and that makes it more difficult to understand the overall organization of a presentation. To compensate for this, stress the organization of your presentation, and make it obvious to your audience.

CREATE VISUALS TO ACCOMPANY YOUR VERBAL DESCRIPTIONS

Just as it is important not to read your presentation to the audience word for word, it is important to create opportunities to communicate through visuals. You will be seen as having given a better presentation if you incorporate visuals. When creating slides using presentation software, limit each slide to around 30 words and to three or four major points. Use a large font—28–32 points—and add graphics from clip art or images from screen captures or picture files to illustrate the points you are making.

Guidelines for giving presentations

When it comes time to actually move to the front of the room, keep these guidelines in mind.

TAKE ADVANTAGE OF THE IMMEDIACY OF HAVING LIVE HUMAN BEINGS IN THE SAME ROOM WITH YOU

While it is stressful to speak in front of people, audiences also offer energy because of the interaction between you and the people you are speaking to. People want you to LOOK THEM IN THE EYE rather than have you not meet their gaze. Identify a few people in the audience, and actually look at them as you speak. You don't have to look at every person in the room—in fact, it may not be possible—so long as you do make eye contact with some of the people in the audience. You will be perceived as having given a better presentation if you make eye contact with your audience.

Related to this is the level of vocabulary that you use when you speak; linguists call this "register." (For more information about register, see Chapter 4.) When speaking in a business setting, use the same level of language that you would use when at a meeting or on the phone with co-workers or customers. Avoid overly formal, stilted language ("I do believe that you are mistaken, Mr. Brown") in favour of the kind of language you would actually use if you were sitting down at a small meeting with other co-workers from another part of the company.

STAND SO THAT YOUR AUDIENCE CAN SEE THE VISUALS THAT YOU DISPLAY ON THE SCREEN

Stand off to one side of the screen on which you are displaying your visuals so that your audience can see them without having to look around you. One consequence of your standing to one side is that you will be less tempted to wander around the room, which is a common tendency. Unless you are the host of a daytime talk show, your audience does not want to watch as you stride around the room and into the audience.

CONTROL THE TIMING OF THE SLIDES SO THAT YOU CONTROL WHEN THE PRESENTATION MOVES FROM ONE TOPIC TO ANOTHER

The slides function as a kind of moving outline of the talk. As soon as a new slide appears, the audience will read it. Don't display the new slide until you want to move the conversation forward. This tactic allows you to take questions during the talk, provided you control when the slides advance from one to another.

BREATHE

It may seem obvious, but one way to make sure you get started well is to pause for a second or two to take a deep breath. Another tactic is to take a look around and say hello to someone you know in the audience before getting started formally. That will get the first words out of your mouth and clear your throat before you try to raise your voice and project it so that everyone in the room can hear you.

The key to a good presentation is preparation. If you prepare handouts and interesting slides, your audience will have something to look at other than you. They will sense that there is value in what you are about to say and encourage you to continue. That will help you get started, and once you get started you have a very good chance of finishing and finishing well.

References

Bawarshi, Anis. *Genre and the Invention of the Writer* (Logan: Utah State University Press, 2003), 17.

Beale, Walter H. *A Pragmatic Theory of Rhetoric*. Carbondale, IL: Southern Illinois University Press, 1987.

Broache, Anne. "Free Speech Under Net Attack, Study Says," *CNET News*, December 5, 2005, http://news.com.com/Free+speech+under+Net+attack,+st udy+says/2100-1030_3-5983072.html?part=rss&tag=5983072&subj=news.

Canadian Intellectual Property Office. "When Copyright Does Not Apply," http:// strategis.ic.gc.ca/sc_mrksv/cip/cp/copy_gd_protect-e.html#4.

Canadian Intellectual Property Office. "Photographs," *Copyright Circulars* 11, (July 1, 1998), http://strategis.gc.ca/sc_mrksv/cipo/cp/cp_circ_11-e.html.

Corbett, Edward P.J., and Robert Connors. *Classical Rhetoric for the Modern Student*. 4th ed. New York: Oxford University Press, 1998.

Crowley, Sharon, and Debra Hawhee. *Ancient Rhetorics for Contemporary Students*. 3rd ed. New York: Longman, 2003.

Department of Health and Human Services (US). "Public Health Service Brochure." http://www.PlainLanguage.gov.

Department of Energy, Office of Science, Office of Biological and Environmental Research (US). "Genetics and Patenting," *Human Genome Product Information*, http://www.ornl.gov/sci/techresources/Human_Genome/elsi/ patents.shtml#2.

Ebel, Hans, F., Claus Bliefert, and William E. Russey. *The Art of Scientific Writing: From Student Reports to Professional Publications in Chemistry and Related Fields*. 2nd ed. Weinheim, Germany: Wiley-VCH, 2004.

The Foundation Center. "Leakey Foundation Offers Funding for Research into Human Origins." *Philanthropy News Digest*. http://foundationcenter. org/pnd/

Government of Canada. "Customer Satisfaction Survey." *Contracts Canada*. http:// contractscanada.gc.ca/en/biddin-e.htm.

Graves, Heather. *Rhetoric in(to) Science: Style as Invention in Inquiry*. Cresskill, NJ: Hampton Press, 2005.

Hamper, Robert, and Sue Baugh. *Handbook for Writing Proposals*. Chicago: NTC Contemporary Publishing Group, 1995.

Katz, Steven B. "The Ethic of Expediency: Classical Rhetoric, Technology, and the Holocaust." *College English* 54.3 (1992): 255–75.

Kinneavy, James L. *A Theory of Discourse*. New York: Norton, 1971.

Kostelnick, Charles. "Supra-Textual Design: The Visual Rhetoric of Whole Documents." *Technical Communication Quarterly* 5.1 (1996): 9–33.

Krug, Steven. *Don't Make Me Think: A Common Sense Approach to Web Usability*. Berkeley, CA: New Riders Press, 2000.

Lakoff, George, and Mark Johnson. *Metaphors We Live By*. Chicago: University of Chicago Press, 1980.

Locker, Kitty O. *Business and Administrative Communication*. 5th ed. New York: Irwin McGraw-Hill, 2000.

Management Working Group of the Interagency Committee on Government Information (ICGI), "Ambiguous Wording Rewritten," *Plain Language* http://www.plainlanguage.gov/examples/before_after/ambigwd.cfm.

Management Working Group of the Interagency Committee on Government Information (ICGI), "Public Health Service, [US] Department of Health and Human Service, Brochure." *Plain Language*. http://www.plainlanguage.gov/examples/before_after/pub_hhs_losewgt.cfm.

McCorduck, P. *Machines Who Think*. San Francisco: Freeman, 1979.

Ministry of Health (Ontario). "Alzheimer Disease." *HealthyOntario.com*. http://www.healthontario.com/english/channel_condition.asp?_Channel_id=4.

Nelson, Wade. "How to Write a White Paper So It Actually Gets Read." http://www.casestudieswriter.com/how2wp.html.

Nielsen, Jakob. *Designing Web Usability*. Indianapolis: New Riders Publishing, 1999.

Peers, Alexandra. "But Martha Made it Look so Easy." *Wall Street Journal*, December 12, 1997, B10.

Plain Language Consumer Contract Act (June 23, 1993), *P.S. 2202*. http://members.aol.com/StatutesPA/73.Cp.37.html.

Schey, J. M. *Div Grad Curl and All That*. New York: Norton, 1973.

Schriver, Karen. *Dynamics in Document Design*. New York: John Wiley & Sons, 1997.

Stewart, Duncan. "Good analysts are good writers," *National Post*, March 9, 2006, FP 9, 10.

Sykes, J.B., ed. *The Concise Oxford Dictionary of Current English*. 6th ed. Oxford: Clarendon Press, 1976.

Toulmin, Stephen. *The Uses of Argument*. Updated ed. New York: Cambridge, 2003.

Tufte, Edward R. *Visual Explanations: Images and Quantities, Evidence and Narrative*. Cheshire, CT: Graphics Press, 1997.

University of Western Ontario. "Student Code of Conduct." http://www.uwo.ca/univsec/board/code.pdf.

Wheildon, Colin. *Type and Layout: How Typography and Design Can Get Your Message Across or Get in the Way*. Rev. ed. Berkeley, CA: Strathmoor Press, 1995.

Williams, Robin. *The Non-Designer's Design Book: Design and Typographic Principles for the Visual Novice*. 2nd ed. Berkeley, CA: Peachpit, 2004.

Index